What
LEFT BEHIND
Left Out

What LEFT BEHIND *Left Out* – *The Truth*

Jeff Canfield

Dan Dyer

Scripture quotations marked (KJV) are from the King James Version of the Holy Bible.
Italics [or Emphasis] in Scripture have been added by the authors.

Publishing services by Selah Publishing Group, LLC, Indiana. The views expressed or implied in this work do not necessarily reflect those of Selah Publishing Group.

ISBN: 1-58930-144-7
Library of Congress Control Number: 2004099931

Acknowledgements

Our heartfelt thanks to all who participated in making this book a reality. We cannot express how much we appreciate your time, talents, and generosity.

Contents

Preface

Have you ever felt as though you cannot understand biblical teaching concerning prophecy and the end times? You have heard teachings, gone to seminars, listened to tapes, read books, and still feel you do not have a good grip on end-time prophecy. Maybe you are a pastor who does not teach prophecy because you feel you do not have a good handle on the subject.

It is our sincere desire to lay out truths concerning end-time Bible prophecy in a way that is easy to understand. We believe by the time you finish reading this book, you will have a firm grip on Bible prophecy relating to the times in which we live. That is what excites us about this material!

In this book we have drawn information from many historic and current events, while putting together parallel passages from Scripture as a basis for our teaching. Our goal is to present a balanced biblical, historic, and modern look at prophecy and the end times.

We pray that as you delve into this material, you will receive understanding and revelation from God's Word.

Jeff Canfield and Dan Dyer

Introduction

Fact, Fiction, or Tradition?

    With so many views alive within Christianity concerning the events of these last days, who are we to believe? That the truth always lies within the Bible seems like an obvious statement. Yet, we often view world events, then try to fit them into our theories of what we believe about the last days, rather than what we clearly see in Scripture.

    If we are not careful, we can become stuck in the rut of tradition. Then each teacher who follows becomes an echo of traditional doctrine.

    The proper way to view Bible prophecy would be as Peter did on the Day of Pentecost. He recognized what was happening because he was familiar with prophetic Scriptures. As the events unfolded, Peter stood up and said, "This is what was spoken by the prophet Joel" (see Acts 2:16). He recognized this major event as a fulfillment of prophecy since he knew the Scriptures and was sensitive to the Spirit of God.

    The following may be a weak example, but in reality it is as simple as this: Imagine that someone prophesied your neighbor would fall off his porch at 8AM next Saturday morning while reading his newspaper. The following Saturday at 8AM you happen to be on your porch drinking a cup of coffee and you witness your neighbor fall off his porch while reading his newspaper. At that moment you remember what had been prophesied concerning your neighbor and you say, "This is what was spoken by..."

History and current events alone do not interpret Scripture. As we will see, Scripture interprets Scripture. However, current events and historical facts can serve us well in a couple of ways:

1. Current events and historical facts help emphasize the soundness of the Scriptures from a natural standpoint, especially to a nonbeliever.

2. Current events and historical facts help determine where we are within Bible prophecy.

What we will find out is that we best understand prophecy as an event occurs or after a major event has occurred that clearly lines up with Scripture. If we preach dogmatically about the interpretation of Bible prophecy before a prophetic event occurs, in reality we are preaching speculation. Would it have meant as much if Peter stood up three years before the Day of Pentecost and preached what he thought Joel's prophecy meant?

This is not to say that speculating about certain aspects of Bible prophecy is wrong. When speaking of future events a degree of speculation will always be involved. All viewpoints of prophetic teaching involve a degree of speculation. At the same time, we must be aware of the problems connected with speculating about prophetic events.

The major problem with prophetic speculation is that sometimes we lack proper discernment when it comes to separating speculation from proper Bible interpretation. Many times Bible teachers do not have the candor to admit when certain aspects of their teaching are simply speculation, leaving their audience with the idea that their teaching is fact. As a result, their listeners share the same speculations with their friends and neighbors as though such speculations are biblical facts. Instead of teaching our prophetic speculations as concrete doctrine, why not just admit that it is speculation?

Another major problem arises if we do not place our speculations upon a solid scriptural foundation, for then our speculations will certainly not hold true. On the other hand, if we have a solid handle on the foundational truths of Bible prophecy, our speculations concerning future events might prove to be correct.

Nonetheless, it stands to reason that the odds of correctly interpreting Bible prophecy increase significantly as we view prophecy in light of an event *as* it occurs, or *after* it occurs.

We will attempt to avoid these pitfalls within this book. This is not to say that we will not speculate concerning certain aspects of Bible prophecy. However, we will freely admit when an idea turns to speculation. At that point it is up to you, the reader, to discern whether a proper scriptural foundation and sufficient evidence exist to support the idea.

Even if you disagree with various speculative analogies, we would encourage you to focus on the bigger doctrinal issues. Do not become sidetracked and miss the solid scriptural teaching laid out in this book through parallel passages and proper Bible interpretation. We must keep in mind several important fundamental truths as we dissect this material.

Scripture Interprets Scripture

We must keep our study in context with Scripture no matter what our favorite TV evangelist may teach. To say, "I do not accept this because Reverend So-and-So does not teach it that way," is to elevate Reverend So-and-So above God's Word. We have a responsibility as Christians to find out what God's Word says, even if it is contrary to the most popular teaching.

We will clearly see in this study that Scripture sheds light on itself. Second Peter 1:20-21 tells us that no prophecy of Scripture is of any private interpretation [origin]. It goes on to say that prophecy never came by the will of man, but holy men of God spoke as they were "moved by the Holy Spirit." The origin of Bible prophecy does not lie with man. Therefore, the only safe and accurate way to interpret Bible prophecy is in light of itself [Scripture].

In each section we will use parallel passages (other Scriptures speaking of the same subject matter) to help us interpret what the passage is saying. Parallel passages help us see the entire picture. If we do not have parallel passages to back up what we are saying, then we will be courageous enough to admit that it is purely speculation.

Technology and Culture Change

How would Daniel, Ezekiel, Zechariah, and the apostle John communicate the events and technology of the times in which we now live? They described images in terms with which they were familiar. Keep in mind the apostle John would not be able to recognize a helicopter, because he had never seen one. Therefore, he would have described it the best way he could, using creatures or images from his era—such as a locust with the face of a man, and a breastplate of iron (see Revelation chapter 9). We will see from Scripture that many of the events spoken of by the prophets happen in *the last* of the last days. (We will examine a biblical definition of the last days in the next section.) Therefore, it is not inappropriate to take the prophet Daniel's or the apostle John's information and relate it to world events of our time.

As we view biblical prophecy in context, allowing Scripture to interpret Scripture, it will help shed light on prophetic symbolism. Understanding this can help bring into focus much of the Bible's prophetic symbolism, bringing clarity to the events and images spoken of in Bible prophecy.

The Proper Way to Handle Speculation

As previously stated, in some areas of our study there will be speculation laid on top of scriptural foundation; speculation that is also supported by world history and current events. We will do our best to support our theories, or speculative analogies, with solid evidence and documentation. Once again, at that point it is up to you, the reader, to digest the information and determine whether the evidence is sufficient.

In the end we will discover that the majority of the creatures, their actions, and the events described in Bible prophecy fall directly in line with modern nations, systems of government, and current world events.

Separate Fact from Fiction and Truth from Tradition

Unfortunately, many Christians today do not discuss end-time doctrine based upon what the Bible says, but rather what the most popular Christian author or speaker says. This is exactly how we become fixed within what the apostle Paul called the traditions of our fathers.

Prophecy is not as difficult to understand as some have proposed—particularly in this generation. When we digest this information, we must accept the truth of God's Word even if we say, "That is not what I was taught before." God's word is our standard—not our traditions.

This is not new and improved doctrine. These truths have been there all the time. We understand prophecy best when we examine it in light of past or present events. Once again, this is the crucial point we are at in history.

Faith, Not Fear

Many Christians have the false impression that God would never allow His Church to go through tough times, or that He would not inform us about those tough times before they came. If that is true, then why did Jesus inform the apostle Peter of what death he would be subject to years before he died? (See John 21:18-19.) Did Jesus do that in order to put fear in Peter's heart? Of course not!

God is a loving Father who does not want His children to be unaware of the signs, seasons, and times in which they live. When we can see what is coming down the road, we can be ready to meet any difficulties in faith and in turn we can minister effectively to others. It is always best to arm soldiers with truth, not teachings that tickle their ears.

Our purpose is not to put fear in anyone's heart. Second Timothy 1:7 says, "For God hath not given us the spirit of fear; but of power, and of love, and of a sound mind." Our desire is a sound biblical examination of prophecy.

We cannot teach a well-rounded view of Bible prophecy and prophetic events in a 150-page book.

In this book we will cover almost every major end-time prophecy in the Bible. We cannot make an accurate assessment of a 1,000-piece puzzle by simply putting together fifty pieces. We must attempt to put all the pieces into place so that we can make a proper assessment of Bible prophecy.

In view of that, do not be intimidated by the size of the book. How do you eat a big sandwich? One bite at a time! We would recommend digesting this material one section at a time, while understanding that each section is simply a piece of the bigger picture. By the time you get to the end, all of the pieces of the puzzle will fall into place.

The exciting part is that this generation is at a pivotal point in history. Our generation has the privilege of doing just as Peter did on the Day of Pentecost in regards to many current facets of Bible prophecy. We are at a place from which we can view prophecy as it happens, or look back at the last several thousand years and see the fulfillment of many prophetic events.

For us to discern the times in which we live is part of God's plan. It also brings us to a firm realization of God's ultimate purpose: to reach the lost and to prepare the bride to meet the Bridegroom. The truth is when we discern the times, we begin to re-examine our lives and ask, "Where do I fit in God's plans?"

The Church has a powerful role to play in this final hour. We must be informed. We must live in such a way that the Word and the power of God are more evident in the body of Christ than in any previous generation!

We believe this information will stir up in the heart of a Christian a renewed sense of urgency and responsibility to fulfill the Great Commission. As you read this material, it is our prayer that a renewed sense of destiny and purpose will be awakened in your heart. God has a great plan for your life!

The question is, will you accept truth over tradition? Will you rise up in faith, breaking any non-scriptural traditional boundaries, and accept the truth of God's Word while submitting to His will in these times in which we live?

Part
I

The Last Days

It is estimated that two-thirds of the Bible is prophecy, and the vast majority of it happens in one generation. In light of that, consider what Amos 3:7 tells us: "Surely the Lord GOD will do nothing, but he revealeth his secret unto his servants the prophets."

We can plainly see that the Lord has revealed His plans and purposes through His prophets. That is an exciting notion, considering it is very possible that the majority of end-time prophecies in the Bible could happen in our generation. On the other hand, one of the great predicaments within Christianity is the interpretation of Bible prophecy.

Can we view biblical prophecies and see the fulfillment of many of them to provide a better understanding of our location in history? Can we discern the times in which we live?

As we study prophecy, we should also consider the words spoken by God through the prophet Daniel: "And such as do wickedly against the covenant shall he corrupt by flatteries; but the people that do know their God shall be strong, and do

exploits. And they that understand among the people shall instruct many" (11:32-33). It is not only God's will that we
understand these times, but also that we instruct many and do
great exploits.

In the twelfth chapter of Daniel we see that God has revealed
many major events of the last days. There we find many references to time. One of the most interesting references comes after
Daniel receives the prophetic words and does not
understand them.

> And I heard, but I understood not; then said I, "O my
> Lord, what shall be the end of these things?" And he
> said, "Go thy way, Daniel; *for the words are closed up
> and sealed till the time of the end.* Many shall be puri-
> fied, and made white, and tried; but the wicked shall
> do wickedly; and none of the wicked shall understand;
> but the wise shall understand."
>
> DANIEL 12:8-10

Daniel lived and died but did not understand the words of
the prophecy. He did not understand simply because it was not
time for those prophetic events to be revealed. Time is one of the
greatest factors we find in Scripture that gives clarity to
prophetic events.

The Bible shows us that prophetic words and events have
time frames. God has preordained certain events to happen at
certain times. For example, Galatians 4:4 says, "But when the
fullness of time was come, God sent forth his Son, made of a
woman, made under the law, to redeem them that were under the
law, that we might receive the adoption of sons." There was a
specific time God had in mind to send His Son into the earth. It
would not have happened any sooner or any later.

We see another clear example of this in Matthew 8:29 where
the demons cried out to Jesus, "Art thou come hither to torment
us before the time?" The time they were obviously speaking of
was the Day of Judgment. Even the demons understand that
God has specific times designed for certain events.

A third example is in Revelation 12:12: "Therefore rejoice, ye heavens, and ye that dwell in them. Woe to the inhabitants of the earth and of the sea! For the devil is come down unto you, having great wrath, because he knoweth that he hath but a short time." In these two passages we see that the devil is aware of the time, and that God has a specific time determined for the devil's fate.

Without a doubt, when the time comes for the fulfillment of prophecy it is as the Lord told Habakkuk, "But at the end it will speak and it will not lie." Why will it not lie? Biblical prophecies cannot lie because God cannot lie. When prophecy comes to pass, it is like a bull in a china shop shouting, "I'm here!"

Recognition of the fulfillment of prophecy is very eye-opening, and very powerful to both the believer and the nonbeliever. The reason for this is that it stirs within us the reality that God is real and His Word is true. Why were Peter's words so compelling on the Day of Pentecost? Because he was revealing to all listeners that the events taking place were a fulfillment of prophecy. His message shouted, "God is real, and He is in control of the times and seasons!" Imagine a generation that can view world events and say, "This is what the prophet Daniel spoke of."

In the book of Revelation we see just the opposite of what the Lord told Daniel. An angel tells the apostle John, "Do not seal the words of the prophecy of this book, for the *time* is at hand" (22:10). The books of Daniel and Revelation go hand in hand. In the book of Daniel we see that prophecy is sealed until the time of the end. In the book of Revelation we see that the time is at hand. Much of what Daniel prophesied concerning the last days is unsealed and comes to pass within the vision the Lord gave the apostle John.

Even so, it is possible that many have not recognized the times in which we live and therefore have missed the fulfillment of key prophetic events. Many of the Jewish religious leaders during Jesus' earthly ministry missed His first advent even though the Old Testament clearly spoke of His coming. In Luke 12:54-56 Jesus gave a stern rebuke to those listening as He said, "When

ye see a cloud rise out of the west, straightway ye say, 'There
cometh a shower'; and so it is. And when ye see the south wind
blow, ye say, 'There will be heat'; and it cometh to pass. Ye hypocrites, ye can discern the face of the sky and of the earth; but
how is it that ye *do not discern this time?*" While Jesus walked
the earth He fulfilled over 300 Old Testament prophecies. He
expected the Jews (those who possessed His word) to understand the times in which they lived.

In Revelation 19:10 we see that the testimony of Jesus is the
spirit of prophecy. Prophecy concerning the last days and the
Second Coming of Christ has Jesus Himself as its source. Prophecy also bears witness of the lordship and majesty of Jesus the
Kings of kings and Lord of lords. The irony is that the One of
whom the prophecies bore witness was rebuking the multitude.

In order to understand prophecy we must first deal with this question: What are the last days?

If the rest of the information in this book is the picture, then
understanding the meaning of the phrase "the last days" is the
picture frame. Getting a handle on what the last days are will
determine our overall view of the events in Bible prophecy and
the time frame in which they occur.

As always, the best way to understand anything biblical is to
go to the Bible. Let us examine several Scriptures concerning the
"last days" so that we may obtain an accurate view of what that
phrase means.

Beginning in Matthew 24:1-3, we see Jesus departing from
the temple and His disciples showing Him the buildings of
the temple.

> And Jesus said to them, "Do you not see all these
> things? Assuredly, I say to you, not one stone shall be
> left here upon another, that shall not be thrown down."
> Now as he sat on the Mount of Olives, the disciples

came to him privately, saying, "Tell us, when will these things be? And what will be the sign of your coming, *and the end of the age?"*

Jesus was prophesying concerning the destruction of the second temple, which happened in AD 70, and the disciples began to ask Him about the sign of His coming and the "end of the age." From that point on in Matthew chapter 24, Jesus answers their questions by explaining the overall scenario for the "end of the age." We recognize from that exchange that the phrase "the end of the age" is another term for the "last days."

In answering the disciples' question Jesus included all things from His ascension forward. How do we know this? Because He begins His description of the end of the age by saying, "Take heed that no one deceives you. For many will come in my name." Jesus was warning his disciples that false Christs would come, and then he continues with a description of the last days all the way to his Second Coming (see Matthew 24:4-31).

We can see in this chapter that false prophets and false Christs were very common in the early church. We can also see that the "end of the age" started at the inception of the church and has included the last 2,000 years.

We have other scriptures to support this teaching. Let us examine Peter's words on the Day of Pentecost: "But this is what was spoken by the prophet Joel: 'And it shall come to pass in the *last days,* says God, that I will pour out of my Spirit on all flesh'" (Acts 2:16-17). Has God's Spirit been poured out? Yes! So we must conclude from Joel's prophecy that the pouring out of God's Spirit on the Day of Pentecost was the beginning of the last days.

It is also interesting that Joel's prophecy described a period of time from Pentecost all the way up until the Second Coming of Christ. At the end of this prophecy it says, "The sun shall be turned into darkness, and the moon into blood, before the coming of the great and awesome day of the LORD." Simply put, the last days are a period of time from the Day of Pentecost (Acts 2) until the Second Coming of Christ.

Confirmation that we have been in the last days since the beginning of the Church can also be found in 1 John 2:18: "Little children, it is the *last time:* and as ye have heard that the Antichrist shall come, even now are there many antichrists; whereby we know that it is the *last time.*"

John wrote this letter around AD 90 and he says clearly that they have already had many false prophets who professed to be Christ. He also recognized that they were in the last time. Again we see that we have been in the last days for almost 2,000 years.

Hebrews 1:1-2 tells us, "God, who at sundry times and in divers manners spake in time past unto the fathers by the prophets, hath in these *last days* spoken unto us by his Son." This is the same thing spoken of in 1 Peter 1:20: "Who verily was foreordained before the foundation of the world, but was manifest in these *last times* for you."

The end of the age, the last days, the last times, and the end times are all the same. The apostles knew very well that they were in the last days, and yet many times we have viewed the last days as the end of the end times. Understanding this basic building block of prophecy will help us establish where we are in history and Bible prophecy.

What about the Six-Day Theory?

We recognize that this is a theory, but we are including it in light of where we are in history. We believe this theory bears some consideration.

Psalm 90:4 and 2 Peter 3:8 tell us that in the eyes of the Lord a day is as a thousand years, and a thousand years as a day. In other words, the Lord does not live within our time. Minutes, hours, days, and years are for our benefit here on the earth, but are not germane in the realm in which God exists. Yet within man's existence, Psalm 90:4 and 2 Peter 3:8 are very interesting when we consider the following:

 ◆ There have been 6,000 years (six days) thus far in God's dealings with man.

- ◆ 6,000 years ago Adam sinned.
- ◆ 2,000 years after Adam fell, God cut a covenant with Abram [Abraham].
- ◆ 2,000 years after Abram, Jesus came and established a New Covenant.

The last 2,000 years have not only concerned the Church, but also Israel. Next will come the seventh day, or a Sabbath (Sabbath means rest). The Sabbath will be the 1,000-year reign of Christ on the earth, which will bring peace to the earth. (We will examine the millennial reign of Christ in a later section.)

How do we know a "Sabbath" (1,000 years of peace) is coming? There is a fascinating passage concerning Israel in Hosea 6:1-3: "Come, and let us return to the Lord; For he has torn, but he will heal us; he has stricken, but he will bind us up. After *two days* he will revive us; on the *third day* he will raise us up, that we may live in his sight."

It is logical to assume that this passage is not speaking of a literal two-day time period, but rather a figurative time period. If it were a literal two-day time period, it would have happened a long time ago. This passage might be speaking about the nation of Israel and how they rejected their Messiah. As a result, God scattered the Jewish people for nearly 2,000 years. That would mean that we are on the verge of the third day when he will raise them up to live in His sight!

We will discuss Israel and God's re-gathering of Israel in another section. For now, it is important to understand that he has times and seasons for his dealings with mankind, and that we have been in the last days for nearly 2,000 years.

As we move into examining the modern nations of the Bible, remember that it is not only God's will that we understand the times, but also that we instruct many and do great exploits.

Let's Review

- Those of the people who understand shall instruct many.
- One of the greatest elements that will help give clarity to Bible prophecy is time.
- We can understand the times we are living in.
- We must conclude from Joel's prophecy that the pouring out of God's Spirit on the Day of Pentecost was the beginning of the last days.
- The end of the age, the last days, the last times, and the end times are all speaking of the same period of time.
- The last days are a period of time from the Day of Pentecost until the Second Coming of Christ.
- The prophet Hosea reveals that we are on the verge of the third day when God will raise Israel up to live in his sight.

Modern Nations of the Bible

As we study this material, there are two reactions we should avoid. One reaction is to say, "This is so simple, and therefore it cannot be true." The fact is, much of what we will learn will seem too simple, but remember that just because it seems too simple does not mean it is wrong.

The second reaction to avoid is one of fear. God allows us to know his plans and purposes. He reveals these plans and purposes through his prophets and apostles because he loves us and he desires that we be prepared to accomplish his will for our lives. However, these truths should not cause us to run out and shout that the sky is falling.

Does the Bible actually speak of nations that are alive and powerful in our generation? Do we see prophecies in the Bible concerning modern nations, systems of government, and events relevant to our times? What we will learn in this section is that it is very likely the Bible speaks of nations that exist in the world today–the 21st century! We will refer to these nations as the modern nations of the Bible.

Since we are in the time of the end, we must conclude that the prophetic seal is off; therefore we can have answers to these questions. We should also keep in mind that much of this information would not have been open to man's understanding 3 or 400 years ago. We will discover as we delve into this material that the events we examine may not have occurred—or the nation mentioned may not have existed—until the last 200 years. Again, what is one of the best elements that give illumination of prophecy? That's right—time. Now let us begin to learn about the modern nations spoken of in the Bible.

In 600 BC, while Daniel laid on his bed, he had a vision. Chapter 12 confirms to us that he had no idea what the vision meant, and that God told him to seal it up until the time of the end.

> In the first year of Belshazzar king of Babylon, Daniel had a dream and visions of his head while on his bed. Then he wrote down the dream, telling the main facts. Daniel spoke, saying "I saw in my vision by night, and behold, the four winds of heaven were stirring up the Great Sea. And the *first was like a lion, and had eagle's wings.* Four great beasts came up from the sea, each different from the other. I watched till its wings were plucked off; and it was lifted up from the earth and made to stand on two feet like a man, and a man's heart was given to it. And suddenly another beast, *a second, like a bear.* It was raised up on one side, and had three ribs in its mouth between its teeth. And they said thus to it: 'Arise, devour much flesh!' After this I looked, and there was another, *like a leopard,* which had on its back *four wings of a bird. The beast also had four heads, and dominion was given to it.* After this I saw in the night visions, and behold, *a fourth beast, dreadful and terrible, exceedingly strong.* It had huge iron teeth; it was devouring, breaking in pieces, and trampling the residue with its feet. It was different from all the beasts that were before it, and it had ten horns. I was considering the horns, and there was another horn, a little one, coming up among them,

before whom three of the first horns were plucked out by the roots. And there, in this horn, were eyes like the eyes of a man, and a mouth speaking pompous words"
DANIEL 7:1-8

In Daniel chapter 7, four beasts rise out of the Great Sea. We will focus on these four beasts in this portion of the study. However, before we discuss them we need to understand the reason God chooses to use symbolism.

Many times the study of prophecy can be somewhat confusing, and even intimidating. Within Bible prophecy we will find a lot of symbolism. Why couldn't God just say, "Here is what this kingdom is, and here is which country this represents?" we ask ourselves.

The disciples questioned Jesus about this same issue. "Why do you speak to them [the multitudes] in parables!" Jesus answered and said, "Because it's given to you to know the mysteries of the kingdom of heaven, but to them it has not been given" (Matthew 13:10-11).

The reason God uses parables and symbols are to reveal truth to those who belong to him and hear his voice while not revealing it to others. He said the same thing through Daniel: "And none of the wicked shall understand, but the wise shall understand" (see Daniel 12:10).

Note: The wicked (as the prophet Daniel says) will experience great frustration concerning prophecy. Prophetic words and parables make no sense to those who reject Jesus as their Lord and Savior. They are also of very little concern to those who do not want to know the truth and to those who are indifferent to the things of God.

What is the Great Sea we read about in Daniel? In most cases when a "Great Sea" is spoken of in the Bible it represents people, and in many cases the Gentiles. Gentile means "those outside," which speaks of unbelievers or unbelieving nations. Otherwise, when God is speaking to the Jews in the Old Testament we typically see words such as "Israel," or "My people." Therefore, in Daniel chapter 7 we are looking at four beasts rising up out of a Great Sea, which represents the Gentile people and nations.

There is also confirmation of this in Revelation 17:1 where we see the great harlot who sits on many waters. Revelation 17:15 tells us that the waters on which the harlot sits are peoples, multitudes, nations, and tongues.

What are the four beasts? Whom do they represent? We will discover that the four beasts become *five* kingdoms.

Let's look at what the Lord reveals concerning these beasts in Daniel 7:15-28:

> I, Daniel, was grieved in my spirit within my body, and the visions of my head troubled me. I came near to one of those who stood by, and asked him the truth of all this. So he told me and made known to me the interpretation of these things: "Those great beasts, which are four, *are four kings* which arise out of the earth. But the saints of the Most High shall receive the kingdom, and possess the kingdom forever, even forever and ever." Then I wished to know the truth about the fourth beast, which was different from all the others, exceedingly dreadful, with its teeth of iron and its nails of bronze, which devoured, broke in pieces, and trampled the residue with its feet; and the ten horns that were on its head, and the other horn which came up, before which three fell, namely, that horn which had eyes and a mouth which spoke pompous words, whose appearance was greater than his fellows. I was watching; *and the same horn was making war against the saints, and prevailing against them, until the Ancient of Days came and a judgment was made in favor of the saints of the Most High,* and the time came for the saints to possess the kingdom. Thus he said: "The fourth beast shall be *a fourth kingdom* on earth, which shall be different from all other *kingdoms,* and shall devour the whole earth, trample it and break it in pieces. The ten horns are ten kings who shall arise from this

kingdom. And another shall rise after them; He shall be different from the first ones, and shall subdue three kings. He shall speak pompous words against the Most High, shall persecute the saints of the Most High, and shall intend to change times and law. *Then the saints shall be given into his hand for a time and time and half a time [three-and-a-half years].* But the court shall be seated, and they shall take away his dominion, to consume and destroy it forever. Then the kingdom and dominion, and the greatness of the kingdoms under the whole heaven, shall be given to the people, the saints of the Most High. His kingdom is an everlasting kingdom, and all dominions shall serve and obey him." This is the end of the account. As for me, Daniel, my thoughts greatly troubled me, and my countenance changed; but I kept the matter in my heart.

God specifically tells Daniel that the four beasts are going to be four kingdoms that are ruling and reigning on the earth in the last days, at the coming of the Messiah. How do we know that these four kingdoms will be alive and powerful in our generation?

Simple Keys that Give Us Understanding

1. The books of Daniel and Revelation present these kingdoms as ruling forces in the last days. Four kingdoms will arise, the last one being the ten-horned beast. Concerning this beast, Daniel's vision specifically speaks of a time when these kingdoms become one kingdom under the authority of one king. After which a little horn (the Antichrist) rises out of the ten-horned beast (ten horns being ten kings that come together as one nation–the terrible beast) and plucks out three kings. (We will learn more about the Antichrist in a later section.)

Daniel speaks of a time when this government (the terrible beast) will attempt to change times and laws, and persecute the saints for time and time and half a time (3 ½ years). As we will see later, this represents the last three-and-a-half years of the last seven-year period before the Second Coming of Christ.

Daniel's vision is speaking of a time when these beasts rise to power and are clearly in existence at the coming of the Lord. At his return, God will seize the kingdoms and turn them over to his Son and the saints. This is evident in Daniel 7:27: "Then the kingdom and dominion, and the greatness of the kingdoms under the whole heaven, shall be given to the people, the saints of the Most High. His kingdom is an everlasting kingdom, and all dominions shall serve and obey him."

2. Remember the seal put on Daniel's words until the time of the end? Remember that we also saw the seal being taken off in the book of Revelation? In this book we see the fulfillment of Daniel's vision happening in the last days.

Also in Revelation (the last days) these beasts become a *unified government* and wage war against the Lord and his saints. Revelation 13:1-2 confirms that these beasts are active on the earth in the last days:

> Then I stood on the sand of the sea. And I saw a beast rising up out of the sea, having *seven heads and ten horns*, and on his horns ten crowns [crowns representing kings or authority], and on his heads a blasphemous name. Now the beast which I saw was like *a leopard*, his feet were like the feet of *a bear*, and his mouth like the mouth of *a lion*. The dragon [the devil] gave him his power, his throne, and great authority.

In Revelation chapter 13 (approximately 700 years after Daniel's vision) the apostle John sees the same beasts rise up out of a sea (Gentile nations), except now they have become one! The beast John describes has seven heads (four heads of the leopard, the head of the lion, the head of the bear, and the head of the terrible beast), and the creature had ten horns. This represents active ruling kingdoms on the earth in the last days.

In Revelation 17:12-14 we see this ten-horned beast again: "The ten horns which you saw are ten kings who have received no kingdoms as yet, but they receive authority for one hour as kings with the beast. These are of one mind, and they will give their power and authority to the beast. These will make war with the Lamb, and the Lamb will overcome them." Later in our study we will discover that the beast is the one-world government.

This also helps confirm two things:

1. The beasts that Daniel and John saw are *nations* or *governments*.

2. They are *Gentile,* or *unbelieving,* nations, which wage war against the Lamb.

In Revelation chapters 13 and 17 we see the same kings and kingdoms that Daniel spoke of coming together to form a one-world government (a unification of nations), which wages war against the Lord. The scriptures in Revelation obviously parallel what Daniel saw.

Now the question is, what governments do the beasts in Daniel represent? Understanding that these kingdoms exist in the times we live in will give us clues as to which nations they are. We will find that the answer is much simpler than we imagined.

Please note that as we study the modern nations of the Bible we are analyzing systems of government and not the masses of individuals within those systems. In short, we are not saying that those who live in the nations mentioned are evil people. We are simply examining the characteristics of nations and their systems of government as we view them in Bible prophecy.

We will also examine the actions of many government officials, and their well-publicized ideologies. World leaders, or those who live within corrupt or ungodly forms of government, have the responsibility of choosing good versus evil. World leaders must do this even if it means taking a hard stance against such government leaders.

Once again, the four beasts Daniel saw are as follows:

1. a lion with eagle's wings,
2. a bear with three ribs in its mouth,
3. a leopard with four heads and the four wings of a fowl, and
4. the great and terrible beast that has ten horns.

According to the Bible we should view these beasts as symbols of countries (kings and nations) that are ruling forces in the last days (the days in which we live). Understanding this will help tremendously in our identification of these beasts.

Now that we have identified the scriptural location and characteristics of the modern nations the Bible speaks of, let us examine them in light of modern times.

The Lion with the Eagle's Wings

One of the definitions given for the word "lion" in the third edition of Webster's New International Dictionary is "the symbol of Great Britain." Does that seem too simple? Is Great Britain a ruling force in the world today? Not only is the answer yes, but Great Britain has been a ruling force for many centuries.

As we have already seen, the Scriptures make it clear that these are symbols of ruling powers and that they exist in our present age. With this in mind it becomes easy to recognize the lion as the modern nation of Great Britain.

Something interesting happens to the lion that helps us validate which nation the lion represents and which nation the eagle's wings represent. In Daniel 7:4 we see that the eagle's wings are plucked off the lion, and it is lifted up from the earth. It stands up and becomes a man and is given the heart of a man. So now we have two nations–the lion and the eagle. The man is in conjunction with the eagle.

Many have questioned whether it is the eagle's wings that stood up like a man, or the lion. In context it was the "it" that arises from the earth and stands up like a man. Think of these nations in terms of identifiable characteristics. What we will find out is that the attributes of each animal or beast coincide with the characteristics of a country.

In other words, the modern nation that has a lion as one of its national symbols does not have a man and an eagle as one of its national symbols. What we are witnessing in Daniel chapter 7 is the formation of a separate nation, apart from the lion. Thinking of it in those terms will help alleviate any confusion about the eagle's wings being the "it."

The next question is, what country has an eagle and a man as its national symbols? That's right, the United States of America! The eagle and Uncle Sam are two of America's most recognized national symbols.

When did the eagle's wings become plucked off the lion? What major event occurred in 1776? The colonies declared independence from Great Britain. In 1776 the eagle's wings were plucked off Great Britain and the United States of America was born. In 600 BC Daniel saw the colonies breaking ties with Great Britain and forming a new nation represented by an eagle and a man.

What do we see on the Great Seal of the United States? That's right–the eagle. On the cover of *Time* magazine, October 27, 1980, an eagle was pictured to represent the United States.

What do we see in times of war? A poster saying, "Uncle Sam Wants You!" During the Vietnam War the United States sold savings bonds by way of an ad saying, "Go with the eagle–the red, white, and blue eagle. Buy United States savings bonds!"

On the cover of *U.S. News and World Report*, December 27, 1999, Uncle Sam was pictured as the "Man of the Century." On July 4, 2004, Uncle Sam appeared on the front page of the Terre Haute (Indiana) *Tribune Star* with the caption "An American Symbol—image personifies freedom, ideals on which the nation was founded." A person does not have to look far to see that we use an eagle and Uncle Sam to represent the United States of America.

Another interesting story concerning the eagle happened in 1991 as the iron curtain fell and the USSR (Union of Soviet Socialists Republics) dissolved. Directly after this dissolution it came to the attention of the United States Secretary of the Interior that thousands of Russian Jews were being persecuted under Soviet rule. Following this discovery, Wings of Eagles Ministries (supervised and backed by U.S. government funding) went into Russia and flew thousands of Jews back to their homeland.[1]

Interestingly, in the book of Revelation we see the eagle's wings only one time. In Revelation chapter 12 we see the Antichrist persecuting the "woman who gave birth to the child." The woman is Israel, and of course the child is Jesus. (We will go more in-depth concerning the woman and the child in a later section.)

Revelation 12:14 says, "And to the woman were given two wings of a great *eagle*, that she might fly into the wilderness, into her place, where she is nourished for time, and times, and half a time." In relation to this passage consider how the United States of America has consistently aided and been a friend to Israel. The great eagle mentioned might possibly represent the United States of America.

One kingdom we see in Daniel has the heart of a man, while the rest of the nations, or governments, have the attributes of an animal or a beast. The United States of America has the heart of a man. Think about how appropriate that is. America is the most compassionate nation in the world. It is the only nation which, when bombing a country, is also feeding the country at the same time.

Some may argue that the United States is not a compassionate nation because they are the ones who dropped two atomic bombs on Hiroshima and Nagasaki during World War II. There are two important points to remember when considering those events. First, we must take into consideration the number of lives saved by bringing a rapid end to the war. And, second, even

---

[1]*Jerusalem Post*, July 13, 1991.

though we bombed those cities, we must remember that we also rebuilt them better and stronger than they were before. Today, Japan not only has a democratic form of government, but it also has one of the most productive economies in the world.

Even in Germany after WW II the U.S. helped rebuild West Germany into a democratic society. America is not like any other country in the world. For the most part, who is the first country that responds with humanitarian aid when other nations experience hardship? What other country on earth gives billions of taxpayers' dollars every year to foreign aid programs? The United States of America truly has the heart of a man.

The Bear with Three Ribs in Its Mouth

In contrast to the relief and restoration of post-war countries by the United States, consider how the Russians went into East Germany after World War II and stripped the factories clean. With that in mind, whom might the bear be that the Bible speaks of in Daniel chapter seven? What country has a bear as its national symbol? Russia!

In Daniel 7:5 we see that the bear has three ribs in its mouth. Not long ago in world history, when Russia was strong and China was not, Russia decided it would take three huge provinces from China–Manchuria, Mongolia, and Xinjiang (pronounced Sinkiang). Russia stripped all three provinces from China by means of treaties, which China feels were unjust.[2] This continues to be a bone of contention between China and Russia yet today.

This passage in Daniel also says that the bear rose up on one side. Russia has fought many wars, but every major war it has won was fought on one side of the country–the West. For a period of fifty years after World War II, Russia exercised control of

---

[2]*Grolier Encyclopedia* © 1993, and *The American Heritage Dictionary of the English Language* © 1969.

many countries on its western side. Those countries include East Germany, Poland, Czechoslovakia, Hungary, Romania, Yugoslavia, Bulgaria, and Albania. Up until the modern era it has been strategically difficult for Russia to conduct any military maneuver from its less populous and more mountainous eastern side. Once it attempted to fight Japan on the east side of the country but had to retreat.

We see that a word came to this bear and it said, "Go and devour much flesh." Russia has been the springboard and the voice for the Communist Manifesto over the entire earth. Of all communist nations, it has devoured much flesh.

Like many countries, Russia has had a hand in killing many people in times of war. However, consider the fact that its leaders have also killed millions of their own people in political purges. For example, the governmental system created by Russian dictator Vladimir Lenin, and perfected by Russian dictator Joseph Stalin, eventually killed more than 60 million of its own subjects![3]

Many of the Russian czars were nothing but evil individuals who ruled with an iron fist while destroying anyone who stood in their way. We can clearly see from its characteristics that the bear spoken of by Daniel aligns itself with the modern nation of Russia.

Even the secular press speaks of Great Britain as a lion and Russia as a bear. A headline in the *Indianapolis Star*, January 4, 1980, read, "After the British Lion, the Russian Bear." On the cover of *Time* magazine, May 21, 1984, there appeared a big bear holding the Olympic rings with a headline reading: "Olympic Turmoil–Why the Soviets Said Nyet."

Many other secular news articles confirm what the Bible already says. On the cover of *USA Today*, September 9, 1988, there appeared a picture of Uncle Sam and a bear. The headline read:

---

[3] R.J. Rummel, *Death by Government* (New Brunswick, N.J.: Transaction Publishers, 1994), p. 79.

"USA/USSR–Glasnost: 'There will be more of this.'" And the cover of *The Economist Magazine*, February 6-12, 1999, is a picture of a bear with the headline, "Russia, financial outcast."

More recently a statement by U.S. Representative Steve Buyer appeared in the Terre Haute (Indiana) *Tribune Star*, December 21, 2003, which said, "The Russian Bear has been replaced by a thousand vipers."

Over and over in the secular press we see these symbols of countries that line up perfectly with Bible prophecy. Yet many Bible teachers will counter, "That is just speculation!" Is it? At what point do we have enough courage to say, "Here's what the Bible says, and here's how it lines up with world history and current world events"?

The Leopard with Four Heads and the Wings of a Fowl

We have learned that the man, the animals, and the creature found in Daniel chapter 7 all represent nations. With that in mind, what would the four heads of the leopard reveal about a nation or a government? As we will see from world history, each head represents a rise and fall of that nation.

Within the last 150 years, three great wars have been staged by the German government. The first was the Franco-Prussian War [1870-71]. This was the first "modern" war of the last two centuries, and it left Germany the most powerful industrial and commercial nation of Continental Europe.

The First World War [1914-18] was Germany's second attempt to rule the world. This is known as "The Great War." And then, of course, Germany's third attempt to rule the world came with the rise of Adolph Hitler's Third Reich, which led to World War II [1939-45]. (Note: *Reich* means "confederation of states.")

Adolph Hitler was an evil person with ungodly ideas of how to create and run a nation. He claimed that his ideas and actions were simply a fulfillment of divine providence. "I believe today that I am acting in the sense of the Almighty Creator, he stated. By warding off the Jews I am fighting for the Lord's work."[4]

Hitler's elitist Nazi ideals led to the annihilation of 6,000,000 Jews and the takeover of many countries with the primary goal of ruling the world. He promised his countrymen that if elected he would give them 1,000 years of peace.[5] It is also interesting that one of the symbols of Hitler's Third Reich was the wing of a fowl.

How does an evil government leader draw so many innocent people into believing and following their evil plans? Three of the major tactics used by Adolph Hitler were: disarming citizens, control of the media, and brainwashing the youth.

Concerning citizens owning guns Hitler said, "The most foolish mistake we could possibly make would be to allow the subject races to possess arms. History shows that all conquerors who have allowed their subject races to carry arms have prepared their own downfall by so doing."[6]

Concerning the media, in the spring of 1933 Hitler outlawed freethinking groups, and with his Enabling Act took control of all the German media.[7] He recognized that tolerance of freethinking and freedom of the press would not afford him the control that he needed.

Of course, that would never happen in America! After all, the mainstream press in America is free to express any ideas it desires…right? A statement by John Swinton, an editor for the *New York Times* [1860-70], might possibly cause us to think otherwise. He is quoted as follows:

---

[4]Excerpt from a speech by Adolph Hitler, Reichstag, 1936. Also found in *Mein Kampf*, by Adolph Hitler, p. 84.

[5]*The Decline and Fall of the Roman Church*, by Malachi Martin, p. 101.

[6]Article by Stephen P. Halbrook, "Nazi Firearms Law and the Disarming of the German Jews," *Arizona Journal of International and Comparative Law*, vol. 17 no. 3 (2000), p. 483.

[7]*New York Times*, May 14, 1993, p. 2.

There is no such thing, at this date of the world's history, in America, as an independent press. You know it and I know it. There is not one of you who dares *to write your honest opinions,* and if you did, you know beforehand that it would never appear in print. I am paid weekly for keeping my honest opinion out of the paper I am connected with. Others of you are paid similar weekly salaries for similar things, and any of you who would be so foolish as to write honest opinions would be out on the streets looking for another job. If I allowed my honest opinions to appear in one issue of my paper, before twenty-four hours my occupation would be gone. The business of the journalists is to destroy the truth; to lie outright; to pervert; to vilify; *to fawn at the feet of mammon,* and to sell his country and his race for his daily bread. You know it and I know it, and what folly is this toasting an independent press? We are the tools and vassals of rich men behind the scenes. We are the jumping jacks, they pull the strings and we dance. Our talents, our possibilities, and our lives are all the property of other men. *We are intellectual prostitutes* [8] (emphasis added).

Concerning the youth, on November 6, 1933, Hitler said, "When an opponent declares, 'I will not come over to your side,' I calmly say: Your child belongs to us already. What are you? You will pass on. Your descendants, however, now stand in this new camp. In a short time they will know nothing else but this new community."[9] As we will clearly see, these are some of the same tactics that the one-world government will use to exercise control on a global scale.

---

[8]*Labor's Untold Story,* by Richard O. Boyer and Herbert M. Morais, (published by United Electrical, Radio & Machine Workers of America, NY, 1955/1979).
[9]*The Rise and Fall of the Third Reich: A History of Nazi Germany,* by William L. Shirer (New York: Crest Books, 1961).

Even though Hitler tried to take over the world, God proved once again that He is in control. An excellent example of this is a notable World War II battle. During this time the Germans developed a military tactic called "blitzkrieg" (or "lightning war"). Lightning war is an accurate description of how Adolph Hitler advanced his war machines across Europe. He advanced so quickly through France that the Allies were within three days of losing the war in Europe. Germany was virtually within days of becoming a dominant world power, and it would have undoubtedly continued to pursue world dominion.

As Hitler blitzkrieged through France, he had over 338,000 Allied soldiers backed up against the English Channel. The speed and destructiveness of his lightning war could have easily pushed the Allies into the English Channel and destroyed any chance at preserving France and mounting an offensive attack against the Nazis.

However, on the brink of victory, Hitler feared that he was falling into a trap because it was all happening too easily. Just as the Nazis were about to destroy the Allied army, he halted the operation and immediately called all of his military generals off the field for a conference. By the time he got his war machine rolling again, the trapped soldiers—all but 40,000 of them—escaped into England to fight another day. This event is called the Miracle of Dunkirk.[10]

Hitler's Third Reich certainly falls in line with Bible prophecy. Even though he desired to rule the world, God said, "Not yet." An old saying tells us "History is *His-story.*" God is in control of times and seasons!

---

[10]*Operation Dynamo: The Achievement of Dunkirk*, The History Net, World Wide Web, and *The Rise and Fall of the Third Reich: A History of Nazi Germany*, by William L. Shirer (New York: Crest Books, 1961).

History reveals that the nation of Germany aligns itself with three heads of the leopard, but what about the fourth head? Does the fact that we see a fourth head indicate that this leopard will rise to power again?

In 1980 Edwin Hartrich published a book called *The Fourth and Richest Reich*, which is all about the modern nation of Germany. The subtitle was "How the Germans Conquered the Postwar World." It would appear as though Germany is being set up to be part of another evil work as a major player in the one-world government.

In Daniel chapter 7 it says, "Great dominion was given to the leopard." Dominion is a driving force to conquer. Germany, and its leaders of the past, has certainly exhibited a driving force to conquer.

An article in *Newsweek*, April 9, 1984, read, "Since the time of Charlemagne, the area that is known as Germany has been the pivot of European history. In the last 120 years the Germans have dominated Europe intellectually, industrially, and militarily." Essentially, that article is saying, "They have got dominion."

What other indications do we have that the four-headed leopard is Germany? The United States has something called Eagle Fighters that are the backbone of U.S. military air superiority.[11] Not long ago Germany began to produce what came to be the number one selling tank in the world. The North Atlantic Treaty Organization (NATO) began using the tanks that Germany produced. Ironically, Germany's number one selling tank is the *Leopard Tank*.

An article about this tank entitled "Great future for the Leopard?" ran in the *German Tribune*, February 20, 1975. This is just another example of how the leopard represents Germany.

---

[11]USAF Fact Sheet, F-15 Eagle, and Encyclopedia of Aviation Scribner's, p. 63.

For many years the world community has not allowed Germany to have a military for the sole fact that they seem to have an itchy trigger finger. Germany has tried to take over the world three times in the last 150 years. Soon it will happen again, along with several other nations.

God will allow a one-world government to rule for a short time in the near future, but as we will see it is simply a fulfillment of prophecy. We can easily see how the leopard with the four heads and the wings of a fowl aligns itself with Germany's First, Second, Third, and soon coming Fourth Reich.

The Ten-horned Beast

Daniel had never seen anything like this beast. It had ten horns on its head, teeth of iron, eyes like a man, and spoke great swelling words against God and against his throne. Scripture says that a little horn rose up in the midst of the horns and took out three of them. Daniel describes the beast as having claws of brass, and everything the beast touches is dashed into pieces.

We know that this represents a kingdom, or government, in modern times. This government is very different from all the others mentioned. This beast does not look like, or even resemble, an animal or a man. It is described as a terrible, dreadful beast. There are a couple of possibilities concerning this government. Admittedly, this brings us to a bit of speculation.

1. Some have speculated that it is the Arab Emirates, which is a conglomeration of Arab states. However, as we will see later, the Antichrist rises out of a revived Roman Empire. In other words, the Antichrist (the little horn) rises to power in Europe. With that in mind, this first choice is not really feasible.

2. Is it possible for Russia to be the bear, and still be part of the terrible beast? This is a possibility. If Russia reunited and formed the original USSR, it would be ten states (ten horns) with enormous military power.

Regardless of whether or not Russia is the terrible beast, we do know that it will play a big part in the one-world government. We will see in another section that Russia (the former Soviet Union) and its socialistic ideas have already played a defining role in the formation of the one-world government.

3. Another possibility, and truthfully a much more likely candidate for the terrible beast, is the European Union (EU). The EU is the uniting of several independent European countries into a smaller version of the United States. In 1957 a treaty was signed–the Treaty of Rome. This was the beginning of the EU and a revived Roman Empire.

Concerning the EU, one man said, "For centuries people have been trying to build one Europe. Napoleon tried to build a Europe, through force. Hitler tried it through force. Now it is up to us–and we are doing it this time by our own choice. If we can build a single Europe, *there will not be war anymore*. At least I hope so"[12] (emphasis added).

When we examine what the Bible has to say concerning the Antichrist, we find that he arises from a revived Roman Empire. In light of that, it is fascinating what we find on the first coin ever made for the EU. The first minted coin is the European Currency Unit (ECU) portraying King Charlemagne, the first king of the Holy Roman Empire. As we examine the EU we see that it is very possible that prophecy is being fulfilled right before our eyes. (We will delve into various aspects of the Roman Empire in another section.)

The EU began with six countries. It was not long before it was a collection of nine countries. On January 1, 1981, the nation of Greece acquired full membership, bringing the total number of countries in the EU to ten, upon which everybody said, "That is it! That is the ten-horned beast!" But that theory seemed to self-destruct when the EU grew to twelve countries, and then later to fifteen.

---

[12]Article, "The New Europe," *National Geographic*, January 2002.

Daniel 7:24 says, "And another [horn] shall rise after them; he shall be different from the first ones, and shall subdue three kings." The beast spoken of in Daniel has ten horns and a little horn that grows out of the ten. Who is the little horn? It is the Antichrist, the leader of the one-world government that persecutes Israel and the saints. The Antichrist rises from the midst of a ten-nation union, then somehow he overthrows three nations (politically or militarily), and the remaining nations arise as one government.

Recently a full-page advertisement in *Time* magazine showed the euro, while stating, "It's our money!" The ad went on to say, "On the first of January 400,000,000 Europeans in twelve countries will wake up to a new currency–the euro."

Wait a minute–twelve countries? As of 2002 there were fifteen countries in the EU. However, as of January 1, 1999, only twelve countries had taken the currency. These are the same twelve countries represented on the EU flag by twelve stars, which the EU says represents "solidarity, harmony, and is the traditional number of perfection."[13] The EU's governing body has stated that even though the number of member states may change, the flag will remain the same.

With that in mind, here is an equation to consider: 12 - 3 (three original EU nations plucked out) = 9 + 1 (the little horn) = 10. That could be it! A little horn rises up, it takes out three founding countries, and then the little horn (the Antichrist) becomes the tenth horn spoken of in Revelation 13:1.

We can come up with many different equations, but we must recognize that right now this is only speculation. Currently there is talk of at least ten more nations joining the EU in 2004-2005. Time will allow us the insight as to whether the EU is the ten-horned beast. Concerning the EU, however, it is obvious that it

---

[13]Europa—The EU at a glance—The symbols of the European Union, World Wide Web.

is quickly becoming a world superpower, and that there is a revived Roman Empire spoken of in prophecy. These are two characteristics of the EU that make us turn our attention toward them in light of Bible prophecy.

The euro is now the common form of currency for the EU. For many decades the U.S. dollar has been the staple currency all over the world. In the early 1920s European investors sunk an enormous amount of money into the American financial market in the hopes that they could gain substantial returns off the American dollar, and control America's banking system. Then, overnight, they pulled all their money out of the market, which aided in the collapse of the American market. This set off what history has dubbed the Great Depression.[14]

In 1933 Congressman Louis T. McFadden also blamed the Great Depression on European investors who controlled the U.S. Federal Reserve. McFadden said, "On account of it, *we ourselves are in the midst of the greatest depression we have ever known. From the Atlantic to the Pacific, our country has been ravaged and laid waste by the evil practices of the Fed [Federal Reserve] and the interests, which control them.* At no time in our history, has the general welfare of the people been at a lower level or the minds of the people so full of despair"[15] (emphasis added). (See more about the Federal Reserve Act in Part III, Section II.)

With great strength of character, America survived the Great Depression. However, repercussions in Europe resulted in the weakening of the franc, the deutsche mark, and all the other European currencies. Germany has had a difficult time generating strength in its own currency due to the wars it has engaged in during the last two centuries. Its indiscretions have caused

---

[14]Article, *The Federal Reserve is a Privately Owned Corporation*, by Thomas D. Schauf.
[15]1978 Arizona Caucus Club.

what amounts to a roller coaster ride of strength and power, then destruction and recovery. Without a doubt these cycles will play havoc with a country's economy.

Today, however, things have changed drastically in France, Germany, and in Europe. The EU is a coalition of countries in which a person can travel freely from country to country. Not only that, but if a person lives in Germany, he can vote in France. For nearly a millennium this type of union in Europe has been non-existent! Once again, it is possible that what we are witnessing is a revived Roman Empire (the heartbeat of a global government) coming together under the guise of the EU.

Much change might occur in the EU in the next decade. At the same time, we see the EU quickly becoming a world superpower. The British historian, Norman Davies, said, "If you are Germany, or France, or the UK, you can't help looking at the American economy and thinking, that's a rather big elephant over there. But if your individual country becomes part of a unified European economy, then you think, goodness—*we could be even bigger*"[16] (emphasis added).

Once again, teaching that the EU is the ten-horned beast is speculation. We must be careful that we do not simply make these horns fit what we believe. We must desire to teach accurately from Scripture. Even though the EU is possibly the ten-horned beast, for the moment we should "put it on the shelf" just as the Lord instructed Daniel to do. We will know more as the EU develops and more unfolds in the natural realm.

In this section we have learned that Daniel saw the beasts as *separate* nations while the apostle John saw them as *unified* nations. We have also learned that the four beasts (which became five nations) make up the dominant superpowers in *the end* of the last days, and that the characteristics of these beasts match those of nations existing in the 21st century.

---

[16]ibid. *National Geographic*, January 2002.

It all comes together in the end of the last days. A one-world government is rising and will soon attempt to rule the earth. Later on we will examine what happens to these superpowers at the return of Christ. We are getting close to the time of his coming. As Christians we must stay alert and recognize prophecy that is being fulfilled right in front of our eyes!

Let's Review

- The beasts Daniel spoke of were kings and kingdoms (nations).
- The nations Daniel saw as separate beasts came together as a unified government in the book of Revelation. Therefore, these are modern-day nations.
- The beast in Revelation rose up out of a sea (Gentile nations).
- Today we see that Great Britain is represented by a lion.
- Today we see that the U.S. is represented by an eagle and a man.
- Today we see that Germany is represented by a leopard.
- Today we see that Russia is represented by a bear.
- The ten-horned beast might possibly be the European Union (a revived Roman Empire).
- At his return, Jesus will subdue all nations and rule the earth.

One-World Government

In Scripture it is clear that God desires to loose understanding in these times. We know that the Gospels are important because they tell us of the work Jesus accomplished. We know that the Epistles are important because they give instruction and understanding to New Testament Christians. Yet, many times we leave the book of Revelation out of our teachings and discussions because it is a mysterious book. However, God has told us not to seal the book up because "the time is at hand."

We have also learned from Scripture what the end times are. We have discovered that the Bible speaks about modern-day nations. We have looked at Daniel the seventh chapter where we saw four beasts:

1. the lion with the eagle's wings,
2. the bear with three ribs in its mouth,
3. the leopard with four heads, and the wings of a fowl, and
4. the ten-horned beast with a little horn rising up in its midst.

We learned that each one of these creatures represented kings and kingdoms. Today we call them nations. We have observed through world history, and even the secular press, that the lion is a symbol of Great Britain. We saw how the characteristics of the eagle's wings and the man exemplify the United States of America. We have examined how the characteristics of the bear align itself with Russia, and that the four-headed leopard could very easily be Germany. We also recognize the possibility of the ten-horned beast representing the European Union.

What is the New World Order?

It is important to recognize that a person can get into a ditch with any teaching. Even though we can easily discern in Scripture that a one-world government will arise to power, there are a couple of ditches we need to avoid.

One ditch is the conspiracy theory ditch. This speaks of those who believe everyone in government is evil and that they are all conspiring to take away our freedoms. This is simply not true.

The ditch on the other side of the road consists of those who think the idea of a global government is ridiculous and will never happen. Unfortunately, many Americans take this stance. Americans often never recognize, or pay any attention to, a sign of trouble until trouble is in their back yard. This is a result of America's self-centered culture. Our goal in this section is to present a balanced biblical and historic view of the one-world government.

Let us begin in our pocketbook. On the back of the U.S. dollar bill we find the Latin phrase *novus ordo seclorum* underneath a picture of the Great Pyramid and the Great Pyramid has an "all-seeing eye" above it. *Novus* means "new," *ordo* means "order," and *seclorum* means "secular." Thus, the literal translation of *novus ordo seclorum* is "the new order of the world [Ages]." In English it is better translated "New World Order." Why would the U.S. dollar bill have "New World Order" on it along with a pyramid (a non-American symbol) with the "all-seeing eye" (an occult symbol) above the pyramid?

Interestingly, the Great Pyramid is the only pyramid in Egypt without a capstone, or cornerstone, at the top. In the year 2000 a very odd gathering of people was to take place at the Great Pyramid. The gathering was to be a collection of several world leaders. These leaders included former President George H.W. Bush (who used the term New World Order over 200 times in the last two years of his presidency), Mikhail Gorbachev, Pope John Paul II, Oprah Winfrey, and other celebrities.

Their plan was to meet on New Years Eve of 2000 and place a two-story tall capstone (intended to catch the first rays of the New Year's sun) on the Great Pyramid. In capping it, they would proclaim that the New World Order that they had worked so hard to achieve was now complete.

Unfortunately for them, the Egyptian government halted their plans to place this capstone. "Pyramid capping," charged critics who cited the back of the U.S. dollar bill, "is a 'Masonic' ritual. Since Freemasonry is just a front for international Zionism," they claimed, "the year began capless in Giza."[17]

The phrase translated as "New World Order" has been on the back of the U.S. dollar bill since the days of Franklin D. Roosevelt in the early 1930s. What is the New World Order? It is a term used to describe the uniting of the world's superpowers to secure and maintain "global peace," or another way of saying one-world government. We are quickly heading toward that government.

Attempts to Institute a One-World Government

A global government is not a new idea. We can see the first attempt at a one-world government in Genesis chapter 11. Here Nimrod tried to build a tower (the tower of Babel) and unite all the people of the earth. However, God intervened and confused the languages.

---

[17]"Artifact: Pyramid Schemes," by Charles Paul Freund, *Reason*, March 2000.

Why did God intervene? Because it was not time for a world government, and because Nimrod had led the people of the world into pagan worship. (We will see later how the coming one-world government will also lead people into pagan worship.) Once again we see that God is in control of times and seasons.

There have been several attempts to create a one-world government since the tower of Babel, but God has brought them to an end. He has a time and season for everything under heaven. Ironically, one of the posters for the EU has a picture of the tower of Babel. In the background a caption reads, "Many tongues... One voice."

God will allow the coming one-world government to flourish for a short period of time, and then it will be destroyed. The only global government that will flourish is the one that Jesus will establish and rule for 1,000 years!

President Woodrow Wilson initiated a more recent attempt at a one-world government. He made this attempt after World War I, and called it the League of Nations. Fortunately, the League never acquired any substantial power, largely due to the fact that America elected not to participate. The Republicans in the U.S. Congress squelched America's involvement and insisted that we remain a sovereign nation.

As we have already learned in Daniel (approximately 700 years before John had a vision of the Revelation of Christ) we see the same beasts (nations), but they are all separate beasts. What is fascinating is that Daniel saw the beasts as being separate nations, but in John's Revelation we see a clearer, more advanced picture of what is happening.

Revelation 13:1-2 tells us:

> And I stood upon the sand of the sea, and saw a beast rise up out of the sea, having *seven heads and ten horns,* and upon his heads the name of blasphemy. And the beast which I saw was like unto *a leopard,* and his feet were as the feet of *a bear,* and his mouth as the mouth of *a lion:* and the dragon gave him his power, and his seat, and great authority.

In John's prophecy these nations come together to form one beast (a one-world government). The picture we have in the book of Revelation is a unification of nations. Today we call it the *United Nations* (UN). Yes, it is prophesied in the Bible!

It is interesting that we do not see the eagle's wings as part of the world government in Revelation 13:1-2. We see the eagle's wings only once in the book of Revelation. We do not see the eagle's wings on the beast (one-world government). Therefore, we would have to conclude that the nation represented by the eagle's wings does not elect to participate in the one-world government during the Great Tribulation.

In Revelation 13:1-2 we see that the mouth of the beast is the lion. What nation does a lion represent? Great Britain! Is it possible that the Bible even reveals the common language for the one-world government? Listed on the UN's website are six official international languages. Listed first is English! Is it any coincidence that the accepted international language is English? It appears that the beast will speak a common language, and that language is English.

The UN claims that they are not a world government. They say that they are simply a coalition of governments. However, when we examine the charter for the UN, it becomes clear that they are a socialistic form of government.

They claim that they do not have free rein and power over nations. In the past, that may have been a half-truth, but in the last thirty years they have begun to exercise great power over nations through economic sanctions. These sanctions serve the purpose of putting the squeeze on a nation's pocketbook through trade limitations or tariffs. The UN has used this tool many times in the past several decades to whip countries into shape. (We will discuss this tactic more in a later section.)

While it is true that many of the UN's member nations are trying to do the right thing, the fact is they are moving themselves right in line with a global government.

History of the United Nations

We can learn a lot about the United Nations by examining their development. Up until the turn of the century the most casualties in any war were no more than 1,000,000. In the First World War, however, more than 8,000,000 died–eight times more than any other war! World War I cost approximately 186 billion dollars! This shocked the world community! Nations came together and said, "We've got to do something about this! This can never happen again!"

After World War I, President Woodrow Wilson met with several other world leaders to launch the League of Nations. It was Wilson [1913] who said, "Some of the biggest men in the U.S., in the field of commerce and manufacturing, are afraid of somebody, are afraid of something. They know that there is a power somewhere so organized, so subtle, so watchful, so interlocked, so complete, so pervasive, *that they better not speak above their breath when they speak in condemnation of it*"[18] (emphasis added).

What Wilson referred to is also found in 2 Thessalonians 2:7, and it is called the "mystery of iniquity," or sins in secret. As we will see, there is a globalist agenda in the world right now that is setting the stage for the one-world government and the Antichrist.

The future of the League of Nations was in the hands of the United States. Once again, the proposal for the League did not sit favorably with the Republicans in the U.S. Congress. Members stood on something that George Washington told this nation: Never get together with other nations and give up national sovereignty. Never put our ability to think for ourselves in the hands of someone else. Without American support, the League of Nations fell apart.

---

[18]*The New American*, "They Dared Call it Conspiracy," 1997.

Many of the nations who desired the League of Nations blamed the U.S. for what happened in World War II. They said that if America had followed through with the League, Adolph Hitler could not have committed such horrible atrocities. His war machine ran through Europe and the Soviet Union with unimaginable brutality. In World War II 61,000,000 people died! The estimated cost of the war was over 1 trillion dollars. The world community stood up once more and said, "We cannot allow this to happen again!"

After the Second World War, President Franklin D. Roosevelt, Joseph Stalin (the Soviet dictator), Winston Churchill (England's prime minister), and several other world leaders met together and proposed the United Nations (UN).

There were many problems within the proposal for the UN that needed resolved. One enormous problem was that America did not want to relinquish its sovereignty. In order to preserve national sovereignty, the framers of the UN charter allowed the five most powerful post-war nations to have veto power in the UN Security Council. This arrangement created somewhat of a democracy.

Note: The permanent members of the UN Security Council are: The Republic of China, France, Russia, the United Kingdom of Great Britain and Northern Ireland, and the United States of America.[19]

The idea was that whenever a nation felt like going to war, they would take their disagreement to the UN which would vote on it. That idea sounds good; however, many of those in the U.S. Congress recognized that even though the UN had the appearance of democracy, the majority of its member nations had

---

[19]United Nations Charter, Chapter V, Article 23 (1).

socialist or communist dictators. As we will see, socialistic leaders have no problem with the idea that the majority rules–as long as they are the majority.

In February of 1945 the leaders of the big three (U.S., Soviet Union, and Great Britain) met at Yalta in the Ukraine. One of the issues addressed at this conference was what to do with all the post-war property that Germany acquired. Who gets what part of Germany? For many post-World War II nations this was like Christmas time.

At Yalta an individual named Alger Hiss was a member of the U.S. delegation. During the negotiations, Hiss gave the Soviet Union a vast amount of post-war property. It turned out that what the Soviet Union could not take in war they took through post-war peace negotiations. Subsequently, Hiss walked away from the negotiations a hero in the eyes of the other nations.

On April 12, 1945, President Roosevelt died and Harry Truman entered the White House. That same month, at the age of 40, Hiss became the director of the Office of Political Affairs. In addition to dividing post-war property at the Yalta Conference, delegates also announced a "conference of United Nations" which convened in San Francisco in April of 1945. Shortly after the Yalta conference, Hiss accepted an appointment as the first secretary-general (pro-tem) of the United Nations. He became the first leader of the UN and even co-authored its charter.

After the conference Hiss flew the charter to Washington in a special military airplane for Truman's signature.[20] When Hiss designed the symbol for the UN, he used the same design as the Soviet Union's national symbol–minus the hammer and sickle. (Using the hammer and sickle would have been too obvious.) History, as well as the UN charter itself, reveals that the UN is the brainchild of socialists.

---

[20]Alger Hiss Timeline, The History Net, World Wide Web.

After the smoke cleared and the dust settled, many members of the U.S. Congress began to examine Hiss' post-war negotiations. They asked, "How did the Soviet Union end up with so much post-war property?" An investigation ensued, and three years later officials seized Hiss for being a communist spy. This was mainly due to the testimony of Whittaker Chambers who was an editor of *Time* magazine [1948]. Chambers had been a Soviet agent and testified that he had received State Department documents from Hiss to give to the Soviets [Russians].[21]

Hiss served five years in prison, all the time denying that he was a spy. After Yalta, and after Hiss went to prison, the Soviet Union gobbled up a huge portion of Europe. America said, "You better stop it!" This was the beginning of the Cold War between the Soviet Union and her allies, and the United States and her allies. The Cold War was a political war with a strong emphasis on espionage and the constant threat of nuclear annihilation.

Within the UN the Cold War produced a stalemate between the Soviet Union and the United States. This was due to the fact that both countries had veto power. Everything the Americans wanted to do, the Soviets would veto. Everything the Soviets wanted to do, the Americans would veto. Subsequently, the UN became a lame duck from 1961-1989.

Reform began in the late 1980s. With the Reagan Administration in the 1980s came compromise on both sides, and not for the good. President Ronald Reagan began negotiations with an individual named Mikhail Gorbachev (the president of Russia) at the same time he was building up U.S. defenses.

The Deadly Wound

And I saw one of his heads as it were wounded to death; and his deadly wound was healed: and all the world wondered after the beast (Revelation 13:3).

---

[21]ibid. *Grolier's Encyclopedia*

In the above verse we see that the deadly wound has to do with the beast, which we have learned is a union of nations. In view of that, this passage is telling us that one of the nations mentioned receives a wound unto death. The Bible reveals that the deadly wound receives healing and the world "wondered after the beast." The question is, which nation receives the wound unto death?

To answer that question let us go back to a period of time directly after World War II. We have learned that Germany instigated the last three great wars. We have also learned how Germany could easily be the leopard with four heads and the wings of a fowl; the four heads representing Germany's first, second, third, and currently fourth rise to power.

After World War II, the world community said Germany could not continue this quest for world domination, therefore they would have to put them underfoot. Why does Germany have this taste for world domination? What does it say in Daniel chapter 7 concerning the leopard? That the leopard has a taste for dominion and a desire to conquer.

Following World War II the newspapers declared, "Germany is dead!" Then, the Russians built a twenty-nine mile wall in order to divide Germany. The "Berlin Wall" separated the Eastern (under Russian control) from the Western portion of Germany (controlled by the post-war Democratic Allies).

In 1968 *Life* magazine ran an article entitled, "Three and a Half Superpowers to Rule the World." In this article, U.S. Undersecretary of State George W. Ball said concerning the Berlin Wall: "This division that festers like a rusty knife wound must someday be healed."

In *USA Today*, August 14, 1986, an article appeared entitled "The Twenty-Nine Mile Wound That Just Won't Heal." This article was speaking of the Berlin Wall.

President Reagan believed and preached that the Russians must tear down the wall. He and Gorbachev both preached world peace and putting an end to the Cold War. Ending this war would become Reagan's biggest legacy.

At the same time, Gorbachev denounced Reagan's preaching of world peace because of Reagan's Star Wars program (a satellite weapons system). Reagan found Gorbachev's weak spot and said, "If you are for world peace, why do you keep your people behind a twenty-nine mile wall?" He challenged Gorbachev by saying, "If you are truly for peace, tear down the wall."

To the world's amazement, Gorbachev responded by tearing down the Berlin Wall on November 9, 1989. On November 20, 1989, an article in *Time* magazine said, "The wall of shame 1961-1989, it was the palpable evidence of a deep wound in European civilization and it is finally healed." Article after article calls the Berlin Wall a wound. In 1989, the wall came down, the deadly wound was healed, and the world marveled!

Within a month after the Berlin Wall had come down, President George H.W. Bush, Mikhail Gorbachev, and Pope John Paul II had a meeting. After their meeting they all came out proclaiming the same thing–this is the beginning of the New World Order.

In the *Indianapolis Star*, September 29, 1991, U.S. Secretary of Defense Dick Cheney said, "The world is in a new era of promise that started two years ago with the collapse of the Berlin Wall." The healing of the deadly wound is like a giant prophetic road sign on the highway to the one-world government!

The United Nations has all the components of a world government.

The UN has an appointed leader called a secretary-general, along with its own Parliament (the General Assembly), an Executive Committee, and a judicial system (the World Court and the International Criminal Court). The UN's judicial system not only has the authority to try individuals, but it also has the power to bring entire nations to trial!

The UN has a global army, also called a "peacekeeping" force. Within the UN we also find the World Health Organization (WHO), the World Trade Organization (WTO), and the World

Bank. The UN also has the United Religions as an arm of their organization. All of this is under the guise of uniting the world for peace!

The United Nations has also proposed a global tax!

The United States of America provides 30 percent of the UN's operational budget. One of the biggest roadblocks for the UN has been that if the U.S. does not like something the UN is doing, the U.S. simply withholds their dues. This political tactic has always presented huge problems. To solve these problems, the UN is examining the possibility of a global tax (the Tobin Tax) in order to fund the organization.

The proposed global tax is only five tenths of one percent of any international transaction. We might think that does not affect most of us, but it is tacked on to whatever we buy from organizations or corporations that do international business (i.e., WalMart, McDonalds, Disney). When the Tobin Tax is in place, the UN's budget will go from 10 billion to 1.5 trillion![22] This influx of funds will propel the UN into a whole new arena of power and independence!

In addition to the proposal of a global tax, as far back as 1972 there have been proposals of a global lottery. The Ministry of Foreign Affairs of Finland is financing research on the concept of a global lotto. In 2001 Martti Ahtisaari, former president of Finland said, "The UN desperately needs financial independence. The steps to launch systems like the Tobin Tax, even if they became operational, might be too long to wait for. I have been thinking about a world lottery, which would partially facilitate the financing of UN activities."[23]

---

[22] The Human Development Report, 1994; and The JBS Bulletin #516, May 2002.

[23] "The Global Lottery," Office of President Ahrisaari, World Wide Web.

For many years the UN operated on donations given by all the countries that are members of their organization. It is likely that they are about to increase their annual budget 150 times compared to what they have had previously. Think of what a global government could do with that kind of budget!

National sovereignty will become a major concern as the financial strength of the UN skyrockets to new levels. In the meantime, the UN has criticized the U.S. because it had withheld funds (nearly 1 billion dollars) payable upon agreement concerning what Senator Jesse Helms called "common sense reforms." Many of these reforms have to do with the issue of national sovereignty.

On January 20, 2000, Senator Jesse Helms (chairman of the U.S. Senate Committee on Foreign Relations) spoke to the UN Security Council. In his speech Senator Helms reminded the UN that the previous year [1999] the U.S. taxpayers contributed 10 billion dollars to support its work, making the point that the U.S. is not a deadbeat nation.

In the conclusion of his speech, Senator Helms said, "If the United Nations respects the sovereign rights of the American people, and serves them as an effective tool of diplomacy, it will earn and deserve their respect and support. But a United Nations that seeks to impose its presumed authority on the American people without their consent begs for confrontation and, I want to be candid, eventual U.S. withdrawal."

The world's language and focus are changing in order to accommodate a world government.

Even the U.S. military is being molded and shaped by global ideologies. James J. Schneider, professor of military theory at U.S. Command and General Staff College, Fort Leavenworth, said, "As an Army we are fortunate to have...a rich web of historical tradition. But our experience is of little use if it cannot be interpreted in light of future operations...[T]he future will be dominated by a single overwhelming presence–the United Nations."[24]

U.S. military personnel are waking up to the fact that they are no longer just U.S. soldiers. In the 21st century our U.S. military personnel will have to be UN soldiers when called upon. In 1996, U.S. soldier Michael G. New was stationed overseas as part of a UN peacekeeping force. A UN commander handed New a blue UN helmet, and Michael told him that he did not agree with what the UN stood for, therefore he would not wear their helmet.

New understood something of which many Americans are not aware. In fine print, it requires UN peacekeeping soldiers to fire upon their own countrymen if so ordered. New told the UN commanders that he was not a UN soldier, but rather an American soldier sworn to uphold the Constitution of the United States of America. As a result of refusing to wear the UN helmet the U.S. military gave Michael New a dishonorable discharge!

Michael New said, "If they kick me out of the Army, if they send me to jail, I want to know, in my mind, after all this is over, I did what I thought was right in the eyes of God."[25] Since then, other U.S. military personnel have taken a similar stand.

The UN keeping world peace sounds wonderful. However, the whole idea raises many serious questions. What happens if an Adolph Hitler gains control of the world government and the global military? What happens if the UN passes laws, as they have in parts of Europe, that if you try to convert anybody to Christianity you will receive a fine or be put in jail? What happens if they make a law saying that a person must have a security mark in order to buy or sell?

---

[24]James J. Schneider, "Ambushing the Future," *Special Warfare*, April 1995, p. 4.
[25]*The New American*, [Article] by William Norman Grigg.

Global Education

The UN is also interested in global education. There are schools in the world now pledging allegiance to the UN. For Americans, that would be a direct assault on the sovereignty of the United States of America.

Two of the UN's principle organizations that deal with issues concerning children are UNICEF (United Nations Children's Fund) and UNESCO (United Nations Educational, Scientific and Cultural Organization).

The motto of UNICEF is "Every Child Is Our Child." Just as Hitler realized, in order for a dictatorship to be successful it must grab hold of the minds of its youth. One example of this is the ten-part series of booklets published by UNESCO called "Towards World Understanding." In UNESCO's very first booklet there is great emphasis on "development in the pupils of an attitude favorable to international understanding, which will make them...ready to accept the obligations which an interdependent world *imposes.*"[26]

Why is it that many Christians do not recognize that we are on the brink of a unified one-world government? How can we possibly miss the fact that a one-world government is being set up right under our noses? It is not even being hidden anymore. It is talked about so openly that we even see it on the covers of *USA Today* and *Time* magazine. Today there is no reason to hide it because most people are indifferent.

Goals of the United Nations

In 1961 John F. Kennedy drafted a government document called *Freedom from War–The United States Program for General and Complete Disarmament in a Peaceful World.* The introduc-

---

[26][Article] Children of the State by Steve Bonta, October 22, 2001

tion of the document reads: "In order to overcome the danger of nuclear war now confronting mankind, the United States has introduced at the Sixteenth General Assembly of the United Nations a Program for General and Complete Disarmament in a Peaceful World."

Three phases are proposed:

- Phase one is "immediate disarmament action."
- Phase two is "all disarmament obligations must be subject to effective international controls."
- Phase three is "adequate peacekeeping machinery must be established."

Within phase three the document states: "This can only be achieved through the progressive strengthening of the international institutions under the United Nations and by creating a United Nations Peace Force to enforce the peace as the disarmament process proceeds." In other words, the UN will be sure to try to confiscate our weapons.

Note: In 1787 Noah Webster (author and statesman) said, "Before a standing army can rule, the people must be disarmed, as they are in almost every kingdom in Europe. The supreme power in America cannot enforce unjust laws by the sword, because the whole body of the people are armed, and constitute a force superior to any band of regular troops that can be, on any pretense, raised in the United States."

The Freedom from War document was written in 1961; thus is not an idea that has just recently surfaced. If we look at the strength and progress of the UN, we clearly see that we are in phase three of the proposed plan!

Not long after the Freedom from War report came *A World Effectively Controlled by the United Nations* [1962]. MIT Professor Lincoln P. Bloomfield wrote this document under contract (No. SCC 28270) with the U.S. State Department. This government-financed study was not intended for public review, and was amazingly candid. In the report Professor Bloomfield explained that the proposed global regime "will occasionally be referred to unblushingly as a 'world government,'" and that the notion of world government is "the basis in recent American policy."

Is the UN's agenda today the same as it was when JFK and Professor Bloomfield wrote those very revealing documents? At the turn of the millennium, UN Secretary-General Kofi Annan submitted a report entitled *Road map towards the implementation of the United Nations Millennium Declaration*. As of 2002, 189 countries in the UN had adopted the Millennium Declaration. Interestingly, the UN no longer refers to its members as "member nations," but rather "member states."

Within the Millennium Declaration are nine different sections:
I. Introduction
II. Peace, Security, and Disarmament
III. Development and Poverty Eradication
IV. Protecting Our Common Environment
V. Human Rights, Democracy and Good Governance
VI. Protecting the Vulnerable
VII. Meeting the Needs of Africa
VII. Strengthening the United Nations
IX. The Road Ahead

The Millennium Declaration affirms the goals of the United Nations and therefore is very enlightening. Some of the goals listed in the aforementioned sections are:

1. Strengthening the rule of law by widening the jurisdiction of the International Criminal Court of Justice and promoting the rapid entry into force of the Rome Statute of the International Criminal Court.

2. Developing a 30-to-90-day deployment capability of the United Nations peacekeeping force.

3. Making progress in disarmament in all areas, including weapons of mass destruction, landmines, and small arms.

4. For the 49 least developed countries, the next steps are implementing a global version of the European "everything but arms" trade program and fully implementing the enhanced Heavily Indebted Poor Countries Initiative and pursuing measures to promote the cancellation of official bilateral debt.

5. In September 2001, will take steps to begin the bridging of the digital divide.[27]

A person does not have to be a political science genius to figure out that the UN has a very distinct agenda. We can also very clearly see that the UN is a socialistic form of government. The UN clearly desires to redistribute wealth, disarm citizens, set up a global military under UN command, and link the world community by means of digital electronics.

In a book by Robert Muller, *My Testament to the UN*, we see one of the most poignant examples of the unmistakable goals of the United Nations. Muller was the assistant to three UN secretary-generals. He is touted as the "Prophet of the UN," not for any Christian reasons, but because of his visionary leadership.

In his book Muller makes some chilling statements such as:

♦   "Tomorrow, it [UN] will be the world's religion...National sovereignty will disappear."

♦   "Anyone who attacks the United Nations is a criminal, because it is the most important institution on Earth."

♦   "The United Nations should have precedence over every nation."[28]

What astonishing statements coming from an individual who was second in command at the UN!

There have been seven secretary-generals in the UN. Alger Hiss was the first (pro-tem), but the UN has distanced themselves from his memory. If a person visits the UN website, or the UN building in New York City, they will find that the organization does not recognize or even mention Hiss.

---

[27]View the Millennium Declaration on the UN's web site, www.un.org.
[28]Robert Muller, *My Testament to the UN*, pgs. 3, 39, 64.

Every secretary-general who followed Hiss has been a socialist! In addition, all fifteen undersecretary-generals for Political and Security Council Affairs in the UN have been Russian. [1946-1993][29]

One of the former socialist secretary-generals of the UN was an individual named U Thant. A quote by Thant in the *Los Angeles Times*, April 7, 1970, reads, "Lenin was a man with a mind of great clarity and incisiveness and his ideas have had a profound influence on the course of contemporary history...His ideals of peace and peaceful coexistence among states...are in line with the aims of the UN Charter."

Thant was referring to Vladimir Lenin who was one of Russia's most notorious and feared dictators. It was Lenin who said, "The scientific concept of dictatorship means nothing else but this: Power without limit, resting directly upon force, restrained by no laws, *absolutely unrestricted by rules.*"[30]

Absolute power is an essential component of Communism and socialism. One of the most disturbing prospects of a global military is the fact that Article 100 of the UN Charter reads: "In the performance of their duties the Secretary-General and the staff shall not seek or receive instructions from any government or from any other authority external to the Organization."

CNN, on April 4, 2004, quoted Russia's President Putan as saying, "The UN is the most efficient organization at solving global problems."

The current UN secretary, General Kofi Annan, said, "Nations have their courts and legislatures. In today's interdependent world, the peoples of the world must have rules and institutions they need to manage their lives."[31] The UN desires to manage our lives!

---

[29]"What the UN Doesn't Want You to Know," by Irvin Baxter Jr., *Endtime Magazine*, March/April 1995.
[30]Ibid. *Death by Government*, by Professor R.J. Rummel, p. 86.
[31]Excerpt from a speech to the Women's International Forum, UN Headquarters, January 14, 2000.

Recently, twelve members of the U.S. Congress voiced their opinion that the UN is the most effective way to manage our country. On July 1, 2004, twelve members of Congress (referred to by many conservative lobbyists as the "dirty dozen") sent a letter to Annan asking him to monitor the presidential election in the United States scheduled for November 2, 2004![32]

Fortunately the UN declined that request. It must be said however, that members of Congress who cannot serve this country by upholding their oath to the U.S. Constitution, and not the UN Charter, need to be voted out of office. Furthermore, when viewed through the eyes of true patriotism, the actions of those twelve members of Congress rank dangerously close to treason.

Call it what you want (New World Order, one-world government, global government), but the fact remains that the information, articles, and the quotations to back up the carrying out of socialistic global agendas are seemingly endless. We could easily fill this entire book with evidence of the UN's goals to implement a powerful one-world government.

When does this worldwide government assume the power and control it desires? What has prompted governments to ban together in past decades to form a League of Nations, or a United Nations? The answer is—*a world war.*

Note: The preamble to the UN Charter verifies this as it reads, "To save the succeeding generations from the scourge of war, which twice in our lifetime has brought untold sorrow to mankind..."

There is a war on the horizon (it is prophesied in the Bible) that is going to kill one-third of the world's population. (We will cover the Third World War in a later section.) In light of past

---

[32]www.laptoplobbyist.com, World Wide Web. Also www.uspoliticstoday.com. (keywords: Congresswoman Eddie Bernice Johnson).

history, it is not farfetched to assume that this war will cause such an outcry by the "world community" that it will easily become the springboard for a one-world government.

Concerning this coming one-world government the Bible tells us:

> And they worshipped the dragon which gave power unto the beast: and they worshipped the beast, saying, *"Who is like unto the beast? Who is able to make war with him?"* And there was given unto him a mouth speaking great things and blasphemies; and power was given unto him to continue *forty and two months*. And he opened his mouth in blasphemy against God, to blaspheme his name, and his tabernacle, and them that dwell in heaven. *And it was given unto him to make war with the saints, and to overcome them:* and power was given him over all kindreds, and tongues, and nations.
> REVELATION 13:4-7

A day is coming when the one-world government will be so powerful that the world will ask, "Who is able to make war with him?"

It is important to keep in mind that we are Christians! (And if you are not...you can be. See the final note at the end of this book.) Our God knew this was coming even before he created the heavens and the earth. This does not mean that we should not stand up for our rights as Americans (rights that are unalienable). However, at the same time we can have confidence that God is still in control of the times and seasons.

God will allow the one-world government to truly flourish (in an evil manner) for forty-two months. As we will see in a later section, this represents the last three-and-a-half years of the final seven-year period.

God has told us to watch for the coming of the Lord. This is not a time for fear, but rather a time to look up for "our redemption draweth nigh." This is a time in which we must teach and train Christians to live by faith, and to stand firm in their convictions. God has revealed these prophetic events so we can prepare our hearts. It is important that we understand and digest this information because these are the times in which we live. God has given this information for this hour.

We can easily conclude that the foundation of the one-world government is in place. The one-world government is the United Nations. What we are watching for now is a formidable leader who will rise up in this New World Order; a leader the Bible calls the Antichrist.

Let's Review

- In Revelation 13:1-2 we see a unification of nations, which is formed in the last days.
- A unification of nations has been proposed after the last two major world wars–the League of Nations following World War I, and the United Nations after World War II.
- The United Nations is a socialistic form of government.
- The deadly wound was the Berlin Wall. Even secular press has called the wall a "rusty knife wound." Revelation 13:3 tells us that when the deadly wound (a wound to a nation) is healed, the world will wonder after the beast. The deadly wound was healed in 1989 and the world marveled.
- In Revelation 13:4-7 we see that there is coming a day when the one-world government will become so powerful that people will say, "Who is able to make war with him?"

The Four Horsemen

A·poc·a·lypse (a•påk'•a•lips) n. an unveiling of hidden things; revelation; disclosure.

For we do not wrestle against flesh and blood, but against principalities, against powers, against the rulers of the darkness of this age, against spiritual hosts of wickedness in heavenly places
EPHESIANS 6:12

Discussion concerning the Four Horsemen of the apocalypse occurs often in many books and movies. Our study will focus on the sixth chapter of Revelation, and the sixth chapter of Zechariah which both speak of the same symbols. As we put these Scriptures together, we will gain a better understanding of the nature and purpose of these prophecies. The two passages we will examine are what we call *parallel passages*, which are very important in proper Bible interpretation. They give us a more complete picture of what God is saying.

In the fifth chapter of Revelation the apostle John saw an angel bring forth a book, then John began to weep because nobody was found worthy to open the seals. Then the only one who is worthy, the Lamb of God, came forth to open the seals. This event leads into chapter 6:

> And I saw then the Lamb opened one of the seals, and I heard, as it were the noise of thunder, one of the four beast saying, "Come and see." And I saw, and behold a white horse: and he that sat on him had a bow; and a crown was given unto him: and he went forth conquering, and to conquer. And when he had opened the second seal, I heard the second beast say, "Come and see." And there went out another horse that was red: and power was given to him that sat thereon to take peace from the earth, and that they should kill one another: and there was given unto him a great sword. And when he had opened the third seal, I heard the third beast say, "Come and see." And I beheld, and lo a black horse; and he that sat on him had a pair of balances in his hand. And I heard a voice in the midst of the four beasts say, "A measure of wheat for a penny, and three measures of barley for a penny, and see thou hurt not the oil and the wine." And when he had opened the fourth seal, I heard the voice of the fourth beast say, "Come and see." And I looked, and behold a pale horse: and his name that sat on him was Death, and Hell followed with him. And power was given unto them over the fourth part of the earth, to kill with the sword, and with hunger, and with death, and with the beasts of the earth
>
> REVELATION 6:1-8

Once again, like the four beasts, whenever we find a beast or a symbol throughout several different places in Scripture, we find that each passage reveals more about that beast or symbol. Each passage gives different details about the same beasts and, in turn, gives us a more complete picture.

A prophet named Zechariah also had a word concerning these same horses. As we examine Zechariah 6:1-8, it will give us a better picture of the significance and the purpose of the horses spoken of in Revelation 6:1-8.

> And I turned, and lifted up mine eyes, and looked, and, behold there came four chariots out from between two mountains; and the mountains were mountains of brass. In the first chariot were red horses; and in the second chariot black horses; and in the third chariot white horses; and in the fourth chariot grisled and bay horses. Then I answered and said unto the angel that talked with me, "What are these, my lord?" And the angel answered and said unto me, "These are the four spirits of the heavens, which go forth from standing before the Lord of all the earth. The black horses which are therein go forth into the north country; and the white go forth after them; and the grisled go forth toward the south country." And the bay went forth, and sought to go that they might walk to and fro through the earth: and he said, "Get you hence, walk to and fro through the earth." So they walked to and fro through the earth. Then cried he upon me, and spake unto me, saying, "Behold, these that go toward the north country have quieted my spirit in the north country."

As we examine these horses, it is important to remember the following:

1.   In Revelation 4:1 John begins to write about events that must take place "hereafter." What does that mean? It is obviously speaking of events that would take place after John had received the Revelation of Jesus (a period of time from approximately 95 AD forward). Revelation 4:1 through chapter 19 has to do with events of the *last days*. Therefore, keep in mind that time frame of these four spirits going forth into the earth is anytime after the apostle John received his vision.

2. The events in the book of Revelation do occur in an orderly fashion within God's time, but they are not necessarily chronological. (We will examine the layout of the book of Revelation more in-depth at the end of our study.)

The Red Horse

What are the four horses according to Zechariah? They are four *spirits* that go out and do what God commands upon the earth. Remember how each of the four beasts represented countries or nations? Clearly these four horses represent spirits, or spiritual systems, that are operating in the earth in the last days.

What were the characteristics of the red horse? The red horse [spirit] "takes peace from the earth, and that the people should kill one another; and there was given to it a great sword." There is a system in the world today that aligns itself with this spirit, and even identifies itself with the color red. That spirit, or system, is *Communism.*

Definitions

Com·mu·nism (kom' yoo-niz' m) n. 1. A social system in which there are no classes and no private ownership of the means of production. 2. The theory of social change on which such a system is based.

So·cial·ism (so' sh·l-iz' m) n. 1. The theory of public collective ownership or control of the basic means of production, distribution, and exchange, with the avowed aim of operating for use rather than profit 2. A political system or party advocating or practicing this theory.[33]

---

[33]*Webster's Dictionary*

By definition, Communism incorporates socialism. The definitions sound harmless. Many world leaders believe socialism is the only way to spawn a fair and just world community. However, human beings prove over and over that they are simply not capable of governing such a system—a system in which a few wield absolute power over the masses. Why? It is called the sin nature. The root problem with Communism and socialism illustrates the old saying, "Absolute power corrupts absolutely."

An atheist believes there is no god. A humanist believes *he* is god.

Humanist Manifesto Points 1 and 2

1. Religious humanists regard the universe as self-existing and *not created.*

2. Humanism believes that man is a part of nature and that he has *emerged* as the result of a continuous process [evolution] (emphasis added).

Characteristically, Communism and socialism are void of God. They are atheistic or humanistic forms of government. The reason is because they express the ideology that man can solve his own problems through proper governmental control. In addition, socialism includes the idea that the majority rules [democracy]. Former Russian president, Mikhail Gorbachev—a staunch Communist, stated in his book *Perestroika* that, "according to Lenin, socialism and democracy are indivisible."[34]

On the other hand, the founding fathers of the United States of America believed that God created all men equal. Therefore, we must have a basis for which we treat all men equal. In America we govern by a rule of law, not by whatever the majority opinion may be. Whatever decisions the U.S. Government makes must

---

[34]From the article, "A Republic, If You Can Keep It," originally appeared in *The New American*, November 6, 2000.

fall in line with the Constitution and the Bill of Rights. Interestingly, the basis for our rule of law is the morals and principles explained in the Bible.

This makes America a republic, not a democracy. An account in the diary of Constitution signer, James McHenry, concerns a woman (Mrs. Powel of Philadelphia) who asked Benjamin Franklin, "Well, Doctor, what have we got, a republic or a monarchy?" With no hesitation whatsoever, Franklin responded, "A republic, if you can keep it."

In a republic the people choose the national leaders. Then, those people govern by a rule of law. The word "republic" comes from the Latin *res publica* which means simply "the public thing(s)," or more simply "the law(s)." In the Pledge of Allegiance we say, "I pledge allegiance to the flag of the United States of America and to the *republic* for which it stands."

Our founding fathers understood that the majority could be wrong. How many times down through history have we seen that to be true? The majority was wrong in the Garden of Eden, at the tower of Babel, in Sodom and Gomorrah, and even in Pilate's court. The Bible itself reveals that mankind needs a standard by which to live, not just whatever feels good to the majority.

Our founding fathers also understood that individuals, not government, are capable of governing their own lives with the understanding that they will have to answer to their Creator. In America individuals choose who governs, and those who elect officials hold those same officials accountable under the law.

In America individuals also have the freedom to choose where they want to work, where they want to live, and how they want to live. The foundation for this is the biblical principle that all are equal in the eyes of God, and each individual has the right to choose his own course in life. Then in the end, each individual will have to answer to the Creator for *how* he lives his life.

In a free society each individual is responsible for his or her own actions and can become anything he desires. This freedom produces growth and strength in many different ways. Freedom allows individuals to create, build, and express their ideas with great passion. America has been the world's leader in all aspects of technology and society because of the godly principle that all men are created equal and are free to pursue life, liberty, and happiness.

Inevitably, what ends up happening in a socialistic and communistic society is that the gap between rich and poor becomes enormous as the centralized government controls the wealth and distribution of wealth. With so much power in the hands of a national leader, also referred to as a dictator, this form of government almost without exception eventually becomes corrupt and oppressive.

Nearly every country that socialism and Communism have been a part of has experienced a revolution to the point that people kill one another! Who inflicted the deadly wound (the Berlin Wall) in Germany after the Second World War? The sword of Communism! Confirmation is found in Revelation 13:15 when it speaks of the beast which "had the wound by a sword, and did live."

As previously mentioned, before the First World War 1,000,000 was the greatest amount of people that had died in any war. In the First World War 8,000,000 died. In the Second World War 61,000,000 people died. The root causes of both of these wars were socialistic dictators whose intentions were to conquer the world.

It is estimated that in China 80 million people were killed in political purges after the Communists took over in 1948![35] Today in China, the government will allow a family to have only one child. Families prefer to have a male child so that they can continue the family lineage. As a result, large numbers of baby girls are abandoned in the streets, or condemned in what are called "dying rooms."[36]

---

[35]*Understanding the End Times*, by Irvin Baxter Jr., copyright 1995, 1999, 2002, p. 125.
[36]Focus on the Family radio broadcast, July 16, 2004.

A friendly form of Communism is nonexistent. What do the Scriptures say about the red horse? It has "power to take peace from the earth and to kill one another with the sword."

We saw earlier that Communism in the former Soviet Union (under the dictatorships of Lenin and Stalin) caused the deaths of approximately 60 million of its own people. Think about that. In just two Communist countries (China and the Soviet Union) their governments have killed approximately 140 million of their own people!

The *Economist* magazine, September 11, 1999, reported that during this century the governments of the Soviet Union, China, Germany, and Japan combined have killed *170 million* in political purges! Without a doubt, wherever Communism has ruled and reigned, it has taken peace from the earth and killed its own people. (Note: Germany and Japan were "pseudo-democracies" before World War II. Germany became a dictatorship under Hitler, and Japan was a dictatorship under the semblance of Imperialism.)

It is also interesting that the color of these horses reveals which of these systems will rule in the one-world government (see Revelation 17:3).

The Black Horse

Once again, Zechariah explains that the horses are spirits, or systems. In Revelation 6:1-8 we see that the black horse has a pair of balances [scales], wheat and barley are being priced, and "it shall not hurt the oil and the wine." What does this activity bring to mind? These are the same decisions being made in the stock market.

On September 24, 1869, the American financial market experienced a crisis, which was dubbed Black Friday. In October 1929, the stock market crashed on Black Tuesday. On October 19, 1987, Wall Street experienced another stock market crisis on what was called Black Monday.[37]

---

[37]ibid, *Encarta Encyclopedia.*

Definition

Cap·i·tal·ism (kapi' tl iz' m), *n.* an economic system in which investment in and ownership of the means of production, distribution, and exchange of wealth is made and maintained chiefly by private individuals or corporations.

We see the color black associated with capitalism in the bad times, but what about in times of prosperity? What phrase do we often hear in reference to a company that is doing well financially? We say that the company is "in the black." (It is also noteworthy that we find a balance, or scale, on the symbol for the United States Treasury.)

Communism is one of the systems that rules the world, and capitalism is another. On December 9, 1966, *Time* magazine ran an interesting article concerning two political parties in Germany. The Christian Democrats were the capitalists, and the Social Democrats were the Communists. These political rivals experienced a tie in their election, so they came up with a compromise.

Concerning the election, *Time* magazine said, "A union of two major parties, the Christian Democrats [capitalists] and the Social Democrats [Communists] that had bitterly fought each other over the years—*a union of black and red.*" The article went on to describe how the union of these political parties was a "marriage of convenience, but a stunning match nevertheless."

America has been the leading capitalistic country in the world. Unfortunately, the tide is shifting from black to red. Currently there are 189 nations in the United Nations. The United States contributes 30 percent of the United Nation's income. If the U.S. does not like something the United Nations does, they walk away with their money. This hurts the United Nations.

Note: In 1995 the U.S. withheld one billion dollars worth of UN dues in an effort to force reforms on the UN's "inefficient bureaucracy." What this really had to do with is the issue of the sovereignty of the United States.[38]

Remember how we learned that the big five post-WW II superpowers have veto power in the UN Security Council? What the United Nations is saying right now is that they want the big five to give up their veto power. The Commission on Global Governance agrees with this assessment as the following statement from *Our Global Neighborhood* illustrates:

Reform of the Security Council is central to reforming the UN system. Permanent membership limited to five countries that derive their primacy from events fifty years ago is unacceptable; so is the veto.[39]

(Interestingly, the majority of items on which the U.S. exercises veto power has to do with Israel.)

Several permanent members of the UN Security Council would be willing to give up veto power for the "betterment of the world community." This will be one of the last hurdles the UN will have to jump (along with financial independence) in order to override the sovereignty of individual nations. One of the big questions for the future is whether the U.S. will remain sovereign, or will they give in to the pressure of the one-world government?

A day is coming when America will not be an influential player in the United Nations. We can easily see in the race toward a one-world government that the red horse of Communism and socialism is overtaking the black horse of capitalism. We can

---

[38]*The People's Chronology, Political Events of 1995*, Henry Holt and Company © 1995, 1996

[39]"What the UN Doesn't Want You to Know," *Endtime Magazine*, by Irvin Baxter Jr. and Eddie Sax. View this article at www.endtime.com.

also see that the colors of the four horsemen represent systems of government, and that these systems operate in the earth in these last days.

The White Horse

The rider of the white horse has a bow, but no arrows. Even though the rider has no arrows, the Bible says he goes forth to conquer. How can a system of government conquer without military might and power? It is obvious that the white horse is fighting and conquering, but not with live ammunition.

The Bible even tells us which direction these spirits go. Zechariah 6:6 says, "The black horses which are therein go forth into the north country; and the white go forth after them; and the grisled [pale] go forth toward the south country."

The white horse has been dominant in the north country, following the black horses. There is another spirit that operates on the earth that is a form of government. As we will see throughout our study of prophecy, the system represented by the white horse is catholicism.

The office of the papacy (the pope) has existed since about 360 AD, and the primary color of this office has always been white. The pope wears white robes, flies in a white jet, rides in a white "pope-mobile," has a white helicopter, and if the pope had a horse it would be white.

When we see the pope get off his airplane in a foreign country, he always gets down on his knees and kisses the ground. Many people think this act is his way of blessing the country in which he is visiting. What the pope is really doing is claiming that nation for the Catholic Church!

The pope is completely sovereign over a church that has a membership of over one billion–nearly one in five people in the world.[40] Think about the amount of power the pope wields over all these people!

---

[40]*Understanding Catholicism*, Second Edition, Bob O'Gorman and Mary Faulkner (2003 Alpha Books, Indianapolis, Indiana) p. 29.

The white horse has gone all over the earth, but particularly in the north country. For example, as of 1991 there were 55,000,000 Catholics just in the United States! That constitutes almost 22 percent of the United States' population (part of the north country).[41]

Important note: This study is not an attack against *individuals*. Odds are that the majority of the people who live in the nations mentioned, or that participate in these systems of government, are good people who believe they are doing the right thing. However, we are coming against *false teachings and systems of government* that the Bible reveals as being anti (or against) Christ.

Remember when John F. Kennedy ran for the presidency? There was a big uproar surrounding his candidacy because he would be the first Catholic president. The problem many people had with that was the fact that the pope is sovereign over all Catholics. One saying heard back then was, "If Kennedy's elected, they will be changing our money to read, 'In the Pope We Trust.'"

The Catholic Church teaches that the pope is Christ's vicar on the earth. In other words the Catholic Church believes that the pope stands in the place of Christ. That means that the pope can even change the reading of the Word of God. In fact, all popes have interpreted the Bible the way they desire. As a result, their interpretation becomes doctrine for all those in the Catholic Church. The scary thing is...no one can dispute it!

In the book *Understanding Catholicism* it says, "Catholics believe that the office of the pope is infallible. Papal infallibility means that *the pope cannot make a mistake when defining a doctrine,* or formal belief, of faith or morals for the Catholic Church"[42] (emphasis added).

---

[41]Ibid. *Grolier's Encyclopedia.*
[42]ibid. *Understanding Catholicism,* Second Edition, Bob O'Gorman and Mary Faulkner, 2003 Alpha Books (Indianapolis, Indiana), pp. 47-48.

We see something interesting about the white horse in Revelation 6:2: "And I saw, and behold a white horse; and he that sat on him had a bow; and a *crown* was given to him."

One of the mile-markers of this prophecy dates all the way back to around 700 AD. The fulfillment of this prophecy came when Emperor Constantine gave the pope a triple-crown tiara. That same crown is still in use today. The pope's crown is one of the most notable symbols of Catholicism. The three-tiered crown even appears on the Catholic flag.

Paul Blanshard (who does not claim to be religious) wrote a textbook for political science called *Communism, Democracy, and Catholic Power*. Blanshard said, "Almost every conflict between nations in modern history has been produced by conflicts among three powers: Communism, democracy, and Catholicism." Those three systems have caused most of the major wars in the world in the last 2,000 years.

Malachi Martin (who died in 1999) was a Jesuit priest–the highest order of priests in the Roman Catholic Church. Martin taught at Vatican College, was an advisor to three popes, and authored many books on the state of the Catholic Church and the world. He was the foremost Catholic writer in the world, as well as a globalist.

One of the many books Martin wrote was *The Keys of this Blood*, describing which geo-political power (capitalism, Communism, or Catholicism) will control the New World Order. The subtitle for Martin's book reads "Pope John Paul II Versus Russia and the West for Control of the New World Order."

Martin not only recognized the ensuing struggle for power in the New World Order, but he also stated, "There will be a one-world government formed in the 90s. The only question is who will rule it?" He goes on to say, "There are three, and only three, geopolitical powers with the necessary structure and doctrine to rule a one-world government. Those three powers are Catholicism, Communism, and capitalism." What amazing statements coming directly from a Vatican insider!

Martin also boldly states, "Willing or not, ready or not we are all involved in an all-out, no-holds-barred, three-way global competition. Most of us are not competitors, however, *we are the stakes.* For the competition is about who will establish the first *one-world system of government* that has ever existed in the society of nations"[43] (emphasis added).

Catholicism is not just a major world religion. It is a powerful world government, which exercises authority over presidents, kings, and ordinary people. (We will take a closer look at the Catholic Church in a later section.)

The Pale Horse

The fourth horse is a little strange. It is a pale horse and the Bible says, "Death and hell follow with it." Also, that the pale horse "kills with the sword, with hunger, with death, and by the beasts of the earth." There is a system that rules in this world right now that does just that.

As we have already seen, Zechariah 6:1-8 tells us which direction each horse rides. The black horse goes to the north country, the white goes after it, and the grizzled (pale horse) goes to the south country. Two worldly systems that quench the Spirit of God in the north country are capitalism and Catholicism. Twenty-two percent of Catholics reside in North America, and nearly 80 percent of the world's wealth is in the northern hemisphere.

As the World Trade Organization meets to decide how to distribute the wealth in the world, there are protesters as we have never seen. These protesters accuse the World Trade Organization of not paying any attention to those in the southern hemisphere–the poorest and unhealthiest hemisphere on the globe. Poverty, famine, and death reign while wild beasts devour.

---

[43]*The Keys of This Blood*, by Malachi Martin, p. 15, © 1990 Simon & Schuster Inc.

The pale horse rode to the south and famine, death, and hell followed. Much of the southern hemisphere is full of disease, famine, poverty, and death. In many African countries, half the population has the HIV virus and in other countries of the southern hemisphere the average lifespan is only forty years. The devil understands full well the sad reality that the faster people die not knowing Jesus, the quicker they experience the fires of hell. Is there any good news in this situation? Yes! Some of the largest revivals are taking place in the southern hemisphere!

Each of these systems operates differently. For instance, the civil liberties and freedoms of a capitalist country are totally opposite of what we find in a Communist society. The freedoms experienced in a capitalist country are also a stark contrast to the incessant coup d'états and governmental corruption that plague many socialistic countries of the southern hemisphere. That is why many times it is difficult for a person from one system of government to adapt to another.

Definition

Oc·cult (ok' ult), *adj., n., v.,* 1. of or pertaining to any system claiming use or knowledge of secret or supernatural powers or agencies. 2. beyond ordinary knowledge or understanding. 3. secret; disclosed or communicated only to the initiated. 4. hidden from view.

The biggest influence of the pale horse that triggers poverty, sickness, death, famine, and hell in the southern hemisphere *are influences of the occult.* The pale horse is a breeding ground and springboard for the operation and influence of occult practices in that hemisphere.

In the north country, we see the effect of capitalism and Catholicism and how they quiet God's Spirit. Likewise, we see the effects of the pale horse (famine, death, and hell) in the southern hemisphere, with the biggest spiritual problem being the dominant presence of the occult.

Occult practices are not only in the hills or the slums where the poor and destitute live. They also exist in high levels of government, and then later encouraged among the common people. There are more occult headquarters in the southern hemisphere than in the northern hemisphere. Because the spirit of the pale horse went to the south, this opened the door for the operation of demonic forces through occult practices which, in turn, takes its victims quickly into death and hell.

However, as we already touched on, the good news is that many major Christian revivals are occurring in the southern hemisphere. In Africa, for instance, millions are being saved in mass crusades. As the apostle Paul said in Romans 5:20, "Where sin abounded, grace abounded much more."

We can easily see that occultism is a ruling force in the southern hemisphere. Again, in his book *The Keys of this Blood*, Martin said that New Age (which is occultism) has the power to be a ruling system in the world. He went on to explain that even though New Age has this type of power and influence "it seems uninterested." Although occultism pales in comparison to these other geo-political powers, we will see that it still plays a major role in the world's system and the coming one-world government.

Does this sound too simple? We should not assume that Bible prophecy has to be difficult. Man is the one who makes it hard to understand. As we will continue to discover, all we have to do is study the Word of God as it is, and these truths become very clear in light of world history and current events.

We can see that these four spirits parallel four distinctive worldly systems that operate in the earth today. As we consider the four horsemen, we must also remember that the last days began nearly 2,000 years ago. Once again, that means that the time frame for the Lord releasing these four spirits into the earth is the last 2,000 years (according to Revelation 6:1-8). Our conclusion then is that the four horsemen are not events that are going to happen—they *are* happening.

Let's Review

- The two parallel passages dealing with the four horsemen are Zechariah 6:1-8 and Revelation 6:1-8.
- The four horses are four spirits of heaven sent into the earth.
- The black horse rides to the north country and aligns itself with the system of capitalism.
- The white horse follows the black horse and aligns itself with the system of Catholicism.
- The red horse was given a great sword, took peace from the earth and caused people to kill one another with the sword. This system aligns itself with Communism.
- The pale horse went to the south country to kill with death, hell, poverty, and wild beasts. This system aligns itself with occultism.
- All these systems have been operating in the earth in the last days (the last 2,000 years).

Part
II

Seventy Weeks of Daniel

Up to this point we have taken a close look at what the Bible has to say about the time frame of the last days, or the end of the age. We have also seen a biblical and historical view of the modern nations spoken of in Scripture, the one-world government, and the four horsemen.

One of the many things we will discover is that there is a final seven-year period spoken of in the Bible. In order to understand the events of the last seven-year time period we must first understand the seventy weeks of Daniel.

This seventy-week period is a marvelous timeline laid out by God. We find this timeline in Daniel, chapter 9. What we are about to dive into is one of the most difficult prophecies in the Bible. Yet, once we begin to dissect it, we will find that we can understand it and that it completes a giant piece of the prophetic puzzle.

Before we dive headlong into the seventy weeks, it is important that we lay a proper foundation. To understand prophecy we must also understand a group of people called the Jews.

The Jews and the Abrahamic Covenant

The Jewish people make up the nation of Israel which is unlike any other nation in the world. It is the nation of people that God chose to bring his covenant through, with Abraham as the father. There was no such thing as a Jew or a nation called Israel at the time God made a covenant with Abram (who later became Abraham) in Genesis chapter 17. God promised Abram that he would have a descendant, and that his offspring would be like the sand of the sea.

Abraham fathered Isaac, and then Isaac fathered Jacob and Esau. Abraham's grandson Jacob had twelve sons. In Genesis 35:10 God changed Jacob's name to *Israel* and Jacob's twelve sons became the heads of the twelve tribes of Israel. So we can see how God fulfilled his covenant with Abraham by bringing forth an entire nation through his offspring, and how Jacob [Israel] literally fathered the twelve tribes.

Note: The Hebrew word for Jew is *Yehuwdiy* (yeh-hoo-dee) which simply means "a descendant of Jehudah (Judah)." Judah was one of Jacob's sons, and the father of one of the twelve tribes of Israel.[44]

As Christians our prophecy came through the Jews, our Messiah came from the Jewish lineage, and the New Testament is the product of born-again Jews as the Holy Spirit gave them inspiration.

First Corinthians 10:32 says, "Give none offense, neither to the Jews, nor to the Gentiles, nor to the church of God." This verse reveals the three groups of people that the Lord deals with in the last days:

---

[44]*James Strong's Greek and Hebrew Dictionary,* #3064

1. the Gentiles (the "world," or unbelievers)–out of which arises the New World Order and the Antichrist,
2. the Jews (who comprise the nation of Israel), and
3. the Church (born-again believers).

Israel is approximately 250 miles wide by 500 miles long. That is not very large! Yet, in this one country there have been more wars fought over one city (Jerusalem) than in any other place in the world. We can watch the Jewish nation because it is one of the most obvious prophetic timepieces that exist today.

Jerusalem was always a prize jewel for any tyrant who set out to take over the world. Interestingly, it is the only capital of all its member states that the UN does not recognize.[45] Jerusalem is not militarily strategic, it is not very fertile, and it does not promise great wealth. Why then have so many desired to capture it?

In order to comprehend why Jerusalem is such a prized jewel, let us go back once again to Abraham. Two thousand years before Christ, Abraham obeyed God and left his home (which today would be in the country of Iraq). He set out on a journey looking for the Promised Land–a land that God would show him.

As God was leading Abraham to the Promised Land, Abraham meets Melchizedek (a priest), and God reconfirms his covenant (a binding spiritual agreement) with him. As we have already seen, God promised Abraham that he would have a son (Isaac), and from Isaac's offspring God would build a mighty nation. When Isaac was a young man, God asked Abraham to sacrifice him on an altar. Abraham obeyed God.

At this point we have to ask ourselves how God was going to make a nation from Abraham's son if Abraham kills him. Hebrews 11:17-19 explains, "By faith Abraham, when he was tried, offered up Isaac: and he that had received the promises offered up his only begotten son, of whom it was said, 'That in Isaac shall thy seed be called': *Accounting that God was able to raise him up,*

---

[45]ibid, *Encarta Encyclopedia.* Also, www.un.org, "Question of Palestine."

even from the dead; from when also he received him in a figure." Abraham went up the mountain to offer Isaac in faith, knowing that God would provide.

Just as Abraham was about to kill Isaac, the Lord sent a ram as a sacrificial substitute. Then, the Lord reconfirmed His covenant with Abraham. Since Abraham would not hold back his only son, God promised to make from him a great nation.

At this point we are going to skip ahead. After Abraham, Isaac, Jacob, Joseph in Egypt, Moses, Joshua, and the judges, we come to Israel's monarchs. Israel's second king was an individual named David. After David's throne was secure, and after he had won many battles, he decided to test his strength by taking a census. In doing this, David mistakenly elevated his own strength and natural abilities, forgetting that it was God's hand that produced his victories. It was God's favor and God's power that brought about David's success.

As a result of David's arrogance, God began to punish him. He sent three different types of punishment, one of them a plague. David responded to the Lord by saying he would rather suffer a plague from God then have evil men come in and take over his country. He made sacrifices to the Lord and listened for God's voice. The Lord spoke to David and told him to go and buy the threshing floor of Araunah and make sacrifices there. David did as the Lord commanded (see 2 Samuel 24:24-25).

After David acquired the threshing floor of Araunah, the Lord instructed him to move the capital of Israel from Hebron to Jerusalem—the exact place where the Lord told him to make sacrifices. (Note: At that time the name of the city was not Jerusalem.) Remember the place where Abraham met Melchizedek, the king of Salem? Salem was ancient Jerusalem. Mount Moriah where Abraham was going to sacrifice Isaac was also in ancient Jerusalem. In Scripture we see that time after time God set forth a covenant in one particular place—Jerusalem.

King David desired to build a temple for the Lord in Jerusalem. However, the Lord did not allow him to build it because he was a man of war. Instead, God chose David's son Solomon, a statesman and an architect.

When Solomon finished building the temple, he celebrated with an enormous dedication ceremony. During this ceremony he prays: "Lord, I know the law of Moses says if we sin and turn our back on you, you will turn your back on us and allow evil men to come in and destroy your temple and take us captive. But Lord if we turn from your ways, and our temple is destroyed, and we're driven out of our land and taken captive, if we turn toward your temple and pray, and turn back to you, will you gather us back into our land and rebuild our temple? (paraphrased)." The Lord answered Solomon in the form of fire falling from heaven, a fire that consumes the sacrifice (see 1 Kings 8; 2 Chronicles 5; Nehemiah 1:8-9).

During a 300-year period in the Old Testament, Israel went through six cycles of: prosperity, disobedience, idolatry, oppression, bondage and servitude, and crying out to God. God sends a prophet, sorrow and repentance, return to obedience, deliverance and salvation. Think about that! The entire nation went through this complete cycle six times. They just couldn't seem to get it right!

Through the prophet Jeremiah, God told Israel (in the book of Lamentations) that because they had done wickedly he would allow them to be held captive in Babylon for *seventy years*. He also said that anyone who resisted King Nebuchadnezzar would die. Likewise, if they were obedient to God in captivity, he would bless them and bring them out of Babylon into their own land.

Upon approaching seventy years in captivity, Daniel began to read the prophets. He read a prophecy by Jeremiah that said God was going to restore Israel back to their nation after seventy years (see Daniel 9:2). Suddenly, Daniel recognized that it was time. *Daniel understood the time in which he lived.*

When Solomon built Israel's first temple, it was one of the seven wonders of the world. When the children of Israel went into captivity, the enemy destroyed this temple. This was heartbreaking for the Jews. A Jew without a homeland and a place to worship feels like half a Jew.

The Medes and the Persians took over Babylon. Next a man named Darius (a Mede) became ruler over the empire. The people in Darius' kingdom were very anti-Semitic. They hated the Jews.

However, when it came to Daniel, King Darius could not find any fault in him. Truthfully, he loved Daniel. Nevertheless, someone tricked Darius into making a decree, a law that Daniel could not keep. He decreed that everyone in the nation must worship an image of him. Of course, Daniel would not obey that law.

When Daniel refused to bow his knee to the image of King Darius, the king had him cast into a den of lions. The irony is, Daniel trusted God and slept very soundly, but Darius could not sleep at all. Early the next day, King Darius checked on Daniel to see if he was still alive. "Daniel, has your God delivered you?" he called. What Darius quickly discovered was that God had delivered Daniel!

As a result, King Darius decreed that no one in the kingdom should serve any other God but Daniel's! In addition the king promised Daniel anything he needed to rebuild the temple. One night in a lion's den paid cash for a new temple!

This brings us to Daniel chapter 9. In Daniel 9:2 we see that Daniel understood how God would keep Israel in captivity for seventy years. Daniel 9:3 says, "Then I set my face toward the Lord God to make request by prayer..." This is a fulfillment of what Solomon prayed.

In Daniel 9:4-14 Daniel confesses Israel's disobedience, and acknowledges that God has done all that he promised concerning the nation's wickedness. Then in verses 15-19 Daniel calls upon the Lord to hear their prayers, remember his covenant, turn from his anger, and deliver them. He also reminds the Lord that he has put his name on Jerusalem (see 1 Kings 8:44 and 2 Chronicles 6:6).

Now we come to the prophecy concerning the seventy weeks of Daniel.

While he was praying, the angel Gabriel comes to him and says that he is to give Daniel skill and understanding. The angel then shows Daniel that there are *seventy weeks* determined for the fulfillment of all prophecy, from the rebuilding of the temple until the Second Coming of Christ.

Two obvious questions are:

1. What is a week?
2. When do the weeks begin?

In the Hebrew, the phrase "seventy weeks" literally means "seventy sevens." It seems obvious that the seventy weeks spoken of in Daniel cannot be seventy literal seven-day periods. If they were, this entire prophecy would be complete. Seventy literal weeks is not quite a year and a half. As we examine this prophecy more closely we realize that Daniel's seventy weeks are seventy *seven-year time periods*.

Gabriel informed Daniel that there is a particular timeline from the "going forth of the command to restore and build Jerusalem until Messiah the Prince." When did the seventy weeks begin? The weeks began when the rebuilding of the temple in Jerusalem was begun. "Know therefore and understand, that from the going forth of the commandment to restore and to build Jerusalem..." (see Daniel 9:25a).

Daniel 9:25b says, "the street shall be built again, and the wall..." When you add up the numbers concerning the events prophesied, we easily understand that there would be *forty-nine years* until Jerusalem's wall and the temple was complete. That prophecy happened just as the Bible describes. This accounts for the first seven weeks, remembering that each week represents one year (7 X 7 years = 49 years).

Daniel 9:26 tells us, "And after threescore and two weeks [62 weeks] shall Messiah be cut off, but not for himself..." According to this passage, it would be sixty-two weeks (62 seven-year time periods) after the rebuilding of the temple that Messiah is cut off (or literally, "suffered the death penalty"). Isaiah 53 is a description of Jesus being despised, rejected, and a man of sorrows acquainted with grief. We also see how he was wounded for our transgressions and bruised for our iniquities. Jesus was cut off from the land of the living as he suffered the penalty of death as the perfect Lamb of God. Daniel prophesied the death of Christ, and the time at which it would happen.

Now let us do the math: 62 x 7 = 434 years. When we add the 49 years that it took to rebuild the wall to the 434 years that it would be until Messiah comes we get *483 years.*

483 years after Daniel's prophecy, Jesus came into Jerusalem riding on a donkey! An interesting thing happened as Jesus approached the city:

> And when he was come near, he beheld the city, and wept over it, saying, "If thou hadst known, even thou, at least in this thy day, the things which belong unto thy peace! But now they are hid from thine eyes. For days shall come upon thee, that thine enemies shall cast a trench about thee, and compass thee round, and keep thee in on every side, and shall lay thee even with the ground, and thy children within thee; and they shall not leave in thee one stone upon another; *because thou knewest not the time of thy visitation"*
> LUKE 19:41-44

What did the Jews do that would cause the Lord to scatter them amongst the nations for nearly 2,000 years? The answer is, they killed their Messiah (see Acts 2:22-23; 5:29-30; 7:51-52).

In reality Jesus died for the sins of the world. His death was a fulfillment of the Father's plan of salvation. Israel had God's word, but they rejected their Messiah. Of all people, the Jews should have known that Jesus was their Messiah. Remember, Jesus himself said, "If thou hadst known, even thou, at least in this thy day, the things which belong unto thy peace! But now they are hid from thine eyes...because thou knewest not the time of thy visitation."

We know that there were sixty-nine weeks until Messiah came. Where is the last seven-year period (the seventieth week)? *The last seven-year period has not happened yet.* Why? What was Solomon's prayer? If Israel sins and turns their back on God, if they do wickedness, God told them that he would scatter them and that they would go into other countries and become captives (also see Leviticus 26:14-33). The Jews had been scattered for nearly 2,000 years! God literally made the Jews a by-word, hence the term "wandering Jew." Furthermore, as a result of rejecting Christ the Jews will receive the Antichrist.

What is happening in Israel right now is all about the devil wanting to put his name in the city where God placed his name. In addition, it is also about the rebuilding of the third temple which will allow the Jews to resume the Old Testament sacrifice.

The Jewish nation is looking toward the rebuilding of their temple. At a Jewish wedding celebration, after the bride and groom take their vows, they wrap a glass in a cloth and then break the glass by stepping on it. To the Jews it is an illustration of the destruction of the first and second temple, and a reminder that they must rebuild the third temple.

We see a brief description of the final seven-year time period in Daniel 9:27. During the last seven-year time period we see that after the end of the war and desolations are determined (Daniel 9:26b), he (the desolator–the prince who is to come) will confirm a covenant with many for one week (seven years). In the middle of the seven years he (the desolator–the Antichrist) will bring an end to the sacrifices and offerings. After this, on the wing of abominations shall be one who makes desolate even until the consummation, which is determined is poured out on the desolate (or desolator). That may sound confusing, but stick with us.

The seventieth week (the last seven-year period) begins with the confirmation of a covenant (a signed peace agreement) between the Antichrist (the leader who rises within the one-world government) and Israel.

In Matthew 24:1-2, while Jesus is looking at the temple with his disciples, he said, "See ye not all these things? Verily I say unto you, there shall not be left here one stone upon another, that shall not be thrown down" (see Matthew 24:2 and Daniel 8:9-12).

Daniel 9:26, "And after threescore and two weeks shall Messiah be cut off, but not for himself: and the people of the prince that shall come shall destroy the *city and the sanctuary.*" That prophecy coincides with what Jesus said concerning the destruction of the temple. In 70 AD the prophecy of Daniel and Jesus came to pass–the destruction of the second temple.

In 70 AD the Roman Emperor Titus came (approximately 37 years after Christ) and destroyed the temple so thoroughly that it took a long time to determine where the original temple stood. The seventy weeks of Daniel began in Nehemiah's day with the rebuilding of the second temple. The last week (the seventieth week) will begin with a peace agreement, which will enable the Jews to begin building the third temple. At that time there will be a peace agreement between Israel and a captivating world leader the Bible calls the Antichrist.

Midway through that final seven-year period is the abomination of desolation, when the Antichrist begins to persecute the Jews (and the saints). Therefore, the first three-and-a-half years of Daniel's seventieth week is not tribulation, but rather a peace agreement. As we will see in a later section, the last three-and-a-half years is *Satan's wrath* being poured out, *not the wrath of God.*

During those first three-and-a-half years of peace, it is possible that many Orthodox Jews might fall into deception thinking the Antichrist is their Messiah. Why? Because the Orthodox Jew believes the Messiah will do two things:

1. Bring peace to Israel.
2. Enable them to build the third temple.

We will delve into the events of the last seven-year time period more in a later section. For now it is important to understand this amazing timeline of prophecy that God has given us through the prophet Daniel. This will help lay a foundation for subjects we will discuss in later sections.

The great news is that after this final seven-year period–Jesus returns!

Let's Review

- The Jews are descendants of Abraham, and God promised the land of Israel to the Jews.
- We see that in Scripture God continually confirms His covenant with the Jews in a particular place, which today is called Jerusalem.
- After the first temple was destroyed (the temple built by Solomon) the Jews were taken into captivity. This was a result of their disobedience, just as the Law of Moses had stated.
- Daniel recognized the time period in which the Jews would be in captivity, and turned himself toward the temple (or where it had previously stood) and prayed.
- The information Daniel received in a vision is a prophetic timeline in which all prophecy will be fulfilled.
- There were forty-nine years determined until the construction of the second temple and Jerusalem's streets and walls were completed.
- Four hundred and thirty-four years after the second temple was built, Messiah was cut off (died).
- After Jesus died (and rose from the dead) sixty-nine of Daniel's seventy weeks were complete.
- There is one final seven-year period left which begins with a peace agreement between Israel and the Antichrist.

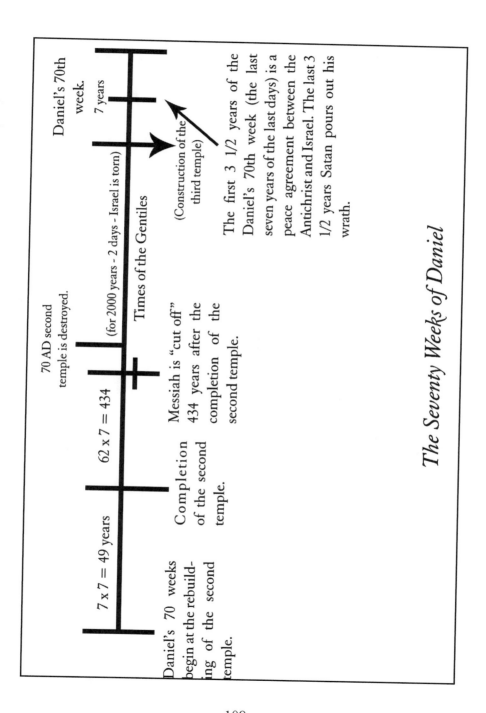

The Seventy Weeks of Daniel

The Regathering of Israel

As we have already seen there are three categories of people talked about in the Scriptures:

1. Israel (Jewish people)
2. The world (Gentiles/nonbelievers)
3. The Church (born-again believers)

We have also looked at some of the history of Israel, especially concerning the temple and the Messiah within the context of the seventy weeks of Daniel.

As we understand more about the Jewish people (the nation of Israel), it will give us a better picture, or history, of what is behind much of the turmoil in the Middle East today. We must also understand that God has made certain promises to the Jewish people, which he will bring to pass.

We learned that Messiah was cut off (crucified) at the sixty-ninth week. Shortly after Jesus was crucified, buried, and rose from the dead, the Jewish temple was destroyed and the Jews were cast out of their land. As we will see, the Jews have been scattered for nearly 2,000 years.

We also learned about the prayer spoken by Solomon at the dedication of the first temple; it concerned foreigners coming in and capturing them while destroying their temple. Solomon prayed that if they repented and prayed toward the temple that God would restore them and rebuild their temple.

Within Christianity there has been teaching that God has forsaken Israel, or that the Church has replaced the Jews. However, the Bible specifically says that God has not forsaken the Jewish people. In fact, there will be a point in time when they will see their Messiah. The Jews who are alive, and who believe in him, when Jesus returns will be born again (see Romans 11:1, 25-27; Revelation 1:7).

The world believed for more than 2,000 years that Israel could never be a nation again because they had been scattered all over the earth. It is interesting to note that even though the Jews had been scattered, wherever they were they stilled called themselves Jews. They also remained within their heritage, most Orthodox Jews not marrying outside Judaism.

Over the last two millennium the Jews have been scattered into many countries. They have even conformed to laws in those countries (as much as possible) in order to live peaceably. Ultimately, however, traditional Jews have adhered to the Old Testament laws. As a result, many peoples and nations have persecuted them.

Think about it. How do we refer to a Jew who lives in America? They are either Jews or American-Jews. Most Jews hold strongly to their belief in Jehovah and will not bend in order to conform to other cultures, and certainly not other religions.

Now, 2,000 years after Christ we have witnessed the Jewish nation being rebuilt. The Jewish people have a homeland for which they continually have to fight. In this section we will see that the regathering of the Jewish people is a fulfillment of prophecy. God said that he would redeem the Jews and bring them back into their land. What is amazing is that most of these events have happened within the last sixty years.

A Scriptural and Historic Look at the Regathering of Israel

They have dealt treacherously against the LORD: for they have begotten strange children: now shall a month devour them with their portions. Blow ye the cornet in Gibeah, and the trumpet in Ramah: cry aloud at Bethaven, after thee, O Benjamin. Ephraim shall be desolate in the day of rebuke: among the tribes of Israel have I made known that which shall surely be. The princes of Judah were like them that remove the bound: therefore I will pour out my wrath upon them like water. Ephraim is oppressed and broken in judgment, because he willingly walked after the commandment. Therefore will I be unto Ephraim as a moth, and to the house of Judah as rottenness. When Ephraim saw his sickness, and Judah saw his wound, then went Ephraim to the Assyrians, and sent to king Jareb: yet could he not heal you, nor cure you of your wound. For I will be unto Ephraim as a lion, and as a young lion to the house of Judah: I, even I, will tear and go away; I will take away, and none shall rescue him. I will go and return to my place till they acknowledge their offense, and seek my face: in their affliction they will seek me clearly. Come, let us return unto the LORD: *for he hath torn,* and he will heal us; he hath smitten, and he will bind us up. *After two days will he revive us: in the third day he will raise us up, and we shall live in His sight.* Then shall we know, if we follow on to know the LORD: his going forth is prepared as the morning; and he shall come unto us as the rain, as the latter and former rain unto the earth.

HOSEA 5:7-6:3

The fifth chapter of Hosea speaks of the horrible atrocities Israel had done to the Lord and how the Lord tore them. He forsook Israel by turning his back on them for a little while.

Hosea also tells us that the Lord smote them in his anger and prophesies, "*After two days he will revive us*; in the third day he will raise us up, and we shall live in his sight."

As we learned in the first section, the two days spoken of by Hosea cannot be a literal two-day time period. We learned that to the Lord a thousand years is as a day, and a day is as a thousand years. This certainly makes sense in light of the Jewish people being scattered and smitten for nearly 2,000 years. At the same time, we know that when God promises something he will bring it to pass.

For nearly 2,000 years we see the Jews stuck in the middle of two covenants. The population of the Jewish race has remained relatively the same. Their numbers did not increase, but God would not allow their numbers to decrease. It is what the Bible calls a remnant—a Jewish remnant scattered all over the earth.

Up until 1850 there were approximately 3,000,000 Jews in the world. However, from 1850-1950 the Jewish population exploded! In 100 years it skyrocketed from 3,000,000 to 15,000,000. The amazing thing is that within that 100-year period Adolph Hitler killed 6,000,000 Jews and Joseph Stalin killed 5,000,000. Still, their numbers increased significantly. That is an amazing miracle. Why did this happen? Because God said, "In two days I will gather you again." In accordance with his word, the Lord began to bring Israel into prominence.

To gain more insight into the regathering of Israel let us look at the following Scripture from Ezekiel 37:1-14:

> The hand of the LORD was upon me, and carried me out in the spirit of the LORD, and set me down in the midst of the valley which was full of bones, and caused me to pass by them round about: and, behold, there were very many in the open valley; and, lo they were very dry. And he said unto me, "Son of man, can these bones live?" And I answered, "O Lord GOD, thou knowest." Again he said unto me, "Prophesy upon these bones, and say unto them, O ye dry bones, hear the word of the LORD. Thus saith the Lord GOD unto these bones; Behold, I will cause breath to enter into you, and ye shall live; And I will lay sinews upon you,

and will bring up flesh upon you, and cover you with skin, and put breath in you, and ye shall live; and ye shall know that I am the LORD." So I prophesied as I was commanded: and as I prophesied, there was a noise, and behold a shaking, and the bones came together, bone to his bone. And when I beheld, lo, the sinews and the flesh came upon them, and the skin covered them above: but there was no breath in them. Then said he unto me, "Prophesy unto the wind, prophesy, son of man, and say to the wind, thus saith the Lord GOD; come from the four winds, O breath, and breathe upon these slain, that they may live." So I prophesied as he commanded me, and the breath came into them, and they lived, and stood up upon their feet, *an exceeding great army.* Then he said unto me, "Son of man, these bones *are the whole house of Israel:* behold, they say, 'Our bones are dried, and our hope is lost: we are cut off for our parts.'" Therefore prophesy and say unto them, "Thus saith the Lord GOD; Behold, O my people, I will open your graves, and cause you to come up out of your graves, *and bring you into the land of Israel.* And ye shall know that I am the LORD, when I have opened your graves, O my people, and brought you up out of your graves. And shall put my spirit in you, and ye shall live, *and I shall place you in your own land:* then shall ye know that I the LORD have spoken it, and performed it, saith the LORD."

The above passage is a parallel passage of Hosea chapter 6. Ezekiel prophesied concerning horrible atrocities done to Israel. During the late 1930s and early 1940s the spirit of antichrist rose up in an individual named Adolph Hitler who promised 1,000 years of peace when he took over the world. This evil dictator began to gather the Jews and bring them into death camps. Could it be that God gave his prophet Ezekiel a glimpse into those camps and crematoriums almost 3,000 years earlier? Could it be that Ezekiel bore witness to a mass annihilation of the Jewish people? God told Ezekiel, "These bones are the whole house of Israel."

After World War II the world thought Israel was dead. One Holocaust survivor said that when the Jews who remained in Germany after World War II sojourned back to their homes (or what was left of their homes) in Berlin, people greeted them with very strange looks, as if they had come back from the dead. The non-Jewish Germans did not expect any Jews to be alive after the Holocaust.[46]

History has vividly recorded the horrifying extermination of 6,000,000 Jews. When we view photographs of the carnage of Hitler's death camps, we see bodies piled so high they had to use bulldozers to push them into enormous ravines for burial.

It is also noteworthy that many of the Jews in Hitler's death camps died from starvation. When a person dies in this manner their body practically dries up after it consumes fatty tissue for energy, then searches for any nutritional substance that will sustain life.[47] When we view scenes of Hitler's massive burials in his death camps, they look like *a valley of dry bones!* Could it be that the valley of dry bones Ezekiel saw were the dried-up, bleached-out bodies of 6,000,000 Jews killed by Adolph Hitler?

In Ezekiel chapter 37 it is very likely that God looks down into Hitler's concentration camps and asked Ezekiel, "Can these bones live?" Ezekiel replies, "Only thou knowest." God tells Ezekiel to prophesy to the bones, and the bones stood up and became *a mighty army.*

So we know that the dry bones represented the nation of Israel. Ezekiel 37:11 says, "Then he said unto me, Son of man, these bones are the whole house of Israel: behold, they say, Our bones are dried, and *our hope is lost:* we are cut off for our parts." The devil tried to eliminate the Jewish people, but he could not get the job done. God breathed life into an entire nation that the world thought was dead.

---

[46]Documentary, "The Long Way Home," Moriah Films.
[47]ibid. *Encarta Encyclopedia.*

When World War II ended there were almost 15 million Jews with no homeland and nowhere to go. As we saw in Ezekiel's prophecy, God used this atrocity to bring his people together from the four corners of the earth. Only three years after the horrific treatment of the Jews in the Second World War, *Israel became a nation!*

The evidence to support that Ezekiel's prophecy is speaking of the Jewish Holocaust becomes stronger when we consider what God has done for the Jews since 1945. When in the last 2,000-plus years has Israel been brought back to its own land, and became a nation? Not only did God bring the Jews into their own land, but as we will see, he also made them a mighty army. As we consider these facts, it becomes more and more apparent that the post-WW II regathering of Israel is exactly what Ezekiel prophesied.

The gathering of the Jews back to their own land was a long drawn-out process. After World War II many of the older Jews who still had assets (mostly American), recognized that they probably would not see the restoration of their homeland. So the older generation began giving the younger generation their in-heritance, explaining to them that they would be the ones who would see the fulfillment of God's promise.

These Jews purchased several large ships so that they could transport Jewish refugees to the shores of Israel. Thousands of Jews from Europe made a trek with their families over a 12,000-foot Alpine crossing into Italy. From there they journeyed to the shores of the Mediterranean where they piled into the ships heading to Israel.

On the shore of Israel, British and Arab soldiers (who occupied Israel after the war) met the Jewish pilgrims. When the Jews got off the boats, the occupying forces began shooting. Only one out of three Jews would actually survive to make it into the land of Israel. Even with such terrible risks there was always a waiting list to make the trip back to Israel. The Jews that survived the trip banded together and literally began to squat in their homeland.

The leading nations of the world got together and voted as to what to do with all the Jewish refugees. By only *three votes* in the UN General Assembly (the U.S. voted in favor of the Jews) they chose to give the Jewish refugees a little sliver of land where their homeland used to be.

After being given this small piece of land, reporters asked the Jewish leaders, "What are you going to call your country?" The Jewish representative stood up in front of the microphone and said, "Our nation is Israel!" The entire world gasped at this stunning announcement![48]

Since that time, the UN as a whole has consistently voted against Israel in various matters. On the other hand, the United States has stood behind Israel and been its friend. President Harry Truman was the first world leader to sign a document officially recognizing Israel as a nation.

On May 14, 1948, Israel became a nation. The very next day millions of Arabs from all sides (Egypt, Jordan, Syria, Lebanon, Iraq, and Saudi Arabia) marched against 600,000 Jews in the newly-occupied Jewish territory. The population of the surrounding Arab nations was 42,000,000. Think about those odds. Forty-two million Arabs against 600,000 Jews! The world community said, "We have done all we can for them, therefore they are on their own."

What happened to the Jews? God fought for His people just as he did in the Old Testament! This band of 600,000 Jews sent millions of Arabs running. After the smoke cleared, the Jews ended up occupying two-thirds more land than originally given.[49] This also coincides with what Ezekiel prophesied when he said, "He commanded me, and breath came into them, and they lived, and stood upon their feet, *an exceedingly great army.*"

---

[48]Ibid. Video Documentary, "The Long Way Home," Moriah Films (highly recommended).
[49]*World Almanac and Book of Facts*, 1997 © 1996. ibid. *Encarta Encyclopedia.*

Time and again when nations attacked Israel, Israel always came out on top. In 1967 the Egyptian leader decided that he would wage an all-out attack on the Jewish people. In just six days Israel defeated the Arab forces again. Thus, history calls it the "The Six-Day War."

During this war, shortly after Egypt rallied the Arab nations to come against Israel, the Arab nations began to lose the war. During a predawn raid the Israelis caught the Arabs off guard and destroyed their entire air force.[50] After this defeat, the opposing army persuaded King Hussein to enter the war by lying to him. They convinced him that the Arabs were not only winning the war, but that they were also about to take over Israel.

Israeli leaders called King Hussein and told him that it was not his fight, and that he should stay out of the war. However, the king believed the Arab nations and entered the fight. When the machine guns ceased, a group of young soldiers stood on the Temple Mount in Jerusalem after nearly 2,000 years! The Jewish military realized what had just happened, and the soldiers began to weep on the Temple Mount.

Note: The Temple Mount is the location in Jerusalem where the first two Jewish temples stood, and where the Jews desire to build their third temple. The biggest problem with this plan is that the Muslims also have a temple on the Mount called the Dome of the Rock. The Dome of the Rock is a dome-shaped mosque, containing a rock with a little dent. The dent, the Muslims say, is where their prophet Mohammed's heel touched when he ascended to meet Allah.

At the time of this victory the chaplain over the Jewish military was an individual named Rabbi Shlomo Goren. Many of the young Jewish soldiers who were weeping on the Temple Mount

---

[50]ibid. *The People's Chronology*

grew up in Russia, and had been indoctrinated with atheistic teachings. As a result, many of them did not even understand why they were weeping.

As Rabbi Goren was watching this, he walked over to the group of soldiers who were atheist and said, "This Temple Mount is holy to us, we understand why it is so important. But this Mount does not mean anything to you, this is just territory we took. So why are you weeping?" The commander said, "We don't know. There is just this feeling here."

The leading commander of that battle over Israeli forces was General Uzi. As an Army chaplain, Rabbi Goren was a firebrand. He continually preached to the soldiers that God was going to restore them, and rebuild the temple.

After taking the Temple Mount, Rabbi Goren ran to General Uzi and said, "Sir, I want you to take some men and go over to the Arab's temple (the Dome of the Rock), and I want you to take one hundred kilograms of dynamite and blow up these heathen places of worship. We must not wait! A few hours from now it will be too late."

General Uzi replied, "Rabbi Goren, be quiet!" "If you destroy the Muslim's temple your name will go down in history." Rabbi Goren told General Uzi. "You will have paved the way for the building of Israel's third temple."

General Uzi said, "My name will go down in history anyway." Rabbi Goren persisted and said, "We have to get rid of the Muslim temple right now!" General Uzi replied, "If you keep talking like this, I will have you arrested and put in jail!" The general made sure that their conversation never leaked out until they both died.[51]

Interesting side note: Over thirty years later, Rabbi Goren's son-in-law began spearheading the fight to build the third temple on the Temple Mount.

---

[51] ibid. *EndTime Magazine.*

Those on the Temple Mount who believed in God said they believed that if they would have destroyed the Muslim temple, it would have prompted the return of their Messiah.

Why was Rabbi Goren so adamant about getting rid of the Muslim mosque? Was it hatred? Was it fear? Could it be something he understood because he had studied the scriptures?

Numbers 33:51-56 says:

> Speak unto the children of Israel, and say unto them, "When ye are passed over Jordan into the land of Canaan; Then ye shall drive out all the inhabitants of the land from before you, and destroy all their pictures, and destroy all their molten images, and quite pluck down all their high places: *and ye shall dispossess the inhabitants of the land, and dwell therein: for I have given you the land to possess it.* And ye shall divide the land by lot for an inheritance among your families: and to the more ye shall give the more inheritance, and to the fewer ye shall give the less inheritance: every man's inheritance shall be in the place were his lot falleth; according to the tribes of your fathers ye shall inherit. But if ye will not drive out the inhabitants of the land from before you; then it shall come to pass, *that those which ye let remain of them shall be pricks in your eyes, and thorns in your sides, and shall vex you in the land wherein ye dwell. Moreover it shall come to pass that I shall do unto you, as I thought to do unto them.*"

Rabbi Goren understood this commandment God had given to Israel "to drive out the inhabitants of the land." Otherwise, those who remain will be pricks in their eyes, thorns in their sides, and will vex them in their own land. Israel continues to have problems with the Arabs when they could have driven the Arabs completely out of their land.

In 1973 another monumental event occurred: A war broke out called the war of Yom Kippur. Yom Kippur is Israel's number one holy day. It is a day when all military people go home to be with their families. It is a day of atonement for sins. It is also considered the Day of Judgment, when God judges Israel.

During Yom Kippur the Arabs marched against Israel on all three sides! They began to invade Israel and destroy her and it seemed as though there was nothing Israel could do! There was a leader during the Six-Day War named Moshe Dayan. As the foreign nations were taking Israel, Dayan looked at Golda Meir (Israel's prime minister) and said, "I fear for the third temple." The third temple is the heartbeat of Israel.

At the same time there was a very unpopular person by the name of Ariel Sharon who was a warrior during the Six-Day War. Sharon, however, was not a politician. He believed that Israel belonged to the Jews, and that they should allow no one to take it.

After the Six-Day War, the Israeli army retired Ariel Sharon because he was like a pit bull. Sharon would not stop after taking a little–he wanted *all* of Israel! The liberal Jews did not like the way Sharon handled things, so they took him out of the picture.

During the War of Yom Kippur, as the Arabs were attacking Israel, the Israeli Army brought Sharon out of retirement. They gave him the southern command, which strategically was the worst command. It was the hot bed of the war.

Sharon took his troops to the southern part of Israel and broke right through the Egyptian lines. Then, he cut off the Arabs from their attempt to escape the country. As a result, Israel had these foreign troops on Israeli soil with no way for them to escape. Israel had them surrounded!

As Israel was winning the war, Russian leaders called the United Nations and demanded a cease-fire. The UN gave in and called for a cease-fire in Israel. Nevertheless, Israel came out of the War of Yom Kippur possessing even more land than before. Since this war there has been constant strife (including bombings and terrorists' attacks) between Israel and the Palestinians.

It seems as though the Arabs realize that they cannot take Israel. As a result, all they can do is initiate terrorist attacks. They continue these attacks in order to provoke Israel to retaliate. Then, when Israel does retaliate, it makes them look like the bad guys. The Arabs are trying to paint Israel into such a bad light that it will force the UN to intervene and bring peace.

From 1989 to the Present

The Berlin Wall fell in 1989. As we have learned, the world recognized the tearing down of the wall as the healing of the deadly wound. After this momentous event, President George H.W. Bush, Pope John Paul II, and Mikhail Gorbachev declared the beginning of the New World Order. Since 1989 we have witnessed many fascinating events taking place concerning the nation Israel.

On May 19, 1993, the leaders of all of Israel's Jewish parties adopted the *Jerusalem Covenant*. In a nutshell this covenant says, "We will never forsake Jerusalem." The signatures on the covenant include the prime minister of Israel, the speaker of the Knesset (Israel's Parliament), both chief rabbis, the mayor of Jerusalem, and most of the other cabinet members. This covenant hangs on the wall in the Israeli Knesset. Israel's leaders have agreed that they will never give up Jerusalem!

In 1993 we had the Oslo Peace Accords where the Palestinians began to speak of wanting their own state. The world community agreed to give them a city named Jericho as part of their Palestinian territory.[52] The problem with that is that Jericho was the first city God instructed the Israelites to capture when they crossed the Jordan.

The agreement the world community made with the Palestinians presented a real problem for the Jews. They had negotiated away the first city God told them to take in the Promised Land to

---

[52]ibid. Encarta Encyclopedia

a Muslim–Yasser Arafat. Until his death in November of 2004, Arafat was the leader of the Palestine Liberation Organization (PLO).

Who are the Palestinians, and why do they think they should have any of Israel's land? The word Palestinian is the same word for Philistine! What the world is witnessing is the same old story–the Israelites against the Philistines. At the Oslo Peace Accords they gave away Jericho to the Philistines!

On November 4, 1995, an ultra-Orthodox Jew assassinated an individual by the name of Yitzhak Rabin as he was leaving a peace rally in Tel Aviv. His reason for the assassination of Rabin is something in the old Hebrew Law that says they should kill anyone who gives away Israeli land. Of course, that does not hold up in court, and Christians cannot condone the killing of Rabin. The fact is, a zealous Orthodox Jew killed Rabin because he was negotiating away land that belonged to Israel.

In 1996 Pope John Paul II came to Jerusalem. During his visit the pope spent very little time with Israel's prime minister, Benjamin Netanyahu. However, he did spend a week with Yasser Arafat and the Muslims, talking about peace for their nation.

Later, he had a very short meeting with Netanyahu. As the pope looked at the city of Jerusalem, and the Temple Mount, he said to the prime minister, "You know this city is holy to three faiths?" Benjamin Netanyahu looked at the pope and said, "*Yes, but it is only promised to one.*"[53]

It is amazing how the Middle East continues to be the hottest bed in the world! What does the Bible say Jerusalem will be? It says that it will be "a burdensome stone, and a cup of trembling to every nation." The one constant problem that the New World Order will face is what the UN calls "the United Nations and the question of Palestine."[54] In other words, how will the UN get a handle on Jerusalem and the Israeli people?

In 1999, the UN invaded Kosovo, deciding that they needed to gain control of a dictator named Slobodan Milosevic. They accomplished their goal!

---

[53]ibid, *EndTime Magazine.*
[54]ibid. www.un.org

While the situation in Kosovo was consuming the UN's time, Ariel Sharon was dealing with an uproar in the Middle East. It was at that time that a UN delegate had some strong words for Sharon, telling him that he better take care of the problem in the Middle East (concerning Jerusalem). Otherwise, the UN was going to come in and do for Israel what they did with Saddam Hussein and Slobodan Milosevic. That information hit the *Jerusalem Post*– "UN Threatens Israel."

What the UN did in Kosovo was a foreshadowing of what they will do someday in Israel. There is coming a day when the UN will invade Israel under the guise of bringing peace.

In the year 2000 we had the Camp David Accords in which Yasser Arafat (the Palestinian leader), Ehud Barak (Israel's prime minister), and President Clinton all met together to talk about peace, or compromise, in Israel.

At that time, Barak was the new prime minister of Israel. He was a compromiser, having given away as much Israeli land as former Israeli prime minister Shimon Peres. Barak (who is now out of office) stated, "One of these days we are going to have to give up Jerusalem and allow it to come under United Nations control."[55] It is hard to believe that an Israeli prime minister spoke those words!

At Camp David, President Clinton said, "We have to find a way that the Jews can have the Temple Mount and the Palestinians can have the Dome of the Rock." Once again, it all came down to the Temple Mount! Clinton even suggested that the UN dig a tunnel so that the Palestinians would not have to pass through Jewish territory to get to their mosque.[56]

The Jews have always been sovereign over the Temple Mount, and that was a constant irritation to Arafat. Following the discussion at Camp David concerning the Temple Mount, a senior Palestinian official said, "The Western Wall is yours (the Israelis) and Haram al Sharif (the Temple Mount) is ours. Stop with your nonsense."[57]

---

[55]ibid. *EndTime Magazine*.
[56]*Current History* (periodical), January 2001.
[57]*Ha'aretz Newspaper*, August 6, 2000.

While Barak was negotiating away Israel, Sharon ran against him telling Israel that if they re-elected Barak he would give away half of Israel. Subsequently, Sharon became Israel's new prime minister. After Arafat said, "No deal," and Sharon came to power in Israel, President Clinton lost his chance at a Nobel Peace Prize and some sort of redeeming presidential legacy.

Sharon is a devout Orthodox Jew and a modern-day warrior for the people of Israel. He prays and believes in the Old Covenant. On one occasion he very boldly went to the Temple Mount and prayed. Since that day there has been terrorist attack after terrorist attack against Israel. Clinton proclaimed, "One of these days we have to divide Israel so that the Palestinians can have the Dome of the Rock, and the Jews can have the Temple Mount."[58] Little did he know that this very thing was addressed in Bible prophecy.

Revelation 11:1-2 says:

> And there was given me a reed like unto a rod: and the angel stood saying, "Rise, and measure the temple of God and the altar, and them that worship therein. *But the court which is without the temple leave out,* and measure it not; *for it is given unto the Gentiles:* and the holy city shall they tread under foot forty and two months."

The old Jewish temple had the court of the Gentiles (where anyone could pray), the outer court, the holy place, and the holy of holies. For so long the Jews thought that they could not build their third temple because the Dome of the Rock sits on the Temple Mount. That is exactly why Rabbi Shlomo Goren wanted to blow up the Dome of the Rock.

The Jews have a "Temple Institute" in Israel, and they have figured out that they can build the third temple right up to the Dome of the Rock. The reason for this is that the Dome of the

---

[58]ibid. *Current History,* January 2001.

Rock sits on the court of the Gentiles. Revelation 11:1-2 says, "But the court which is without the temple leave out, and measure it not; for it is *given unto the Gentiles.*"

Right now the Temple Institute has gathered most of the articles for the third temple. In gathering these articles, they found that certain garments had to have special dyes and in order to get these dyes, they had to go to the ocean and extract them from oceanic vegetation. In addition, the Temple Institute had to use a computer to figure out how to make the seamless garments for the priests.

They have the menorah, they have made the instruments for the temple, and young men are being trained in temple sacrifices. They even have many of the stones for the third temple cut.

God has supplied what the Jews need down to the last detail. For instance, the Temple Institute needed a red heifer for the temple sacrifices. After this red heifer is sacrificed, the ashes make a sort of lye that the priests mix with water and sprinkle on themselves for cleansing before they perform their priestly duties.

The red heifer was thought to be extinct until a few years ago. Anytime someone has reported having a red calf, a priest from Israel would examine the calf to see if it was pure. This type of animal has not been around for almost 2,000 years, since the destruction of the second temple.

A person in Mississippi said, "I think I have one of those cows." The leading rabbis of Israel flew to Mississippi and found their pure red heifer![59] God has ordained these things for this time.

Many believe that the Jews' third temple will be the eighth wonder of the world. Up until now they have had a compromise problem. God has clearly instructed them, "If you do not drive the Gentiles out of your land, they will be thorns in your eyes and thistles in your side."

---

[59]*Mystery of the Red Heifer,* by Chaim Richman (The Temple Institute).

The stage is being set in Israel for the building of the third temple. Will the Jews risk building it until there is a viable peace agreement in Israel? Certainly not! Therefore, this will require a peace agreement, most likely through the UN. The Bible tells us that a world leader will rise in the one-world government and bring peace in the Middle East. According to Scripture, this will mark the beginning of the final seven-year period. (We will delve more deeply into the final seven-year period in a later section.)

When we see a viable peace agreement between the UN and Israel, we know we have seven years left. We must keep our eyes open, and recognize the signs of His coming!

Let's Review

- In prophecy we see that Israel would be torn. Israel had been scattered for nearly 2,000 years.

- God began to increase the number of Jews from the middle 1800s to the middle 1900s. This was the beginning of the fulfillment of God's promise to bring the Jews back into their land–Israel.

- In Ezekiel 37 we see that the valley of dry bones represents the whole house of Israel. Even Ezekiel perceived that Israel was dead in this prophetic view. After WW II the world thought that Israel was dead.

- Only three years after WW II God raised Israel up to become a nation. He also caused them to become a mighty army.

- The third temple is the heartbeat of Israel. The preparations have been made for its building. All the Jews need is a viable peace agreement to begin.

Times of the Gentiles

In this study we are painting a picture, and each topic is a portion of the overall picture. It sure would be nice to cut to the chase and know the exact moment when Christ will return. Even though he clearly told us that no man knows the day or the hour of his return, we can see that it is God's desire that we understand prophecy. Prophecy reveals why Jesus is coming back, as well as the time frame of his return.

What we will learn in this section is that God has revealed another prophetic timetable concerning the duration of man's government. Let us take a look at Luke 21:19-28 to help us understand the times of the Gentiles:

> In your patience possess ye your souls. And when ye shall see Jerusalem compassed with armies, then know that the desolation thereof is nigh. Then let them which are in Judea flee to the mountains; and let them which are in the midst of it depart out; and let not them that are in the country enter thereinto. For these be the days of vengeance, that all things which are written may be fulfilled. But woe unto them that are with child,

and to them that give suck, in those days! For there shall be great distress in the land, and wrath upon this people. And they shall fall by the edge of the sword, and shall be led away captive into all nations: *and Jerusalem shall be trodden down of the Gentiles, until the times of the Gentiles be fulfilled.* And there shall be signs in the sun, and in the moon, and in the stars; and upon the earth distress of nations, with perplexity; the sea and the waves roaring; Men's hearts failing them for fear, and for looking after those things which are coming on the earth: for the powers of heaven shall be shaken. And then shall they see the Son of man coming in a cloud with power and great glory. And when these things begin to come to pass, then look up, and lift up your heads; for your redemption draweth nigh.

What are the times of the Gentiles? Once again, this is important to understand because it gives us another prophetic time clock toward Jesus' return.

When the abomination of desolation occurs, Jesus warns that those who are in Judea should flee without even going back for their coat. It is at this time that Jerusalem is trampled underfoot by the Gentiles "until the times of the Gentiles be fulfilled." Simply put, the times of the Gentiles is the time period in which God allows human government to rule on the earth.

It is at the end of this time (the times of the Gentiles) that God pours out His wrath, and then Jesus sets up His earthly government. How do we know this? In Luke 21:19-18 we see:

1. Israelis fleeing to save their lives.

2. A time of vengeance, that "all things which are written may be fulfilled."

3. Signs in the sun, moon, and stars, and distress of nations on the earth, the sea and the waves roaring, men's hearts failing for fear, and the powers of heaven being shaken. (We will see in a later section that this describes the time of the pouring out of God's wrath.)

4. The Son of man coming in the clouds (the Second Coming of Christ).

In this section we will examine some prophetic words that the Lord spoke through the prophet Daniel concerning dominant world governments. As we dig into this prophecy we will see:

1. These governments become easy to identify.
2. The revealing of a prophetic timetable.
3. These governments cover a time period from Daniel's day up until the return of Christ.

Nebuchadnezzar's Dream

We must go to Daniel chapter 2 in order to get a firm grasp on which Gentile kingdoms have ruled, and which ones will rule until Jesus returns. In Daniel chapter 2 we see something strange happening. The ruler at that time, King Nebuchadnezzar, had a dream from God and he does not know the interpretation. He called for all the wise men, soothsayers, and magicians in his court, but none of them could tell him the meaning of the dream. Therefore, the king had all of his wise men killed because they could not interpret the dream.

Nebuchadnezzar's men also sought to kill Daniel and his companions. Daniel asked for a little time, and then he would interpret the dream. He sought the Lord concerning the dream and the Lord revealed the secret to him.

What we see in Daniel 2:27-45 is that the interpretation of Nebuchadnezzar's dream reveals the major kingdoms that would rule on the earth until the coming of the Lord. This is the prophetic timeline for the times of the Gentiles.

The Prophecy and its Context

Daniel 2:27-45 says:
> Daniel answered in the presence of the king, and said, "The secret which the king hath demanded cannot the wise men, the astrologers, the magicians, the sooth-

sayers, shew unto the king; But there is a God in heaven that revealeth secrets, and maketh known to the king Nebuchadnezzar what shall be in the latter days. Thy dream, and the visions of thy head upon thy bed are these; As for thee, O king, thy thoughts came into thy mind upon thy bed, what should come to pass hereafter: and he that revealeth secrets maketh known to thee what shall come to pass. But as for me, this secret is not revealed to me for any wisdom that I have more than any living, but for their sakes that shall make known the interpretation to the king, and that thou mightest know the thoughts of thy heart. Thou, O king, sawest, and behold a great image. This great image, whose brightness was excellent, stood before thee; and the form thereof was terrible. This image's head was of fine gold, his breast and his arms of silver, his belly and his thighs of brass, his legs of iron, his feet part of iron and part of clay. Thou sawest till that a stone was cut out without hands, which smote the image upon his feet that were of iron and clay, and brake them to pieces. Then was the iron, the clay, the brass, the silver, and the gold, broken to pieces together, and became like the chaff of the summer threshing floors; and the wind carried them away, that no place was found for them: and the stone that smote the image became a great mountain, and filled the whole earth. This is the dream: and we will tell the interpretation thereof before the king. Thou, O king, art a king of kings: for the God of heaven hath given thee a kingdom, power, and strength, and glory. And wheresoever the children of men dwell, the beasts of the field and the fowls of the heaven hath he given into thine hand, and hath made thee ruler over them all. *Thou art this head of gold.* And after thee shall arise another kingdom inferior to thee, and another third *kingdom of brass*, which shall bear rule over all the earth. And the fourth kingdom shall be *strong as iron*: forasmuch as iron breaketh in pieces and subdueth all things: and as iron that breaketh all these, shall it break in pieces and bruise. And whereas thou sawest *the feet and toes, part of potter's clay, and part of iron, the kingdom shall be divided;* but there shall be in it of the strength of the iron, forasmuch as thou sawest the iron mixed with miry clay. *And as the toes of the feet were part of iron, and part of clay, so the kingdom shall partly strong and partly broken.* And whereas thou sawest iron mixed with miry clay, they shall mingle themselves with the seed of men; *but they shall not cleave one to another,* even as iron is not mixed with clay. And in the days of these kings shall the God of heaven set up a kingdom, which shall never be destroyed: and the kingdom shall not be left to other people, but it shall break in pieces and consume all these kingdoms, and it shall stand forever. Forasmuch as thou sawest that the stone was cut out of the mountain without hands, and that it break in pieces the iron, the brass, the clay, the silver, and the gold; the great God hath made known to the king what shall come to pass hereafter: and the dream is certain, and the interpretation thereof sure."

Daniel begins by explaining that Nebuchadnezzar's kingdom is the first kingdom (the head of gold). This gives us the starting point of this prophecy. We see that the end of the last kingdom comes when a small rock is hewn out of the mountain without hands. The small rock will smite the image on the feet, and the image will turn to dust. After the Lord strikes the image, it will look as chaff on the summer threshing floor and will blow away as the small rock grows and fills the whole earth.

Jesus is the Rock hewn out of the mountains without hands. Jesus is the stone that the builders rejected, which became the Chief Cornerstone. Jesus spoke of himself as the Chief Cornerstone. He also said, "And whoever falls on this stone will be broken; but on whomever it falls, it will grind him to powder" (see Matthew 21:42-44). Therefore, the context of this prophecy is from Nebuchadnezzar's kingdom until the Second Coming of Christ.

The Head of Gold

Daniel interpreted the dream and explained that Nebuchadnezzar (the Babylonian kingdom) was the head of gold. At the time when Daniel interpreted the dream (604 BC), Nebuchadnezzar ruled the known world. His architecture and hanging gardens made Babylon one of the seven wonders of the ancient world. Some historians purport that there has never been another city like King Nebuchadnezzar's Babylon. Daniel's interpretation proclaimed that an inferior kingdom would come and take away Nebuchadnezzar's kingdom.

The Arms of Silver

The king who ruled after Nebuchadnezzar was Belshazzar. He did not possess the same wisdom as Nebuchadnezzar who had put Daniel, Shadrach, Meshach, and Abed-nego in charge of all the wise men, magicians, and governors. Daniel's stature was great. Even though he and his friends were in Babylon, *Babylon was not in them.*

When Belshazzar became king, he began to defile the holy things of the Jewish temple by partying with them. Daniel 5:3-4 says, "Then they brought the gold vessels that had been taken from the temple of the house of God which had been in Jerusalem; and the king and his lords, his wives, and his concubines drank from them. They drank wine, and praised the gods of gold, and of silver, of brass, of iron, of wood, and of stone."

As they were doing this, a finger of a man's hand (without the man) came out of nowhere and began to write on the wall– ME'-NE, ME'-NE, TE'-KEL, U-PHAR'-SIN. None of Belshazzar's magicians or wise men could interpret the saying.

Belshazzar's wife said, "I heard there is a man named Daniel in whom King Nebuchadnezzar confided. Maybe he can make the interpretation known." So they called Daniel in order that he might give the interpretation to Belshazzar's dream.

Daniel said, "I feel sorry for you, because I did get the interpretation." The interpretation of ME'-NE, ME'-NE, TE'-KEL, U-PHAR'-SIN is this: "God has numbered thy kingdom, and finished it. Thou art weighed in the balances, and art found wanting. Thy kingdom is divided, and given to *the Medes and Persians.*"

Belshazzar had promised Daniel half of his kingdom if he could interpret the dream. After Daniel's interpretation Belshazzar put a gold chain around his neck and made a proclamation that he should be the third ruler of the kingdom, but of course Daniel knew better. God was stripping the kingdom from Belshazzar. That very night Belshazzar was slain, and his kingdom overtaken by the Medes and the Persians. The arms of silver were the Medio-Persian kingdom, which would rule for a time.

The Belly and Thighs of Brass

In Daniel chapter 2 we see another kingdom rise after the Medio-Persian Empire. This kingdom would be inferior to the Medio-Persian Empire, yet it would be stronger than the Medes and the Persians. This next kingdom would be the belly and the thighs of brass. This was the *Grecian kingdom.* Historically, we know that Alexander the Great (the Greeks) defeated the Medes and the Persians. By the age of thirty, he had conquered the known world. He then sat down and wept because there were no more worlds to conquer.

We also read about this in the eighth chapter of Daniel where a ram represents the Medes and the Persians. We also see Greece represented by a he-goat, and a great horn, which grew out of the midst of the he-goat. Scriptures tell us that this horn would knock the ram on its side and defeat it. It also says that the horn is broken and *four* notable ones come up in its place.

Alexander the Great died at the age of thirty from pneumonia and inebriation. He never married or had any children. He was simply a warmonger. Four parts of his kingdom rose up and took his place. The four horns that rose up were Egypt, Syria, Spain, and Greece.

The Legs of Iron

Next, a stronger kingdom arose and took over Greece, and eventually all of Europe. The leg as strong as iron (the fourth kingdom) that "breaketh into pieces and subdueth all things" was the *Roman Empire.*

Who occupied Jerusalem in Jesus' day? The answer is Rome. Today Roman occupation would be equivalent to the UN going into and occupying a country (subduing all things). The Romans allowed the Jews to live, do business, and worship in the temple, but all under the watchful eye of Rome which would punish the Jews if they stepped out of line.

At that time, the Roman Empire was second to none in government, art, and science. Kings and kingdoms have tried to revive the empire since its fall. Much of this is due to the fact that many historians and intellectuals have glorified the empire as if it was the greatest government the world has ever seen. This is typical of secular people who exalt intellectualism–as well as the customs and trappings of a culture–above godly morals and ethics.

The Roman government was very oppressive. It has been said that there was a time when the Roman government had crucified so many Jews in a certain river that the crosses practically blocked the river. It is reported that in AD 70, when Titus entered Jerusalem, there were so many crosses with Jews crucified on them along the road leading to Jerusalem that it looked like modern power poles alongside the road! The Roman government was a very evil, cruel, and godless government! Sadly, it is proclaimed by many as one of the best governments the world has produced.

There are, however, a few things we can learn from the decline of this government. The book, *The History of the Decline and Fall of the Roman Empire,* speaks of several reasons why the Roman Empire died:

1. increase in taxes,
2. troops scattered on foreign soil,
3. deterioration of religion,

4. deterioration of the family unit, and

5. increase in games (entertainment).

Do these social elements sound familiar? America is on that same path! Elements of the Roman government survived, even though the government itself died. As we will see, there have been other failed attempts at recreating a Roman Empire.

The Feet of Iron and Clay

After the Roman Empire, another kingdom arose that still had the iron element from the Roman era, but with an additional element–clay. We also see that the iron and clay would not be able to cleave to one another. The ratification of this government occurred in AD 800.

First, in AD 700, there was an emperor of Europe named Constantine who fulfilled a portion of the prophecy concerning the white horse. As we have already seen, the rider of the white horse received a crown. Up until AD 700 the pope never had a crown. Yet, in AD 700 the Roman Emperor Constantine crowned the pope as Christ's vicar (or substitute) on this earth. The crown, a beautiful three-tiered crown, is still presented to popes today at their coronation.

In AD 800 an individual named Charlemagne became king of the Roman Empire, and today he is immortalized in Rome through great statues. Charlemagne was the Roman emperor over all of Europe. The biggest problem he faced was being able to restore the great power of the Roman Empire.

The pope and the Roman emperor put their heads together and discovered that with combined forces they could restore and strengthen the Roman Empire–and that is exactly what they did! Pope Leo III crowned Charlemagne as the ruler of the *Holy Roman Empire* in AD 800. Within the Holy Roman Empire the political and the religious powers came together. From that point, those who ruled the Holy Roman Empire were always the pope and a European king, the king usually being German.

The problem with this religious and political union was the question of who had the most power. There was a time in European history (AD 500-1500) when the pope had so much power that he would appoint kings and leaders at will.[60]

The pope could also have people killed at will. One example of the absolute power of the papacy happened in July of AD 1209 when an army of orthodox Catholics attacked Beziers and murdered 60,000 unarmed civilians. The whole city was sacked, and when someone complained that Catholics were being killed as well as "heretics," the papal legates told them to go on killing and not to worry about it "for the Lord knows His own." [61]

Another example was at Minerve where 14,000 Christians were put to death in the flames, and ears, noses, and lips of "heretics" were cut off by the "faithful."[62]

Interestingly, according to *Webster's II New Riverside University Dictionary*, a heretic is "one who holds or advocates controversial opinions, especially one who publicly opposes the officially accepted dogma of the Roman Catholic Church." Even today we can see that both papal power and European power have been very influential on the world's stage.

History reveals that pride got in the way every time the pope and a European leader came together to rule, as both desired absolute power. We know from Scripture that pride always precedes destruction. The pope would insist that the temporal should not rule over the spiritual. The king would reply, "If you are so dominant, let's take our militaries out to battle and find out who is going to rule!" They would rule the world together for a season, but in the end the iron and clay just would not mix. This is what Daniel was talking about when he said the clay (religious) and the iron (political) would not be able to stay together.

---

[60]*Pontiff*, by Gordon Thomas and Max Morgan-Witts, pp. 201-255, 274, also Encyclopedia Americana, Volume 14, p. 313.
[61]*The History of the New Testament Church*, by Peter S. Ruckman, Ph.D. (Bible Believers Bookstore; Pensacola, Florida; 1989).
[62]ibid. *The History of the New Testament Church.*

Revival of the Holy Roman Empire

A more recent attempt at a revived Holy Roman Empire happened not long after the turn of this last century. In the 1930s an evil leader by the name of Adolph Hitler promised that if elected he would provide 1,000 years of peace. While Hitler was climbing the political ranks, a pope named Pope Pius XII signed an agreement with the German government.

This pope became known as Hitler's pope. In Rome in 1933 the Vatican and the German government signed an agreement called a concordat. Three of those at the signing were Cardinal Pacilli, Franz von Papen, and a little known Vatican prelate named Montini. The agreement stated that if the Germans conquered Europe, together they would institute a new Holy Roman Empire.

Von Papen, a sinister Nazi and devout Roman Catholic, became instrumental in setting up the concordat between Nazi Germany and the Vatican. He was also Hitler's ace diplomat and the Vatican's agent in bringing Hitler to power. Von Papen said, "The Third Reich is the first world power which not only acknowledges, but also puts into practice the high principles of the papacy." [63]

Cardinal Pacilli, then the Vatican secretary of state, later became Pope Pius XII. Montini later became Pope Paul VI. Cardinal Pacilli, after becoming Pope Pius XII, was noticeably silent while Hitler exterminated 6,000,000 Jews!

During World War II we see another agreement among three men–Francisco Franco (dictator of Spain), Benito Mussolini (dictator of Italy), and Pope Pius XII. These three agreed that when Hitler took over Europe they would institute a new Holy Roman Empire.

---

[63]*Volkischer Beobachter* (German Newspaper), January 14, 1934.

The book, *The Secret History of the Jesuits*, tells about the financing and building of Hitler's war machine by the Vatican in order to conquer the world for Roman Catholicism. Hitler, Mussolini, and Franco were to be the defenders of the faith. Their goal was to win and conquer the world while setting up a millennium for the pope.

Hitler, a devout Catholic, stated, "I learned much from the Order of the Jesuits. Until now, there has never been anything more grandiose on the earth than the hierarchical organization of the Catholic Church. I transferred much of this organization into my own party." [64]

In his book, *The Decline and Fall of the Roman Church*, Malachi Martin wrote, "Adolph Hitler and Pope Pius XII planned a 1,000 year 'Reich,' but thankfully, they were defeated."[65]

History reveals to us that Pope Pius XII desired to have a hand in the one-world government that Hitler tried to create:

> The next pope came April 6th, 1951. The pope who presided over the church during World War II and the Holocaust had a joint meeting with World Federalist delegates who had just come out of the Fourth Congress of the World Movement for World Government. Of this movement Pope Pius XII said, "Your movement dedicates itself to realizing an effective political organization of the world. *Nothing is more in conformity with the tradition and doctrine of our church.*" [66]

Hitler truly believed that God's providence was on his side. One notable incident, in which he was fortunate enough to escape death, involved a German colonel named Claus von Stauffenberg. Stauffenberg was fully aware of Hitler's evil intentions, and was sick of seeing what he was doing to Europe.

---

[64]*Mein Kampf*, by Aldof Hitler, p. 478.
[65]*The Decline and Fall of the Roman Church*, by Malachi Martin, p. 101.
[66]ibid. *EndTime Magazine.*

Stauffenberg conceived a plan to kill Hitler. In order to carry out his plan, he gained access to Hitler's high level meetings. After gaining access to these meetings Stauffenberg said, "Fate has offered us this opportunity, and I would not refuse it for anything in the world. I have examined myself before God and my conscience. It must be done because this man [Hitler] *is evil personified.*"

Stauffenberg sat down next to Hitler in one of his top secret meetings wherein they discussed covert operations and their plans to take over Europe. What Hitler did not know was that Stauffenberg had come to the meeting with a bomb concealed in a briefcase. Colonel Stauffenberg got up from the table to use the restroom just two minutes before the bomb exploded. After the colonel left, Hitler had a gut level intuition about the briefcase. Hitler took it and moved it to another part of the room, thus surviving the explosion with only a few minor injuries.[67]

Hitler pointed to that incident to convince those around him that he was fulfilling the will of God. Had Hitler succeeded with his plans to take over Europe, the world would have witnessed a revived Holy Roman Empire.

One of the many horrifying events that took place when Hitler was in power happened on a night that the Jews refer to as "the night of broken glass." On that night, Hitler's men gathered all the Jews out of the Jewish ghetto–a ghetto which Hitler created. He gathered the Jews and placed them in concentration camps, claiming that he was finishing what Titus began in 70 AD. What did Titus do in 70 AD? He destroyed the temple and began killing the Jews.

Hitler modeled many of his governmental symbols after early Roman government symbols; however, he modeled much of the *form* of his government after the Catholic Church and the Jesuit priesthood. What Hitler recognized was that the Catholic Church is formed like a world government.

---

[67]Colonel Claus von Stauffenberg, The History Net, World Wide Web.

143

Francisco Franco was the dictator of Spain during World War II. His press published a statement on May 3, 1945 (the day Hitler died), which said, "Adolph Hitler, son of the Catholic Church, died while defending Christianity." It went on to say, "Over his mortal remains stands his victorious moral figure. With the palm of the martyr, God gives Hitler the laurels of victory."[68] Hitler's regime was clearly an attempt at reviving a Holy Roman Empire, an empire that was part political and part spiritual.

Once again, this is not to say that the people involved in the Catholic Church are evil. There are people who believe in a one-world government who are very sincere in their desire for world peace. But a person can be sincere, and still be sincerely wrong. The apostle Paul said many things to the Christian church that were hard to hear, but he did it because he loved them. Our motive is the same!

Note: Jesus told us that if his kingdom were of this world then his servants would fight. His kingdom is not of this world! As Christians we are not looking to institute a perfect, or friendlier, world government. Jesus will handle that when he returns. Our calling is to preach Christ, and Christ crucified. Jesus is the One who changes people, lives, and governments.

The latest initiation of a revived Roman Empire came in 1957 with an event called the Treaty of Rome at which time the world witnessed the first six nations of the European Union coming together. At the same time the Cold War had begun between the United States and the Soviet Union.

In centuries past, Europe had dominated the world. However, because of the divisions in Europe, the United States and the Soviet Union were now the dominant forces in the world. As

---

[68]*The Secret History of the Jesuits*, by Edmund Paris.

a result, several countries in Europe began to band together and form a union that would eventually become a world superpower. As we have learned, European leaders believe that with the 400,000,000 people in their countries (collectively) they could again become a dominant world power.

Concerning the modern nations of the Bible, we have learned that just before Christ returns there will be a terrible beast with ten horns. In Scripture we also see that the Antichrist will rise out of that terrible beast, which is a ten-nation union. We have speculated that the ten-nation union might easily be the European Union (EU).

In the book of Daniel we also see that Christ will come and set up his kingdom (of which there will be no end) at the time of these ten toes. The ten toes of the feet will consist of both iron and clay (see Daniel 2:42-44). Obviously, this kingdom that exists at the time of Christ's coming is a revived Holy Roman Empire. This idea comes from the fact that its elements are the same as the previous Holy Roman Empire, and it is an extension of the feet of iron and clay. Therefore, we can see the definite possibility, and parallel, between the ten-horned beast (the EU) and the ten toes of iron and clay (possibly the EU and the Roman Catholic Church).

The image that exists on the first coin of the EU also speaks of a revived Holy Roman Empire. The EU's first coin, the European Currency Unit (ECU), has a picture of Charlemagne on it, the first king of the Holy Roman Empire. It is easy to see that the EU is trying to create a revived Roman Empire; however, they cannot do it without the *religious* aspect.

Representatives of the United Nations and the EU have said, "We have come as far as we can in a New World Order right now politically." All they need is someone to bring it together religiously. It is interesting that in all the high level meetings at the UN or the EU, as well as at any peace summit or peace negotiations, Rome sends a representative of the pope. The pope is also the only religious leader allowed to address the UN General Assembly.

In July of 2004 the General Assembly voted to expand the role of the Catholic Church within the UN. The following announcement appeared on the Catholic Family and Human Rights Institute's website.

Vatican's Role at UN Unanimously Endorsed by General Assembly

The General Assembly (GA) of the United Nations last week decided unanimously to confirm and expand the status of the Vatican at the United Nations. The GA document adopted last week was the first major clarification of the prerogatives of the Vatican as a *"permanent observer state,"* which has held this status at the UN since 1964. Not only did the General Assembly endorse the long-standing role of the Vatican, it decided to grant it new privileges, "in order to enable the Holy See (the Vatican) to participate in a more constructive way in the Assembly's activities," according to a UN press release. Perhaps most importantly, the Holy See will now possess the right to participate in the general debate of the GA, the right to circulate documents and the right to reply in debates. One diplomat told the Friday Fax that the Holy See's status could now be likened to a *"full member state, just without the vote"*[69] (emphasis added).

Whom do we see precipitating and celebrating the tearing down of the Berlin Wall? After the healing of the deadly wound we see a meeting between President George H.W. Bush, Mikhail Gorbachev, and Pope John Paul II. After the meeting they all came out proclaiming the same thing–New World Order!

---

[69]Catholic Family and Human Rights Institute (www.c-fam.org), volume 7, number 29.

All this is leading into a latter-day government (the heart-beat of which is the revived Holy Roman Empire), out of which the Antichrist will rise. Scripture tells us that the Antichrist will be partners with a spiritual leader that does signs, wonders, and miracles. The Bible says he will look like a lamb, but speak like a dragon.

It is intriguing to note a true story of what happened when a minister presented this material to a Catholic bookstore for sale. A bookstore representative called the minister and said, "If you are saying that the pope is the Antichrist, then we cannot sell your material." The minister replied, "I am not saying that the pope is the Antichrist. But, to be fair with you, I am saying the pope will be *partnered* with the Antichrist."

The response the minister received from the bookstore representative was astonishing! She told the minister, "Oh, I have no problem with that. Our Catholic prophecies have told us for years that there is an evil pope coming."[70]

In the twelfth century, St. Malachy had a vision of every pope all the way up to the last one, each receiving a coat of arms that represents his reign. This priest also saw the coat of arms of every pope up to the last one. This same priest prophesied that the last pope would be evil.[71]

A saying about the Roman Catholic Church goes, "When it is the minority it is like a lamb. When it is at equity it is like a sly fox. When it is the majority it is like a tiger that tears to pieces."

We have seen that Babylon was the head of gold and Medio-Persia the arms of silver. The belly and the thighs of brass were Greece, and the legs of iron represented the Roman Empire. We have also seen that the feet of iron and clay represented the Holy Roman Empire–a religious and political combination. Historically speaking, we are quickly entering the time of the ten toes in which we will see a revived Holy Roman Empire.

---

[70]ibid. *EndTime Magazine.*
[71]*The Book of Catholic Prophecies*, by Yves Dupont, p. 19.

The time of the ten toes is the same time period that a small rock (hewn from the mountain without hands) will smite the image and destroy all human government, as we know it. We are coming to the end of the "times of the Gentiles" (man's government) spoken of in Scripture when Christ will come and set up his earthly kingdom!

Let's Review

- The time of the Gentiles is the time period of human government on this earth.
- The times of the Gentiles will end when Jesus returns and sets up his earthly kingdom.
- The head of gold in Nebuchadnezzar's dream was Babylon.
- The arm of silver was the Medio-Persian Empire.
- The belly and thighs of brass were the Greek Empire.
- The legs of iron were the Roman Empire.
- The feet of iron and clay (that would not cleave together) were the Holy Roman Empire. This empire was a combination of political and religious power.
- We see the same type of empire present on the earth at the Second Coming of Christ. This empire is represented by the ten toes of iron and clay–a revived Holy Roman Empire. This appears to be happening today in the form of the European Union.

Part
III

The Antichrist

Up to this point we have referred many times to the leader of a one-world government who will rise to power through a revived Holy Roman Empire. One of many names the Bible uses when speaking of this individual is the Antichrist.

This section will attempt to answer many questions concerning this ungodly world leader, such as: What does "antichrist" mean? Is the Antichrist an actual person, or just a spiritual system or way of thinking? What are the characteristics of the Antichrist? What actions will we see that unveil his identity? When does the Antichrist come on the scene? Does the Antichrist exercise control over the entire world?

First John 4:3 explains, "Every spirit that confesseth not that Jesus Christ is come in the flesh is not of God: and this is that spirit of antichrist, whereof ye have heard that it should come; and even now already is it in the world."

According to Scripture, if anyone says that Jesus Christ did not come in the flesh, they are antichrist. That is a standard underlying feature of the system, ideology, or thought process called the spirit of Antichrist.

The Bible also speaks of *the* Antichrist as a distinct, specific person, with certain identifiable characteristics. He has a definite way of thinking and speaking, and an evil agenda that is inspired by Satan. We are even told where the Antichrist comes from.

There are fifty specific references to the Antichrist in the Bible. One passage, 2 Thessalonians 2:1-9, speaks of the Antichrist when it refers to the "man of sin" and the "son of perdition [destruction]." This same passage also tells us that he will oppose and exalt himself above all that is called God, or that is worshipped "So that he sitteth in the temple of God, showing himself that he is god" (verse 4). Then further in verse nine, "Even him, whose coming is after the working of Satan with all power and signs and lying wonders."

This passage is talking about a specific person, "the son of perdition," and describes a person as being controlled by the spirit of antichrist. The Antichrist is a distinct individual who will rise on the scene in the last days.

Daniel 9:26-27 says,

> And after threescore and two weeks shall Messiah be cut off, but not for himself: and the people of the *prince that shall come* shall destroy the city and the sanctuary; and the end thereof shall be with a flood, and unto the end of the war desolations are determined. And *he* shall confirm a covenant with many for *one week.*

In Daniel 9:26-27 we see that the "he" who confirms the covenant for one week (Daniel's seventieth week–the final seven-year period) is the "prince that shall come." His (the Antichrist's) people are the ones who destroyed the second temple after Messiah was cut off. Who were these people? It was the Roman Emperor Titus who marched into Jerusalem in 70 AD and destroyed the second Jewish temple. The Antichrist will arise from among the same people–a revived Roman Empire.

Some have posed an interesting question: Since the Antichrist enters the temple of God, professing himself as God, would it not be safe to say that he is a Jew since he sits in the temple of God? We learned earlier that the beast with seven heads and ten horns is a unification of modern-day Gentile nations. One of those nations is the ten-horned beast spoken of in Daniel 7:8, out of which a little horn rises (the Antichrist). So Scripture reveals that the Antichrist is a Gentile and not a Jew.

Another passage that helps give us clarification is Revelation 17:10-12 which reads:

> And there are seven kings: five are fallen, and one is, and the other is not yet come; and when he cometh, he must continue a short space. And the beast that was, and is not, even *he is the eighth, and is of the seven,* and goeth into perdition. And the ten horns which thou sawest are ten kings, which have received no kingdom as yet; but receive power as kings one hour with the beast.

At the time John received this vision, six major kingdoms had ruled the earth: Assyria, Egypt, Babylon, Medio-Persia, Greece, and the Roman Empire. In John's day, five dominant kingdoms had come and gone. Therefore, at the time he received his vision the Roman Empire would have been the one that "is." The one that came after John's vision was the Holy Roman Empire (the seventh kingdom–the feet of iron and clay), and that is the one that had "not yet come."

Revelation 17:11 explains that the Antichrist will be the *eighth* king, and would be "of the seven" prior to him. So, once again, we know that the Antichrist is a real person and that he rises out of Gentile nations.

Important Scriptural Truths Concerning the Antichrist

1. He rises on the world's scene at a specific time in history (2 Thessalonians 2:6).

2. He shows up as a prominent peacemaker at the beginning of Daniel's seventieth week, which is the last seven-year period before the return of Christ (Daniel 9:27). The fact that the Antichrist is a peacemaker in Israel also tells us that he must establish trust with Israel.

3. The "day of the Lord" and our "gathering together unto Him" do not happen until *after* the revealing of the Antichrist (2 Thessalonians 2:1-3).

4. He springs onto the scene as a world leader, or dictator who destroys marvelously with peace (Daniel 8:25).

As we examine Bible prophecy in light of current world events it would not be far-fetched to assume that the Antichrist is alive right now. It is also very possible that within the not-so-distant future he will rise on the scene and show his true colors. According to the Scriptures this happens "in his time." This brings us to a very important question...

What is restraining the Antichrist from being revealed?

Second Thessalonians 2:6 says, "And now ye know what withholdeth that he [the Antichrist] might be revealed in his time."

What held back Jesus from coming into the earth? Was it the mystery of iniquity? Was it the unbelief and spiritual degradation of the Jewish people that held Jesus back?

Scripture very clearly explains what held Jesus back the first time he came to the earth. Galatians 4:4 says, "When the fullness of *time* had come, God sent forth His son, born of a woman." Time (the proper time in the Father's plan) is what kept Jesus from coming into the earth. Ecclesiastes 3:1 confirms this. "To *everything* there is a season, a time for every purpose under heaven."

There are many glaring examples of this in Scripture. Daniel 7:25 speaks of the Great Tribulation when it says, "And he [the Antichrist] shall speak great words against the most High, and shall wear out *the saints* of the most High, and think to change times and laws: and they [the saints] shall be given into his hand until a time and times and the dividing of times [3 ½ years]."

A second example is Revelation 13:5, which reveals that the Great Tribulation lasts for forty-two months (3 ½ years).

A third example is Revelation 12:6 that tells us that the Great Tribulation lasts 1,260 days (3 ½ years). Clearly we see Satan rising within the Antichrist three-and-a-half years into the last seven-year period.

We learned in Part II that God had a specific time in mind for Jesus to come to the earth. God also has a specific time for the revealing of the Antichrist so that he may do his evil deeds. According to Daniel, seventy weeks are determined until sin passes away. Once again, God has everything lined out, and his word says that he does *nothing* unless he reveals it to his servants the prophets.

Since we understand that there is a specific time for the Antichrist to do his horrible deeds, we know that he cannot do it early, nor can he do it late. Like everything else in God's prophetic plan, Satan also has an appointed time. In his time, the Antichrist will emerge from a revived Roman Empire.

Former CBS anchorman Walter Cronkite said, "We are in a leaderless world, and we desperately need one."

Economist Julian Snyder said, *"We soon have a rendezvous with a world dictator."*

And Henry Speck (one of the founders of the EU) said, "We don't want another committee. What we want is a man of stature to lift us out of the economic morass into which we sink. Send us such a man, *and be he man or devil*, we will receive him with open arms."

As we examine the events of the last century, it is logical to assume that the rise [revealing] of the Antichrist will not occur until something devastating happens. What precedence do we have for this type of speculation? As it has been twice in this past century, history reveals that the springboard for the Antichrist and the one-world government will be a world war.

We will soon learn that the Bible speaks of a war that kills one-third of mankind. After that event, the world will cry out for peace and a leader they believe can give them world peace.

Note: Something else that we can learn from history is that America has experienced great Christian revivals *after* major world wars!

First Chronicles 12:32 says, "And of the children of Issachar, which were men that had understanding of the times, to know what Israel ought to do..." Just as the sons of Issachar had understanding, we also need to understand the times in which we live, enabling us to have scriptural answers as these world events occur.

Here are several of the names the Bible gives for the Antichrist:

- Antichrist (1 John 2:18)
- The Little Horn (Daniel 7:8)
- The prince [governor] that shall come (Daniel 9:26-27)
- The wicked one, the man of sin, and the son of perdition (2 Thessalonians. 2:1-8)
- The beast (Daniel 7:11, Revelation 13:11-12)
- The king of the North (Daniel 11:5-45)
- Gog, the chief prince [governor or ruler] of Meshech, Tubal, and Rosh (Ezekiel 38)

The places mentioned in Ezekiel 38 are in Russia. Meshech became Moscow, and Rosh became Russia.[72] In Ezekiel chapters 38-39 we read about two invasions of Jerusalem by Magog, Meshech, Tubal, and Rosh. The first invasion is at the Battle of Armageddon, and the second is after 1,000 years of peace (the millennial reign of Christ).

At the end of the 1,000-year reign of Christ, these armies will march against God (Jesus and his saints in Jerusalem). The second time they march against the Lord, fire will come down from heaven and consume them. It is after that event that we see God create a new heaven and earth. (We will cover that in-depth in a later section.)

The beast in Revelation 17:3 has a specific color, which is scarlet, or red. What did the spirit of the red horse represent? It represented Communism, which incorporates socialism. Is it any coincidence that all eight general secretaries of the United Nations have been Socialist?

Richard Wurmbrande (founder of Voice of the Martyrs) was tortured while imprisoned in Russia. He said, "The Russian Christians had such beautiful souls. They said, 'We know that the star with the hammer and sickle which we wear on our caps, is the star of Antichrist.' They said that with much sorrow."

Within three books of the Bible there are fifty specific prophecies about the Antichrist and his characteristics! Of course we understand he must have all of the characteristics and not just a few.

Many have speculated as to the identity of the Antichrist. For instance, in the book, *The Antichrist and a Cup of Tea*, the author speculates that the Antichrist might be Prince Charles. However, as we will see, if we have a good handle on the basics of Bible prophecy concerning the Antichrist and his characteristics, we can easily dismiss this idea.

---

[72]*Ezekiel, Art Scroll Tanach Series* (Brooklin: Mesorah Publications, Ltd. 1988), p. 581.

Some have speculated that it might be someone like Juan Carlos, king of Spain. Juan Carlos fits a few of the characteristics of the Antichrist. The Catholic Church even endorses Juan Carlos. Interestingly in the past, the pope always christened the king of Spain as the "King of Jerusalem." Spain is also within the realm of the revived Roman Empire. Once again, however, the Antichrist must have *all* the characteristics given in the Bible and not just a few.

Some consider Joerg Haider another viable candidate. In 1999 CBS news reported,

> The inexorable rise of Joerg Haider throughout the 1990s has put him and his far right Freedom Party on the threshold of power. As an occult neo-Nazi, Haider has been criticized for calling veterans of the Nazi SS "men of character," and for once praising Hitler's "orderly employment program." Nowadays Haider presents a more acceptable image trying to reposition himself. He hobnobs with American academics and lawmakers. He is a handsome, telegenic, clever campaigner. Haider, a youthful 49, has a long career ahead of him. He and his party are a force to be reckoned with in the next century."

Haider certainly has the attitude and influence to be an Antichrist candidate, but as we will see he is missing a vital characteristic.

There seem to be many dynamic politicians on the world's stage that might fit the mold of the Antichrist. The glaring problem with all of the candidates that we have mentioned so far is that they are not Russian. Ezekiel 38:2 tells us that the Antichrist is the "prince [governor or ruler] of Rosh." In other words, the Antichrist will be someone who has been a leader in Russia. If we gain an understanding as to the biblical qualifications of the Antichrist, then he may not be that difficult to recognize as he rises to power.

As we examine some of the key characteristics of the Antichrist, we will also include an example of a person who fits the Antichrist mold very well. Our point in giving an example of a person who fits the characteristics of the Antichrist is to drive home the point that there are those in the world who have these characteristics right now! As we said in the introduction to this study, there is nothing wrong with speculation, as long as we can admit that it is simply speculation and do not attempt to make it doctrine. So even though the "what" is fact, we must remember that right now the "who" is speculation.

The Antichrist will be a great peacemaker.

In 1986 Irvin Baxter Jr. wrote a book called *A Message For the President.* Baxter surmised that whoever was responsible for tearing down the Berlin Wall (the deadly wound) would probably be the Antichrist. The wall fell in 1989. The person who was responsible for tearing down the wall received a Nobel Peace Prize [1990] for his "Foreign Policy Initiatives."

This famous peacemaker also got together with other world leaders and headed off something called the Velvet Revolution. World leaders personally counted him responsible for tearing Communism into pieces. They asked him how it felt to have singlehandedly destroyed Communism. He replied, "You think that is what I did? I assure you I am still a Communist and that is the furthest thing from the truth."

What is the truth concerning the fall of the Iron Curtain? Could it be that it was the greatest conquest *for* Communism? Could it be that the fall simply set Communism and socialism loose? What common policies drive many governments today? Many governments implement the policy of caring for the less fortunate via the redistribution of wealth, centralized healthcare, disarming citizens, and government control of education. Could the fall of the Iron Curtain truly be as one article heading suggested, "Faking the Death of Communism?" Biblically speaking, the Antichrist will be a great peacemaker, and he will also be socialistic in his political ideals and pursuits!

In 1998 this well-known peacemaker received one of Israel's highest awards–the Gates of Freedom Award. He was personally responsible for setting 600,000 Jews free from Russia, and sending them back to their homeland! When addressing a State of Israel Bonds dinner, this peacemaker recalled that when Russian Jews first "responded to the call of their homeland," he regretted their leaving. "After all, they had done so much for our country," he said, citing Jewish contributions in science, culture, medicine, and law. "Nevertheless, I could not tell them not to go," he told the 1,200 supporters of Israel Bonds assembled at the New York Hilton. Former Israeli Prime Minister Yitzhak Shamir, who also spoke at the dinner, credited this man with giving "new life to the Jewish people" and enriching "the life of the state of Israel."[73]

This great peacemaker is doing all these wonderful things, and yet he still freely admits that he is a Communist. As mentioned earlier, there has never been a friendly form of Communism. With that in mind, it stands to reason that there must be a higher agenda.

This charismatic world leader basically ran the Arab nations for a very long time. He has exercised great control over the media, and in 1987 was *Time* magazine's "Man of the Year." Three years later *Time* magazine named him one of their "Men of the Decade."[74] Ted Turner said "This politician is the greatest man in the last two thousand years."[75]

---

[73]*Jewish Telegraphic Agency – Jewish News Weekly of Northern California*, Friday October 30, 1998.
[74]*Time* magazine, January 1, 1990.
[75]Article, "The Men Who Run the World," by Irvin Baxter Jr.

The Antichrist will help establish and promote the New World Order.

This individual, along with several other individuals on his board, is responsible for drawing out the charter of this New World Order. The charter is in the form of a book called *Perestroika*, which means restructuring. This peacemaker speaks about a thing called "glasnost," meaning openness, or a new way of thinking.

Openness in the New World Order means to be open to other governments, faiths, and peoples. This man who preaches "glasnost" is a globalist, and his heart is bent on bringing forth a one-world government.

According to the plan in his book he says, "We have to eliminate all ties of national sovereignty, all economic sovereignty, all people's loyalty to family and religion." In addition to punishing people who commit genocide and crimes against humanity, he believes in punishing anyone with a narrow-minded view of religion (that is, fundamental Christians).

You have probably guessed by now that this world leader we are speaking of is Mikhail Gorbachev. Not only is Gorbachev Russian, but he is also one of the most celebrated world leaders of the last two decades!

Professor Reo M. Christenson, a respected American professor of political science at Miami University in Ohio, published an article in the *New York Times* on April 27, 1990. In the article Professor Christenson wrote, "Mr. Gorbachev has probably made greater contributions to the well-being of humankind than any other political figure in history...I can think of no statesman in history to have done so much."[76]

---

[76]*The Keys of This Blood*, Malachi Martin, p. 30.

Interestingly in *The Keys of this Blood,* (the aforementioned book by Malachi Martin) the inside title page reads, "The Keys of this Blood–The struggle for world dominion between Pope John Paul II, Mikhail Gorbachev, and the capitalist west."

In 1987, Gorbachev recalled the aim of the Bolshevik Revolution, saying, "In October 1917 we parted the Old World, rejecting it once and for all. We are moving toward a new world, the world of Communism. We shall never turn off that road."

Gorbachev, as the chairman of the State of the World Forum, said, "Those who hope that we shall move away from the Socialist path will be greatly disappointed. Every part of our program of perestroika–and the program as a whole, for that matter–is fully based on the principle of more socialism and more democracy. We will proceed toward better socialism rather then away from it."[77]

The Antichrist will be an environmentalist, and pro-abortion.

One of the many goals of the UN is managing the environment. In order for the Antichrist to appeal to the world community (ideologically), he will have to be, or pretend to be, an environmentalist.

Coincidentally, Gorbachev is the founder and president of an environmental organization called Green Cross International. The UN has awarded Green Cross International their highest accreditation as a general consultant with the Economic and Social Council of the United Nations. In other words, Green Cross International is the world's environmental agency from which the UN seeks advice![78]

There are many very interesting articles on Gorbachev's Green Cross International website, including one entitled, "A Leading Role for the Security Council." Gorbachev unashamedly states

---

[77]"In their own words," *Eco-logic,* May/June, 1996, p.20f.
[78]Green Cross International's website, World Wide Web.

that he believes the United Nations Security Council should take the lead in fighting terrorism and other global problems. Within this article Gorbachev also states, *"Globalization cannot be stopped, but it can be made more humane for those it affects."*

Green Cross International even has a plan for peace in the Middle East, which interestingly involves the environment. On Saturday, December 9, 2000, *The International Herald Tribune* ran a piece by Gorbachev with the title "A New Middle East Peace Initiative." Within this article Gorbachev calls for:

1. internationalization of the peace process,
2. a "Marshall Plan" to reduce inequalities in the region, and
3. the use of *water* as a natural vehicle for peace in the Middle East.

He says, "Whatever the political climate, the people of this region need to drink water and to grow their crops."

In forming Green Cross International, Gorbachev managed to enlist the help of many celebrities and world leaders, including Yoko Ono, Olivia Newton John, the late John Denver, the late Carl Sagan, and even Javier Peres de Cuellar (ex-secretary general of the UN). All of these people serve, or have served, on Green Cross International's board of directors. Gorbachev's two presidential advisors are CNN's Ted Turner and actor Robert Redford.[79]

Green Cross International argues the case that despite repeated efforts, the international community of nation states has not yet been able to agree on "an effective international treaty, which guarantees the rights of the Earth."

Green Cross International views the creating of international law as a slow and tedious process. In a 1997 interview with the *Los Angeles Times*, Gorbachev said:

---

[79]ibid. "The Men Who Run the World," and Green Cross International's website, World Wide Web.

We also need a new international environmental legal code rooted in an *Earth Charter*–a covenant similar to the United Nations Declaration on Human Rights. The idea of an Earth Charter was first conceived at the Rio Summit. During the Rio evaluation meeting this March, the Earth Charter Commission, which I chair, drafted such a document with the aim of presenting it to the UN General Assembly for approval by the year 2000. "Do not do unto the environment of others what you do not want done to your own environment," reads one charter item. "Adopt modes of consumption, production, *and reproduction* that respect the regenerative capacities of the Earth," said another. "My hope is that this charter will be a kind of *Ten Commandments, a Sermon on the Mount,* that provides a guide for human behavior toward the environment in the next century and beyond"[80] (emphasis added).

When world leaders meet at global world summits and discuss the environment, much of it has to do with population control and a "final solution." One world leader proclaimed, "We need to decrease the human population by about two-thirds."

The goals of the New World Order include population control, which goes hand-in-hand with environmentalism. Therefore, it also stands to reason that the Antichrist will be pro-abortion. The Bible says that the Antichrist will not regard "the desire of women" (see Daniel 11:37). Traditionally, and biblically, a woman's desire is to have a family. A reasonable interpretation of that Scripture is that the Antichrist will be pro-population control, which would include abortion.

---

[80]*Los Angeles Times*, May 8,1997.

The Antichrist will even gain the respect of religious people.

True Christians need to be aware of the Antichrist's agenda so they do not fall to his deception! The Bible plainly tells us that the Antichrist will not regard "the God of his fathers, nor any god; for he shall exalt himself above them all" (see Daniel 11:37).

Today, New Age is creeping into every nook and cranny of religion. New Age is a conglomeration of many different religions including Buddhism, Hinduism, eastern mysticism, Wicca, witchcraft...you name it. The only thing you cannot say within New Age religion is that there is only one way to God. This makes New Age void of the only true and living God. This also means that those who participate in New Age forms of religion are proclaiming that *they* are god because *they choose* their own pathway to salvation.

Mikhail Gorbachev hosted the "New Age Forum" in his headquarters in San Francisco. Funded by the United Nations, the purpose of the forum was to gather together all of the world's major religions. This meeting was called the United Religions Initiative. (We will examine this more in a later section.)

The Antichrist will have the support, and be partnered with, the most powerful religious leader in the world. Pope John Paul II said, "I believe there must be a United Europe formed from the Euro Mountains to the Atlantic Ocean, and I believe my most frequent pen pal [referring to Mikhail Gorbachev] would be the ideal presiding officer."[81]

Pope John Paul II also referred to Gorbachev as a "crypto-Christian" (crypto means secret).[82] There is no such thing! Jesus told us that if we do not confess him before men, he will not confess us before the Father (see Matthew 10:32-33).

---

[81]*U.S. News and World Report*, May 18, 1992.
[82]ibid.

As previously mentioned, the pope is the only religious leader allowed to speak at the UN. The first time Pope John Paul II spoke before the UN [1979] he called for significant wealth redistribution. When he spoke at the UN in 1995 he called for socialistic world reform. He also stressed the need to strengthen the United Nations.[83]

On March 9, 1992, in the *New York Times*, an article ran entitled "My Partner the Pope." In this article Gorbachev said:

> I have carried on an intensive correspondence with the pope since our meeting in the Vatican in 1989. I believe ours will be an ongoing dialogue. We both share mutual affection and understanding of our meetings also related in our letters. I cannot help but to say that we share a desire to complete that which we have began together. Personally, I'd be glad to take any opportunity to continue working with the pope, and I believe that this desire should prove mutual and lasting.

The Antichrist will be ruthless (as bad as he is good).

In 1985, a man named Andrei Gromyko nominated Gorbachev for the Proletariat Bureau in Russia. When speaking of Gorbachev during his nominating speech Gromyko said, "This man has a nice smile, but he has teeth of iron."[84]

Coincidentally, the Bible describes the ten-horned beast as having teeth of iron. This may not only apply to the union of nations in Daniel chapter 7, but also the leader of this union.

American billionaire Armand Hammer, who was a friend of the Soviets and a critic of the U.S. during the Cold War, said of Gorbachev, "His weakness is that he has a temper, and that he flares up; he has a lot of pride, of course, and self-confidence."

---

[83]*EndTime Magazine*, November/December 1995.
[84]"Gorbachev: The Man With a Nice Smile and Iron Teeth", *Reader's Digest*, October 1987.

Wait a minute! Some may say that Gorbachev does not fit the persona of the Antichrist that is taught by many prophecy teachers. What about the teaching that the Antichrist will be a very handsome, photogenic person?

The Bible does not describe the Antichrist in that fashion. In Daniel 7:20 it says, "His look will be more *stout* than his fellows." In the New King James Version the same passage reads, "Whose appearance was *greater* than his fellows." This passage could be speaking of his physical appearance, but a more likely interpretation would be his political stature. Keep in mind, in a one-world government a person's political influence is worth much more than his outward appearance.

A person might also argue that because Gorbachev is advancing in years that he will not be effective in the political arena. Let us remember, one of our most effective and beloved U.S. presidents was in his late seventies when he governed. We must also consider that one of the most beloved religious figures of this century–the pope–is also well advanced in years.

Once again, our point in sharing this information is to alert Christians to the reality that there are those on the world's stage right now that fit that mold. However, even if we identify a world leader who fits the mold of the Antichrist, the fact is at this point in time it is still speculation.

What else do we know about the Antichrist?

This one-world dictator will rise out of a revived Roman Empire as a much welcomed, and highly respected, man of peace. After a third world war that kills one-third of mankind, the world community will more than welcome someone whom they believe can bring peace into a desperate situation.

In addition, after the next world war, there will be one major hot spot left in the world–the Middle East. Nevertheless, the Bible warns that when they say "Peace and safety," then sudden destruction comes (see 1 Thessalonians 5:1-3).

Remember how one week in Daniel chapter 9 equals seven years? When the Antichrist steps on the world scene, he will initiate a peace agreement between the Arab nations and the Jews. More than likely this will come through, and be enforced by the United Nations.

If you asked the Jews what their Messiah will do for them, most will tell you the same thing: He will allow them to build their third temple, and he will bring peace to Israel. The Antichrist will bring a false sense of peace to Israel because there will be three-and-a-half years of tranquility. It seems logical that during that time of peace the Jews will build their third temple.

In Revelation chapter 12 we see the woman [Israel] who gave birth to the Child [Jesus]. (We will study Revelation chapter 12 more in depth in a later section.) Then we see the woman given two wings of a great eagle that she might fly into her place where she is nourished for three-and-a-half years. The educated guess concerning the eagle's wings is that it is very possible that the eagle's wings represent the United States of America. This idea is reinforced by the fact that Israel truly has only one friend in this world–the United States of America. The U.S. has consistently stood behind Israel since it became a nation in 1948.

An article in the *Jerusalem Post*, dated July 13, 1991, said, "U.S. Christians rally behind Israel. Jack Kemp, Secretary of the U.S. Housing and Urban Development, last week led more than one thousand Christians in a spectacular gathering to support Israel and to raise funds for the continued immigration of the Soviet Jews to the Holy Land. The rally was held under the banner 'On the Wings of Eagles.'"

As we have learned, it seems evident in Scripture that the eagle's wings represent America. If that is the case, then it also seems likely that America (as a nation) does not give in to the wishes of the Antichrist and his one-world government. It appears as though America still has the power and means to aid and support Israel.

Does the Antichrist dominate the world from corner to corner?

Does the Antichrist rule the entire world? Is everyone in the world forced to take the mark of the beast? These are very valid and troublesome questions. It is helpful to note that the Antichrist rises to power as the head over a ten-nation union. World leaders may also call upon him to lead the UN. It seems logical then that many nations would be under his thumb, but does the Bible say that *every* nation is dominated by the Antichrist?

Daniel 11:41 says, "He [the Antichrist] shall enter also into the glorious land [Israel], and many countries shall be overthrown: but these shall *escape* out of his hand, even Edom, and Moab, and the chief of the children of Ammon."

It appears in Scripture that modern day Jordan [Ammon], modern day Arabia [Edom], and Moab never fall under the hand of the Antichrist. Scripture also indicates that when the Antichrist tries to destroy Israel, 144,000 Jews escape into Edom.

Scripture reveals that Israel is cut in half when the Antichrist invades (see Zechariah 14:1-2). For some reason, after the invasion Israel is still standing. It is clear that Israel is still a nation at the time of Christ's return. This is supported by the fact that the Antichrist has to march against them at the Battle of Armageddon. Therefore, we see that Israel is not totally defeated at the end of the last three-and-a-half years.

We can also discern from Daniel 11:44 that all the nations of the earth do not come under the Antichrist's control. In the book of Daniel, nations from the North and East trouble him, then the Antichrist goes forth with great fury to destroy. The fact that the Antichrist has to go forth with fury tells us that he is not in complete control.

Before Armageddon we see other nations rise against the Antichrist's government. It appears as though a couple of wars are fought in the Antichrist's efforts to conquer Israel and the world, with Armageddon being the final battle that brings the Antichrist's reign to a close.

This information tells us that the Antichrist controls the world's *system* while making every effort to be the dominant world superpower. Also, we can readily see in Scripture that the Antichrist is able to flex his governmental power, might, and muscle while destroying many people and establishing a new economic system. This system will include the mark of the beast. It is also obvious that the Antichrist does not gain complete control of all nations.

As previously mentioned, historically the greatest revivals in America have occurred after a major world war. (We will discuss the third world war in a later section.) We also see that America has continually backed Israel. While the Antichrist persecutes Israel and the saints, it is very possible that a great spiritual awakening might occur in America.

Heavy persecution has always served to identify those who are with Christ and those who are not. Heavy persecution causes revival among those who are truly serving the Lord—Christians who are willing to put their lives on the line for the gospel. True revival among the saints (God begins with his own house) causes a renewed sense of passion for the presence of the Lord, the fear of the Lord, and hunger for his Word.

When the elements of revival are permeating the church, evangelism is a natural outgrowth. This is exactly what happened to the early church in the book of Acts. The more persecution the church suffered, the more the church prayed and worshipped. The more they prayed and worshipped, the more the church grew (see Acts 2:42-47; 4:13-33).

We also must keep in mind that the saints will still be here during Satan's wrath—the last three-and-a-half years. Therefore, we see a body of believers being brought together in power by a common thread—*passion and persecution.*

At the return of Christ, we also see that there are sheep nations and goat nations. The sheep nations retain their dominion, and the goat nations lose their dominion. We can speculate from Scripture that America will be a sheep nation because it appears as though they continue to aid Israel. Pray that they will continue to do so.

As we move forward in our study we will plainly see that the Great Tribulation is not a seven-year period of God's wrath being poured out, but rather a time of Satan's wrath. The Great Tribulation is a time when the Antichrist will rise to power, and persecute Israel and the saints. It is also a time when the Antichrist dominates the world's economic system, and rules over a ten-nation union while proclaiming peace, yet actually bringing sudden destruction. If the Great Tribulation sounds scary, just remember that it is only three-and-a-half years. That is less than one U.S. presidential term!

As we conclude this portion of the study, let us also remember a very important piece of Daniel's prophecy. "But the people that do know their God *shall be strong, and do exploits. And they that understand among the people shall instruct many*" (Daniel 11:32-33).

Let's Review

- The Antichrist is a man with specific characteristics mentioned in the Bible.
- The Antichrist is a Gentile.
- The Antichrist does not regard the desire of woman. Biblically this means that he will probably be pro-abortion (anti-family).
- He will seek to change times and laws.
- The Antichrist will be a globalist and an environmentalist.
- He will destroy marvelously with peace.
- He is "more stout" than his fellows (more than likely speaking of his political stature).
- The Antichrist is the "little horn" that rises out of a ten-nation union (most likely a revived Roman Empire).
- He will persecute Israel and the saints for the last three-and-a-half years of Daniel's seventieth week.
- Considering where we are in prophecy, it is very possible that the Antichrist is alive and active today.

Mark of the Beast

And he causeth all, both small and great, rich and poor, free and bond, to receive a mark in their right hand, or in their foreheads: And that no man might *buy or sell*, save he that had the *mark*, or the *name* of the beast, or the *number* of his name. Here is wisdom. Let him that hath understanding count the number of the beast: for it is the number of a man; and his number is six hundred threescore and six [666].

REVELATION 13:16-18

In this section we will not only examine the mark of the beast from a biblical standpoint, but also from the world's point of view. When many people consider the mark of the beast within the last several decades, it has become rather obvious that the initiation and perpetuation of the mark of the beast will be accomplished through technology. This is one of the many things we will find out in this section.

Something else we will see is that from the world's perspective the mark of the beast will be about global economics and financial security. Nonetheless, spiritually speaking, the mark of the beast is about *who* and *what* we worship.

The True Cause of War

As we have already seen, the world has experienced more casualties from war during the last century than any previous century. Why? As technology increases so does our capability to kill mass amounts of people. We have also witnessed many evil dictators rise and employ genocide and political purges as a vehicle to exercise absolute power over the masses. The fact is, we are living in perilous times!

Once again, the world community cites three causes for war—politics, economics, and religion. Global politicians believe that if we have one government in control and one global army, we could eliminate war. The problem is, what if another Adolph Hitler gained control of the global army? A humanistic globalist does not recognize that the true cause of war is sin.

James 4:1-4 tells us,

> From whence come wars and fightings among you? Come they not hence, even of your lusts that war in your members? Ye lust, and have not; ye kill, and desire to have, and cannot obtain; ye fight and war, yet ye have not, because ye ask not. Ye ask, and receive not, because ye ask amiss, that ye may consume it upon your lusts. Ye adulterers and adulteresses, know ye not that the *friendship of the world is enmity with God?* Whosoever therefore will be a friend of the world is the enemy of God.

Wars and striving come from within our members; it is a condition of the heart. In order to truly stop war people must change on the inside—within their own members. There is only One who is capable of doing that kind of inward work, and his name is Jesus.

James 4:1-4 also touches on economics. In this world are those who have, and those who have not. Every major war has been the result of a national leader lusting after something, which they cannot have unless it is taken by force.

The world community believes that if they could get people to agree politically, economically, and religiously, we could put an end to all war, thus providing world peace.

Several critical elements are needed, however, in order to establish effective global control:

- ◆ To obtain global governance the "world community" [UN] would have to bring everyone under some sort of common global ethic, or ideology.

- ◆ For a global government to be truly effective, member nations will have to give up their national sovereignty.

- ◆ A unification of religions is also necessary in order to manipulate religious ideologies in a world government. Control of religions will ensure a world government that there will be no interference from radical fundamentalists. (We will examine this element further in the next two sections.)

- ◆ Another major roadblock on the path to a global government is *economics*.

In order to establish an influential one-world government, world leaders will have to entice peoples and nations to give up their economic ties. For the one-world government to work, there must be either a common currency, or a common system for financial transactions. World leaders believe they must have some type of universal system through which they can effectively manage the economy of a global community. Ultimately this type of system cannot totally dominate due to two innate factors: 1. human desire, and 2. the laws of supply and demand. Nevertheless, world leaders will try to institute a worldwide economic system.

Many powerful economic unions are already in place around the globe. There is even a single organization that exercises authority over all the others. Let us take a quick look at these powerful economic unions.

The European Union

A century ago the average person would have never dreamed that the world might be on the verge of uniting under a global government and a worldwide economic system. Most would have considered that idea futile simply because everybody has a different currency, everybody has a different product, and most nations covet their sovereignty. Sixty years ago people would have never imagined that over ten nations would come together and have one currency as Europe has succeeded in doing.

An article in *Time* magazine, January 2000, said, "On the first of January, 300,000,000 Europeans in twelve countries will wake up to a new currency—the Euro." (Note: *National Geographic*, January 2002, says the EU has 380,000,000 people.)

There are several major financial systems in the world today. The European Union (EU) is one of those large economic unions. Currently, the EU Common Market has close to 400,000,000 people. It does an exchange of 7 trillion dollars per year!

APEC

Another enormous financial body is the Asian Pacific Economic Corporation (APEC), which consists of eighteen nations amassing 1.6 billion people, with a yearly trading volume of 15 trillion dollars! China is one of the founders of APEC.

NAFTA

A more recent economic union is the North Atlantic Free Trade Association (NAFTA), which came into effect in 1994, and consists of 381,000,000 people in thirty-four nations throughout North and Central America. NAFTA has a yearly trading volume of 6.3 trillion dollars!

When free trade opened up between the U.S., Canada, and Mexico it was supposed to increase jobs in the United States. The ratification of NAFTA in the U.S. Congress infuriated many Americans. Instead of producing jobs in America, many companies–including RCA, Otis Elevator, and Westinghouse–jumped ship and went outside the U.S. to produce their goods. As a result, thousands of Americans lost good paying jobs due to the fact that large corporations moved in order to obtain cheaper labor. This is one example of the fallacy of global economics.

Another side of the institution of NAFTA is the political aspect. GATT, which later became the World Trade Organization, placed numerous companies under great pressure (through tariffs) to move to second and third world countries. In retrospect, this was the UN's way of trying to "spread out the wealth."

Because we are coming into a time of global economics, the United States of America (or any other country) cannot depend upon loyalty from large corporations. The bottom line is, big corporations will go wherever they feel they can flourish. In addition, corporations will continue to feel the pressure from the world community to disperse their wealth around the globe.

The WTO

Another large global economic system is the World Trade Organization (WTO), which is also an arm of the United Nations. The WTO (formerly GATT) oversees *all* these other economic unions. It is a global economic body that supervises world trade, tariffs, and economic treaties.

Not long ago a meeting was held in New York City called the World Trade Summit. When the WTO convened this meeting, a massive demonstration took place outside the meeting. Why? Because third-world countries wanted to know what the WTO was going to do about poverty in their countries. What is evident to some, but the world does not understand, is that global economics is not the answer.

Many people are not aware that the WTO meets in total secrecy, not allowing the average citizen of a country to view their proceedings. What is truly frightening is that within the WTO there is no veto power![85] Each country has one vote regardless of the size of the country.

The charter for the WTO consists of 22,000 pages. When President Clinton quickly pushed the ratifying of this document through the U.S. Congress, only one member of the U.S. Senate had read the entire document. This lone senator voted against it![86]

In a nutshell, the purpose of the WTO is that when disagreements arise between countries concerning tariffs or trade, the WTO steps in and decides what each country will do. Consider the implications of these WTO decisions. What we are witnessing is global powers meeting in secret, and world leaders having no veto power over global trade decisions.

The number one tool that the UN uses to get countries to conform to the New World Order is *economic sanctions*. Before the 1960s, Cuba used to be a popular resort location for many Americans. However, after the Cuban Missile Crisis the United States placed economic sanctions on Cuba. Because of these sanctions it is illegal to buy Cuban cigars. Guess what happened to Cuba after the United States placed economic sanctions on them...Cuba's economy took a nose-dive!

---

[85]*Final Warning*, Grant R. Jeffrey, (Harvest House Publishers, 1996) p. 338. Also see The Phyllis Schlafly Report, June 1994.
[86]ibid. *Final Warning*, pp. 336-337.

By all appearances the UN has used economic sanctions to manipulate national elections. One example of this is the pressure the UN, via the WTO, placed on South Africa. UN sanctions against South Africa aided in placing a man named Nelson Mandela into power.

Many years ago U.S. tax dollars, through the UN and the WTO, placed economic sanctions on Haiti and succeeded in putting a Catholic priest named Bertrand Aristide into power.[87] Aristide was a liberation-theologist who believed that if Jesus were alive on the earth today he would be a Marxist (Communist). Liberation Theology is a union between Catholicism and Marxism.

UN economic sanctions were also extremely effective after the first Gulf War. It was then that the UN placed economic sanctions on Iraq because Saddam Hussein refused to comply with their demands to allow UN inspectors to inspect Iraq's weapons. The UN basically said, "We are going to come in and do what we want to do, or else..." The next thing we saw on the news was Saddam's people starving.

We might think, "That is fine as long as it is Iraq." Yet, what if the UN put sanctions on the United States of America? They know that the most effective way to get nations to comply with their demands is to hit them in the pocketbook. If nations refuse to do what the global government wants them to do, they place economic sanctions on them so that they cannot effectively buy or sell. The purpose of global economic sanctions is to whip countries into submission.

At this point, veto power within the UN Security Council is the only thing that protects the sovereignty of the United States of America. On the other hand, in the WTO *no one* has veto power!

Furthermore, when the proposed global tax is in place, the United Nations will not need the United States or its money any longer. What happens if the United States chooses to remain

---

[87]ibid. *EndTime Magazine*, and *Encarta Encyclopedia*.

sovereign? What happens when America says, "We are not going to give up our rights! We are going to trade with who we want, and sanction who we want!" The UN is going to say, "No you are not!"

It has been said that those who do not learn from history are destined to repeat it. George Washington warned America never to give up its national sovereignty! He learned from the Bible that if you lay with dogs you are going to get fleas!

America needs to be ready for persecution if we ever decide to pull out of the WTO. Why? The U.S. does the majority of its business through world trade. If the WTO puts economic sanctions on the U.S., and cuts off a portion of its importing and exporting, the results could be much worse than the Great Depression. In addition, we do not live in an agrarian type society as Americans did in the 1920s when many families kept a garden.

Some might say, "Oh that will never happen!" On the contrary, in the fall of 2002 the Associated Press (Geneva) reported, "WTO Allows Sanctions Against United States." The article said, "The World Trade Organization ruled today that the European Union can impose trade sanctions of up to $4 billion against the United States in a tax dispute, the biggest penalty it has ever allowed." The article went on to say, "The sanctions were *twenty times* the amount levied in any previous WTO dispute."

For many decades America has enjoyed being the leader in the world's financial market. If we did not like something the UN was doing, we would take our ball and go home. That is no longer the case. Today, America rises or falls (as do most countries) according to the global market.

Is it possible that the moral and ethical decisions of Americans (even Christians) will be steered according to global economics? Will Americans decide to institute the mark of the beast so that they can buy and sell in a global market in order to maintain their comfortable way of life? Will comfort and moneymaking outweigh our devotion to God? We need to ask ourselves these questions because that is where our society is heading.

According to the Scriptures this approaching economic power will be so broad that it will not only affect individuals, but also nations.

In Revelation 13:11-18 we are told:

> And I beheld another beast coming up out of the earth; and he had two horns like a lamb, and he spake as a dragon. And he exerciseth all the power of the first beast before him, and causeth the earth and them which dwell therein to worship the first beast, whose deadly wound was healed. And he doeth great wonders, so that he maketh the fire come down from heaven on the earth in the sight of men, and deceiveth them that dwell on the earth by the means of those miracles which he had power to do in the sight of the beast; saying to them that dwell on the earth, that they should make an image to the beast, which had the wound by a sword, and did live. And he had power to give life unto the image of the beast, that the image of the beast should both speak, and cause that as many as would not worship the image of the beast should be killed. *And he causeth all*, both small and great, rich and poor, free and bond, to receive a mark in their right hand, or in their foreheads: And *that no man might buy or sell, save he that had the mark*, or the name of the beast, or the number of his name. Here is wisdom. Let him that hath understanding count the number of the beast: for it is the number of a man; and his number is six hundred threescore and six.

Why does the devil want people to take this mark? Again, it is all about whom we worship, what we have faith in, and whom we are going to follow!

Technology and the Benefits of the Mark

Technology, like anything else God gives us, can be used for good or for evil. The mark of the beast will control and manipulate people's lives in a global economy. Think about the fact that the mark (in terms of technology) will impact the economies of entire nations. That was not even possible until the last quarter of the last century.

Some might argue that this type of manipulation and control could never happen in this day and age. Remember, it was not that many years ago that Lenin and Stalin gathered up all those who would not comply with their Communist government in the Soviet Union. Then those evil dictators killed those they gathered, or confined them to prison and work camps. Joseph Stalin beat and tortured people until they either conformed to his wishes, or until they died. Mao Tse-tung did the same thing in China.

Then there was Adolph Hitler who gathered up the Jews, put a mark on them (the Star of David), placed them in prison camps, and killed 6,000,000 of them. All these things happened within the last century! Once again, we are living in perilous times.

Why would anyone desire to take the mark of the beast? Surely great benefits will be presented in order to entice a person into taking the mark. It seems logical that the world will advertise the mark in such a way that a person would be crazy to refuse. God's Word warns that if possible, even the elect will be deceived (see Matthew 24:24). The world will consider a Christian who refuses the mark of the beast as a fundamental religious weirdo.

In 1986 the infamous attorney F. Lee Bailey proposed a law that no one could have over $200 cash at any one time. Bailey said, "Only drug dealers and criminals need cash."[88] If we conducted all of our transactions electronically, why would anyone need cash? This is the first time in history when that type of system has been possible. It is becoming obvious that we are quickly heading toward a cashless system.

------

[88]*South Bend (Indiana) Tribune*, June 5, 1986.

Not that long ago President Clinton was pushing hard for a national medical identification card for the purpose of security. After the September 11 attack on America, rhetoric had already begun concerning a national ID card to make Americans safer. In *Time* magazine, January 2002, an article ran that explained, "Big Brother already knows where you live. Why not let him make you safer?"

Already in Denmark everyone has to have a national ID card,[89] and in many European nations you have to have a national ID card in order to conduct any type of business. Prime Minister Tony Blair is pushing hard for a national ID card in England, and he was even pushing President Bush to implement one in the United States. This idea is not new. There was a proposal as far back as the early 1980s for such a card.[90]

There could be many benefits with an ID card (security card or security mark). It would eliminate the need for paper money. In a cashless system there would be less robbery and crime. The IRS and the banks would love such a system!

Some banks do over two million transactions in a single day! Every paper transaction (checking accounts, etc.) cost fifty cents to a dollar to produce. A paper trail generates large amounts of expense for the banking system. In the future, electronic financial transactions will be the way to go because they only cost an average of three cents a piece.

Furthermore, with a paper trail there are always floaters– transactions where the "check's in the mail," but the transaction takes much longer than preferred by the banks or the customers. At times there might be millions of dollars floating around in the banking system. Electronic transactions eliminate floaters with the push of a button.

---

[89]*Indianapolis Star,* November 11, 1978.
[90]*U.S. News and World Report*, September 15, 1980, and USA Today, September 12, 1984.

There is a system now called SWIFT (Society for Worldwide Inter-bank Financial Transmission), a part of the WTO. A person who is a part of SWIFT can make a transaction in any bank in the world. Security, speed, and accessibility will be the big selling points for the cashless one-world system. New Guinea is one of the most underdeveloped countries in the world. Less than half of the people there have shoes. Yet, they are fully functioning on electronic transactions!

Another great benefit to the cashless global economy is that it eliminates all the sundry numbers in our lives. For example, most people have anywhere from six to ten very important numbers, ie. Social Security, driver's license, checking account, medical insurance, credit card, phone, birthdate, and address. Some of these numbers are so important that if anyone stole even one of them, it could severely disrupt our lives.

Identity theft is one of the biggest problems in America. In Michigan City (Indiana) Prison, at one time one-third of the prisoners were incarcerated for check fraud. Imagine being presented with one number, which is an extremely secure form of identification, for *all* worldwide transactions. The world will be ecstatic over such a system!

Think about the great benefits of a security mark when it locates missing children or adults. NBC News, June 17, 2003, reported on two products developed by Digital Angel to help locate missing children. One is a child's watch with a Global Positioning Satellite (GPS) device, and the other a beeper-type product with a GPS device. *Good Housekeeping* magazine endorsed these products with the only noted concern that they did not work well around tall buildings.

Those products sound good, except that now that they are in the public eye, any child abductor will immediately check for, and then rid a child, of these devices. Once these products are proven not to work as well as expected, we will simply be one step closer to the mark.

Hypothetically, imagine *Good Housekeeping* being willing to endorse the best child protection product yet...the electronic chip. Imagine the advertisement: "Allow Digital Angel to watch over your child! Our angelic protection has the *Good Housekeeping* seal of approval with one notable concern–opposition from fundamental Christians!" This idea could become an easy sell to parents in the twenty-first century! If a child that was missing had received an electronic implant, authorities could instantly track them by way of Global Positioning Satellites.

In *Popular Science*, July 1995, Ronald Kane, vice president of Cubic Corporation, the number one producer of Smart Card Systems for terminals, said, "If we had our way we would place a chip behind the ear of every child that comes out of the maternity ward."

The tragedy that struck America on September 11, 2001, drove home this idea of electronic identification. Workers at the Twin Towers site said that most of the concrete blocks of the buildings were reduced to pieces of rubble not much bigger than the human hand. After tragedies like this, we hear talk of how identification of victims in this type of situation would be much easier if people had received an electronic chip implant.

There are so many plusses involved with an electronic identification system. A security mark or microchip implant would be a logical solution for providing peace and security in these perilous times. Those in the world will say that a person would be stupid not to take the mark.

Why will the one-world government desire to force the mark on people? If the world views the mark as the greatest device yet to produce safety and security, then logically the only people (in their eyes) who would refuse the mark would be criminals or terrorists. However, those who understand what God's Word has to say about these issues will boldly refuse the mark.

What is the mark of the beast going to be?

Is it just going to be a chip implant? Is it going to be a card? Is it going to be a biometric, or retina-scan (scanning of the eye)? The Bible gives three ways that the mark of the beast is implemented:

1. on the forehead,
2. on the right hand,
3. receiving the name of the beast, or the number of his name (see Revelation 13:16-17).

According to Scripture a person could receive a mark another way besides on the forehead or right hand. Revelation 13:17 speaks of receiving the *name* or *number* of his name. There will no doubt be individuals who cannot receive the mark in the form of an electronic chip under their skin due to physical or medical restrictions. The world will make it suitable and beneficial for *all* to receive the mark in other ways.

In 1996 a U.S. Patent (App. No.: 709,471) was acquired for a method for verifying human identity during electronic sales transactions. The abstract for the patent reads:

> A method is presented for facilitating sales transactions by electronic media. A bar code or a design is *tattooed* on an individual. Before the sales transaction can be consummated, the tattoo is scanned with a scanner. Once verified, the seller may be authorized to debit the buyer's electronic bank account in order to consummate the transaction (emphasis added).

Several years ago a Visa commercial showed an individual walking around a store sticking groceries in his pockets. At first the viewer has the idea that the person is shoplifting, especially as the man walks out the front door and is stopped by a police officer. The officer shouts, "Hey mister! You forgot your receipt!" The man turns and takes a receipt out of a sensor by the doors, then turns to the officer and says, "Thanks!" The commercial ends with the announcer saying, "Visa...Smart Money!" These advances in technology will drastically cut time at airports, banks, grocery stores...you name it.

Currently, veterinarians use a special needle to insert computer chip implants a little bigger than a grain of rice under the skin of pets. In Spain this identification chip is mandatory in cattle. The implant can hold around 10,000 pages of information on a person and be scanned by a computer!

In 1999 CNN did a report on Professor Kevin Warwick, the director of cryogenics at the University of Reading. On Monday, August 24, 1998, Warwick became the first human host of a microchip. During a twenty-minute procedure, described as a routine silicon implant by Dr. George Bilious, doctors inserted into Warwick's arm a glass capsule not much bigger than a pearl. The capsule holds several microprocessors.

When asked how he felt, Warwick replied, "In my building I feel much more powerful, in a mental way. Not at one with the computer, but much, much closer."

Why did Warwick say this? Because now when he walks up to his house the doors unlock. When he leaves his house, the doors lock and the alarms set. When he walks into his office the lights come on and the computer says, "Hello, Mr. Warwick." That is the mental power of which Warwick speaks. He went on to say that without this power he would feel as if a part of him were missing.

Warwick proclaimed that this implant has real world implications. He envisions enormous medical applications such as helping paralytics to walk, and that is just the beginning.

On February 13, 2002, a Florida couple took the chip. This couple told the press that they wanted to be the first to have a Radio Frequency Identification Chip placed in their bodies, mostly as a means of dealing with medical issues. Around the same time a Brazilian official announced that he is traveling to the United States to be fitted with a personal RFI Chip as a deterrent to kidnapping.

An article ran in *Time* magazine, March 11, 2002, called "Meet the Chipsons." The subtitle read, "Jeffrey, Leslie, and their boy Derek will be America's first cyborg family. Are you ready to 'Get

Chipped?'" In the article Jeffrey explained, "The advantage of the chip is that the information is available at the time of need. It would speak for me, give me a voice when I don't have one."

If that is not sobering enough consider the closing words of the article:

"Here [in the U.S.] we're still dealing with FDA, privacy, and civil liberties issues," says Bolton (vice president of Applied Digital Solutions). "But we're not stopping. We're going into South America right now!" Technology has a way of moving faster than legislation, and if it comes down to a race between cyborgs and senators, guess who will win? Resistance is futile.

Applied Digital Solutions, which holds the patent rights to Digital Angel, says that with Digital Angel they can track every living person on the planet.

Currently VeriChip has a "Chipmobile" that is on the move giving anyone who is interested an opportunity to "get chipped." Interestingly, the U.S. Department of Commerce and the globalist World Economic Council have thrown their weight behind VeriChip.[91] On the VeriChip website they offer visitors the opportunity to "Pre-Register for your personal VeriChip." VeriChip also lines out the two greatest benefits of the chip: *security identification and financial identification*. (View their website at www.adsx.com.)

Is it possible to take the mark of the beast without knowing?

A couple of questions will undoubtedly arise within the Christian community concerning technology and the mark of the beast.

---

[91]*Understanding the End Time*, Irvin Baxter Jr., copyright 1995, 1999, 2000, p. 176.

1. Technology like the VeriChip obviously is a wonderful advancement to the security of children, finances, medical issues, etc. Why would it be wrong to take it if the government is not saying that I cannot buy or sell without it?

2. If I did take a mark (tattoo, chip, number) and the government came along later and said, "Now you have to have a mark so that you can buy or sell," could I not just have it removed at that point?

Many people might have thought when credit cards came out that it was the mark of the beast. We know that the credit cards in and of themselves are not the mark of the beast. Yet, what if the government said that we could not buy or sell unless we have the proper credit card? Now we have a problem!

The VeriChip may not be the mark of the beast, but it seems obvious that it is the type of technology that will help *facilitate* the mark of the beast. In other words, the world stage is being set for the coming global economic system, and the technology we are witnessing (e.g. SWIFT, tattoos, chip implants) will no doubt play an enormous role. Therefore, the trap that we must be aware is (we will use the chip as an example):

a) A person takes the chip.

b) That same person becomes used to the chip.

c) Then they enjoy their comfortable lifestyle with the chip.

d) Afterward they cannot *give up* the chip.

Follow-up questions: How easy will it be for that person to give up the chip after they have acclimated themselves to the comfort and ease of having it? Will the person who takes the chip be able to give it up even when they are told they could not buy or sell without it? Will they succumb to the enemy's trap, just as Adam and Eve did in the Garden of Eden while agreeing with the devil as he asked, "Did God really say…?" This has always been the devil's subtle way of snaring believers.

Revelation 14:9-11 tells us:

> And the third angel followed them, saying with a loud voice, "If any man worship the beast and his image, and receive his mark in his forehead, or in his hand, the same shall drink of the wine of the wrath of God, which is poured out without mixture into the cup of his indignation; and he shall be tormented with fire and brimstone in the presence of the holy angels, and in the presence of the Lamb: And the smoke of their torment ascendeth up forever and ever: and they have no rest day nor night, who worship the beast and his image, *and whosoever receiveth the mark of his name.*"

Revelation 13:14 shows us that the beast deceives those that dwell on the earth. Will there be Christians who take the mark so that they can buy, sell, and continue their comfortable lifestyles? That is very possible, and unfortunately, it is also very likely. Remember this is all about whom, or what, we worship.

The mark of the beast is easy to recognize in Scripture. When the world says, "You cannot buy or sell unless you have this particular name, number, or mark," guess what? That is the mark of the beast! This aspect of identifying the mark of the beast should be obvious to those who stay informed.

It is possible that Christians who waver may be deceived into taking the mark while hoping that God will forgive them in the end. The Bible makes it clear, however, that those who take the mark of the beast are lost for eternity. It cannot be emphasized enough that the mark of the beast is all about who we worship. The bottom line is, if we are not *living* for Christ we will never *die* for Christ!

Will all be forced to take the mark or suffer the consequences?

Revelation 13:16 says, "He causeth all, both small and great, rich and poor, free and bond, to receive a mark." In this verse, the word "all" is clearly speaking of groups or classes of people. The mark of the beast will affect all *classes* of people–small, great, rich, poor, free, and bond.

We have already learned that Edom, Moab, and Ammon will not fall under the Antichrist's rule. We have also learned that not every nation follows the beast. Scripture reveals that the Antichrist never fully subdues the world, but he does gain control of the world's system. The mark of the beast (a global economic system) will certainly impact the entire world. Nevertheless, it is still our choice as to whether or not we accept the mark. We need to be ready in our hearts to make the right choice.

To most in the world community the UN's economic sanctions, the UN's peacekeeping army subduing any unruly nations, and the EU superpower flexing their muscles will become business as usual. Most people will simply learn to bend with the breeze and look unfavorably upon those who choose not to conform. For most, taking the mark of the beast will be as casual as applying for a credit card or receiving a Social Security number.

Even though the Antichrist and the coming one-world government may not control every nation, they will be the dominant world superpower. It seems clear in Scripture that the Antichrist's system will be the major influence in the global economy. This will make it very difficult for all those who do not wish to do business through the mark of the world's system. It is also apparent in Scripture that the Antichrist will force those under his control to take a mark or be put to death.

In the times that are quickly approaching, if a person loves their job more than they love God, they will probably take the mark. If those who are under the thumb of the Antichrist love their children more than God, they will probably take the mark of the beast.

A line is being drawn in the sand. We must remember that strength for these times comes from the Spirit of God! Also, that He has not given us a spirit of fear, but of power, love, and a sound mind (see 2 Timothy 1:7).

Those who take the mark of the beast, or worship the beast, are damned for eternity. We must not be ignorant of the devil's devices. The mark of the beast will not be presented with a pitchfork, a red devil suit, and a person saying, "If you take this you are condemned!" At first the mark of the beast will be subtle; more than likely it will come in phases. When we are mindful of our location in Bible prophecy, then we can see what is coming down the road and we can make decisions that will please the Lord and not man.

According to worldly philosophies, money and power go hand in hand. The individuals involved in creating a one-world government have understood for many decades that they must gain control of our pocketbooks. If they can do this, they can manipulate economic ties, politics, and even religion. A cashless society allows for complete control, such complete control that the government can say, "You cannot buy or sell unless..."

We are going to finish this section of teaching with some economic information that hits much closer to home. In America the manipulation of economics began many decades ago in the form of the Federal Reserve, a central bank. Many Christians are unaware of the behind-the-scenes power brokering that has occurred in a grand effort to control the masses through the control of U.S. currency. It will be worth your while as a Christian, as a student of end-time prophecy, and as a patriot to understand the following information. As we will see, the Federal Reserve in America has helped pave the way for global economic power, and quite possibly the mark of the beast.

The Federal Reserve Bank

Rothschild, a London banker and major Federal Reserve investor, wrote a letter saying:

It (Central Bank) gives the National Bank almost complete control of national finance. The few who understand the system will either be so interested in its profits, or so dependent on its favours, that there will be no opposition from that class... The great body of the people, mentally incapable of comprehending, will bear its burden without complaint, and perhaps without even suspecting that the system is inimical [contrary] to their interests.[92]

One enormous concern to America in this new world of global economics is the value of the dollar. In the United States the Federal Reserve regulates the value of the dollar. Before the turn of the last century [1900] the value of the U.S. dollar would rise and fall based upon how much gold the United States had in its reserve.

After the establishment of the Federal Reserve our paper dollar is worth whatever the Federal Reserve, as well as investors and foreign currency traders, says it is worth. This is called fiat money. The value of fiat money is based upon how much confidence the user has in the government–the one issuing the money.

In order to understand how easily America could be swept up, or swallowed up, in a global economy we need to have understanding of how the U.S. dollar is regulated and who actually owns it. The banking dynasties listed below have exercised a significant amount of control over the New York Federal Reserve District, which controls the other eleven Federal Reserve Districts. These banks also are partly *foreign owned* and control the New York Federal Reserve District Bank.

---

[92]ibid. *The Federal Reserve is a Privately Owned Corporation*, by Thomas D. Schauf.

The ownership of the twelve central banks was a very well-kept secret for many decades. Since 1914 the secrecy, operation, and ownership of the Federal Reserve was so great that the primary owners were not known until recently.[93] The following are the banking dynasties and primary stockholders and owners of the Federal Reserve Banking system:

Rothschild (found in five pivotal nations of Europe)
Warburg (Germany and Holland)
Sassoon (cousins of the Rothschilds operating in the Far East)
Lazard Freres (France)
Mendolsohn (Amsterdam)
Israel Moses Seif (Italy)
Kuhn Loeb (New York)
Goldman Sachs (New York)
Lehman Brothers (New York)[94]

When England lost America's War of Independence, they planned to control us by controlling our banking system, the printing of our money, and our debt. It was Rothschild who said, "I don't care who the government is, let me control the money and I will control the country." The bankers listed above were connected to London Banking Houses, which ended up controlling the Federal Reserve.

How did it happen? After previous attempts to push the Federal Reserve Act through Congress, a group of bankers funded and staffed Woodrow Wilson's campaign for president. Wilson had committed to sign this act. In 1913 Senator Nelson Aldrich, maternal grandfather to the Rockefellers, pushed the Federal Reserve Act through Congress just before Christmas when much of Congress was on vacation. When elected, Wilson passed the Federal Reserve Act. Later, he remorsefully replied, *"I have unwittingly ruined my country."*[95]

---

[93]ibid. *One World*, by Tal Brooke, p. 243.
[94]ibid. *One World*, by Tal Brooke, (End Run Publishing), © 1989 & 2000, pp. 230-234.
[95]*Repeal the Federal Reserve Banks*, by Rev. Casimir Frank Gierut, p. 31.

The Federal Reserve Act became law the day before Christmas Eve, in the year 1913, and shortly afterwards, the German International bankers Kuhn Loeb and Company sent one of their partners to the U.S. to run it. Paul Warburg was the first chairman of the Federal Reserve until it was revealed that his brother Max Warburg was head of the Central Bank of Germany.[96]

Thomas Jefferson warned, "If the American people ever allow private banks to control the issue of their money, first by inflation and then by deflation, the banks and corporations that will grow up around them, *will deprive the people of their property until their children will wake up homeless on the continent their fathers conquered.*" Thomas Jefferson also said, "I believe that banking institutions are more dangerous to our liberties than standing armies."

Congressman Charles A. Lindbergh of Minnesota said: "This [Federal Reserve] Act establishes the most gigantic trust on earth. When the president [Wilson] signs this bill, the invisible government of the monetary power will be legalized... the worst legislative crime of the ages, perpetuated by this banking and currency bill."[97]

On May 23, 1933, Congressman Louis T. McFadden brought formal charges against the Board of Governors of the Federal Reserve Bank system, the Comptroller of the Currency, and the Secretary of United States Treasury for numerous criminal acts, including but not limited to, conspiracy, fraud, unlawful conversion, and treason.

In his speech to Congress McFadden explained the following concerning the Federal Reserve:

> Some people think that the Federal Reserve Banks [are] United States Government institutions. *They are private monopolies*, which prey upon the people of these United

---

[96]ibid. *One World*, by Tal Brooke, p. 234.
[97]*The Most Secret Science*, (Betsy Ross Press, P.O. Box 986, Ft. Collins, CO 80522), p. 33.

States for the benefit of themselves and their foreign customers; foreign and domestic speculators and swindlers; and rich predatory moneylender[s]. In that dark crew of financial pirates there are those who would cut a man's throat to get a dollar out of his pocket; there are those who send money into states to buy votes to control our legislatures; there are those who maintain international propaganda for the purpose of deceiving us into granting of new concessions which will permit them to cover up their past misdeeds and set again in motion their gigantic train of crime.

These twelve private credit monopolies were deceitfully and disloyally foisted upon this country by the bankers who came here from Europe and repaid us our hospitality by undermining our American institutions.

We were opposed to the Aldrich plan for a central bank. The men who rule the Democratic Party then promised the people that if they were returned to power there would be no central bank established here while they held the reins of government. Thirteen months later that promise was broken, and the Wilson administration, under the tutelage of those sinister Wall Street figures who stood behind Colonel House, established here in our free country the worm-eaten monarchical institution of the "King's Bank" *to control us from the top downward, and from the cradle to the grave (emphasis added).*[98]

---

[98]ibid, 1978 Arizona Caucus Club, and *The Federal Reserve Bank*, by H.S. Kenan, published by The Noontide Press.

In McFadden's speech he also said, "The Federal Reserve Board, a government board, has cheated the government of the United States and the people of the United States out of enough money to pay the national debt several times over." Since its inception, the Federal Reserve has not been audited!

How dangerous is the agenda of those behind the Federal Reserve? On February 17, 1950, the Council on Foreign Relations (CFR) member James Warburg (banker, and architect of the Federal Reserve System) stated before the Senate Foreign Relations Committee, "We shall have one-world government whether or not you like it, by conquest or consent."

If the U.S. does not do something to reform and refurbish the infrastructure of its economy, the European Union (the Euro) will become the standard and dictate what the U.S. dollar is worth. More than likely that is exactly how the *twelve private credit monopolies* will continue to marionette the U.S., while maneuvering us directly in line with the one-world economic system.

The Federal Reserve Banking system also gives powerful globalist bankers the leverage they need to threaten the sovereignty of the United States of America through the possibility of economic collapse. True reform must include America pulling out of the United Nations, and an audit and restructuring of the Federal Reserve System.

Christians must get involved in initiating reform in America. Christians must stand up and be a voice in every arena—including the political and economic. Otherwise America, along with the Christian church, will be swept up into a global society that includes immense economic pressure.

Christians understand that God is the answer and not politics. Yet, it is because of the sovereign plan of God that we can enjoy unalienable rights as citizens of the United States. Those who have been given such great freedoms must also endeavor to be brave stewards of those freedoms. Edmund Burke said it well when he said, "The only thing necessary for the triumph of evil is for good men to do nothing."

Concerning the mark of the beast, we must remember that when we are born again, we pledge allegiance to God! We say with our mouths and believe in our hearts that Jesus is Lord! When a person takes the mark and worships the beast (the world's system), they are pledging allegiance to the world and what it has to offer. They become a friend of the world, and an enemy of God. When a person takes the name of the beast, they receive his spirit.

In Revelation 20:4 we see the rewards for those who remain faithful to Christ:

> And I saw thrones, and they sat upon them, and judgment was given unto them: and I saw the souls of them that were beheaded for the witness of Jesus, and for the word of God, and which had not worshipped the beast, neither his image, neither had received his mark upon their foreheads, or in their hands; *and they lived and reigned with Christ a thousand years.*

This is not a game we are playing. We cannot shrug off the seriousness of these scriptures. We must settle these issues in our hearts, and we must remain loyal to Jesus at all cost no matter what happens in the global economy. In the end, those who remain loyal to Christ will reign with Him on the earth for a thousand years, then experience eternal life with Him.

Let's Review

- The mark of the beast is about whom we worship.
- The one-world government will exercise authority over all classes and races of people. The global government will make it extremely difficult for those who do not take the mark to buy or sell.
- There will be areas of the world where the Antichrist exercises complete control and tries to force everyone to take the mark.
- It is an individual's choice as to whether they receive the mark.
- According to Scripture there are three ways to receive the mark: The forehead, right hand, or the name of the beast.
- All those who take the mark are lost for eternity.
- Those who remain loyal to Christ, born-again believers who do not take the mark, will rule and reign with Him one thousand years.

Mystery, Babylon the Great

We have examined the political and economic side of end-time prophecy, and now we will take a look at the religious aspect of end-time prophecy.

The number one cause for war is religion. Religion is closer to people's hearts than their politics. As a result, they become offended when we talk about religion. Nevertheless, we must be mature enough to discuss religion or politics without absorbing offense.

We do realize that in writing this material we encountered a choice. We could have simply skipped over this topic; however, this topic covers *two entire chapters* in the book of Revelation. The other choice we have is to speak what we believe is the truth. Out of all of these end-time lessons, this may be the hardest lesson to teach and the hardest lesson for people to receive. Nevertheless, we will attempt to speak the truth without malice. The purpose of truth is to instruct, to correct, and to guide. The most important aspect of biblical truth is that it makes us free.

It is important to note that we are not coming against individuals in this teaching, but rather doctrine and a religious system that is clearly unscriptural and as a result has caused much harm.

Jesus experienced great difficulties with the dominant religious system of His day. The Jewish doctrine had become perverted and corrupt. We see this in Scripture when Jesus confronted the Pharisees. The Pharisees were the hardline sects of the Jewish religious leaders, and Jesus told them that they were of the "synagogue of Satan." Those words were very confrontational! Jesus did not commit sin when He spoke those words to the Pharisees. He walked this earth without sin, and was the expressed image of the Father (see Colossians 1:15; Hebrews 1:3).

Jesus spoke those poignant words in love to His own people, to the Jewish leadership in His Father's house (the temple) because His true desire was change. He told us that it is the truth that makes us free (see John 8:31-32).

In Scripture we see that Jesus and His disciples were not afraid to speak out against false doctrine. Therefore, we also should not be afraid to speak the truth in love, even if it is not politically correct!

Jesus said, "Many shall come in my name, and shall deceive many" (see Matthew 24:5). Too many times we can easily accept what a person says simply because they speak or come under the covering of Christianity. Many times we receive teaching [doctrine] without question just because a person may talk about Jesus. It is vitally important that we study the Word of God so that we may have discernment when it comes to biblical truth versus false doctrine.

Revelation 13:11-15 tells us:

> And I beheld another beast coming up out of the earth; and he had two horns like *a lamb,* and he spake *as a dragon.* And he exerciseth all the power of the first beast before him, and causeth the earth and them

which dwell therein *to worship the first beast,* whose deadly wound was healed. And he doeth great wonders, so that he maketh fire come down from heaven on the earth in the sight of men, and deceiveth them that dwell on the earth by the means of those miracles which he had power to do in the sight of the beast; saying to them that dwell on the earth, that they should make an image to the beast, which had the wound by a sword, and did live. And he had power to give life unto the image of the beast, that the image of the beast should both speak, and cause that as many as would not worship the image of the beast should be killed.

In Revelation 13:11 we see a creature that looks like a lamb, but speaks like a dragon. Who is the dragon? It is Satan (see Revelation 12:9). He has a doctrine of devils, but he *looks* like a lamb. He looks like a peacemaker. This passage is talking about someone who goes out before the Antichrist and his system while exercising power in accordance with the beast–the false prophet. We see in Scripture that a spiritual leader will rise (the false prophet) and will lead the world into something called a one-world religion.

We learned in previous lessons that two figures ruled the Holy Roman Empire–a political leader and the pope. When the pope is crowned, several titles are proclaimed over him at his coronation. Those titles include father of kings and princes, the pastor of the universe, and the vicar of the earth of our Lord Jesus Christ[99] (vicar means that the pope stands in the place of Christ[100]).

According to their prophecies the Catholic Church believes that Jesus Christ will not *physically* return. They believe that He will empower the Church to take over the world's system and bring 1,000 years of peace on the earth. At that time the pope

---

[99]*Encyclopedia Britannica*, 1971, Volume 22, p. 907.
[100]*Understanding Catholicism*, Second Edition, Bob Gorman and Mary Faulkner; (2003 Alpha Books, Indianapolis, Indiana), p. 46.

will become something called "king of kings" and will rule over the kings of the earth. Catholicism teaches that this is the spiritual ruling over the natural for 1,000 years until the Judgment Day.[101]

In Revelation chapters 17 and 18 we see a detailed description of this spiritual system, or spiritual government, called Mystery, Babylon the Great. Before summarizing these two chapters, we would encourage you to stop and read these two chapters in their entirety.

In these chapters we see the following description of this religious system:

- The great whore sits upon many waters (Revelation 17:1).
- The kings of the earth have committed fornication with her, and have been made drunk with the wine of her fornication (Revelation 17:2).
- The woman sits upon a *scarlet* colored beast (Revelation 17:3).
- The woman is arrayed in *purple* and *scarlet* color, and decked with gold, precious stones, and pearls having a golden cup in her hand full of abominations and filthiness of her fornication (Revelation 17:4).
- The name on her forehead is, MYSTERY, BABYLON THE GREAT, THE MOTHER OF HARLOTS AND ABOMINATIONS OF THE EARTH (Revelation 17:5).
- The woman was drunken with the blood of the *saints*, and with the blood of the *martyrs of Jesus* (Revelation 17:6).
- She rides upon the beast (the scarlet colored one-world government) (Revelation 17:7).
- She sits upon seven hills (Revelation 17:9).
- She sits upon the waters, which are peoples, multitudes, nations, and tongues (Revelation 17:15).

---

[101]*The Book of Catholic Prophecies,* by Yves Dupont, pp. 91, 117.

- The woman is a great city, which reigns over kings of the earth (Revelation 17:18).
- She becomes the habitation of devils, and the hold of every foul spirit, and a cage of every unclean and hateful bird (Revelation 18:2).
- The merchants of the earth have waxed rich through the abundance of her delicacies (Revelation 18:3).
- She glorifies herself, and says, *"I sit as a queen"* (Revelation 18:7).
- She has the voice of the bride and bridegroom in her (Revelation 18:23).
- She deceived nations by her sorcery. (Revelation 18:23)
- She possesses the souls of men (Revelation 18:13).

As we begin to dissect Revelation 17 and 18 we must ask ourselves many questions. Who is the "woman" of whom this passage speaks? What does she do? From where does this woman come? Where do true believers fit in this picture? We can also note that it appears as though the ten kings (possibly the prominent nations of the European Union) rebel against this woman and burn her with fire and destroy her in all of her glory. That scenario coincides with the same old conflict we saw in the Holy Roman Empire–the political clashing with the religious (see Revelation 17:16).

In examining this prophecy we will hit on the major portions that pertain to this powerful worldwide religious organization. As you will see, several of the descriptors mentioned fit together. Thus, there is no need to be redundant in our examination. The characteristics we do not dissect have either been spoken of in an earlier lesson, or they will become obvious as we examine the more prominent characteristics.

The first thing we should understand is that the woman is a *city*, and that she rides upon the *beast*.

In Revelation 17:7 we are told that the beast, which has seven heads and ten horns (the one-world government), carries the woman. Then, in verse 9 we see that the seven heads, which were the seven heads of the one-world government, transform to reveal the location of the woman, rather than putting the emphasis on the beast. The heads in this prophecy also represent seven hills on which the woman sits.

In other words, one fascinating aspect of this prophecy is that the woman (this religious harlot) not only sits upon the beast that has seven heads and ten horns, but she also is a city that sits upon seven hills. Now we understand that this religious organization has a strong connection, or relationship, with the one-world government, which includes the European Union, and is a city on seven hills.

As we examine this passage we need to answer several questions.

1. Is there a city in the world today that is seated on seven hills, which is also the headquarters of a religious organization that affects [influences] people from every kindred, tongue, and nation?

2. Is this city a partner with the political system of the New World Order?

3. Do the city and its religious organization fall in line with all the other criteria described in Revelation chapters 17 and 18?

One city fits this description very well! Rome is famous for being "the city of seven hills." The seven hills are so famous that they each have their own name: Aventine, Palantine, Capitoline, Quirinal, Viminal, Equiline, and Caelian.[102]

---

[102]*World Book Encyclopedia*, 1976, Volume 16, p. 405

When we examine the Catholic Church we are looking at an international system of government seated on seven hills. As we continue in our study we will also see that she is the Mother of Harlots, Abominations of the Earth, Mystery, and Babylon the Great.

Next let us examine the phrase "Babylon the Great."

The Catholic Church believes that Peter was the first pope,[103] Christ's successor on Planet Earth, and that he wrote a letter to them giving them a greeting from "Babylon" (see 1 Peter 5:13). The early Catholic Church believed that Babylon was the apostle Peter's secret name for ancient Rome. They not only believe Peter was speaking of Rome when he used the word Babylon, but they also believe it was during that time that he was the bishop of Rome.

Because the Church believes Peter was the bishop of Rome [Babylon], and the first pope, they set up their headquarters in Rome. In doing so they view themselves as following the model established by their first pope. So we see that the headquarters of the Catholic Church is on seven hills, and even the name Babylon the Great fits the Catholic Church. By the way, you will never find the word "pope" in the Bible. It simply does not exist. The papacy is an unscriptural office.

"The woman was arrayed in purple and scarlet."

Within the Catholic Church are cardinals, archbishops, bishops, and priests. These positions (under the authority of the pope) make up the Church's governing body. It is set up like an earthly government. What is even more interesting is that Scrip-

---

[103]ibid. *Understanding Catholicism*, Second Edition, pg. 47

ture reveals that the clothing of the harlot is scarlet and purple. Within the governmental system of Catholicism, they clothe the cardinals in scarlet [red] and the bishops in purple![104]

Why were these colors chosen? When Jesus was taken before Pilate and Herod, the Roman guards mocked Him by throwing a scarlet and purple robe on him while calling him the "King of the Jews." Essentially, the Catholic Church set their system up much like the Roman government, while using many of the same colors the Romans used. Keep in mind, however, that the Roman government participated in pagan worship, and many of the Romans brought pagan rituals into Catholicism.

The waters that the woman sits upon are all peoples, tongues, and nations.

Recognizing this characteristic within the Catholic Church is simple! For more than 1,500 years the Church has exercised power over peoples, tongues, and nations. Even today presidents and kings visit Rome to pay homage to the pope. As we have already learned, during the latter parts of the first millennia AD popes appointed kings as they willed. In this present era we have seen the pope's presence as the Berlin Wall fell, and he has even been invited to speak to the United Nations.

There are one billion Catholics in the world—nearly one of every five persons. Catholicism is the largest world religion, and is present on every continent in the world.[105] We do not have to look hard to see that Catholicism is a spiritual system that has infiltrated every kindred, tongue, and nation.

---

[104]Article, The Criterion, July 1, 1988.
[105]ibid. *Understanding Catholicism*, Second Edition, p. 29.

She says in her heart, "I sit as a queen."

When examining the Catholic doctrine it becomes clear that they believe Mary the mother of Jesus is deity, along with the Father, the Son, and the Holy Spirit. The "Assumption of Mary" was an edict handed down by Pope Pius XII (1950). Catholic doctrine teaches that Mary was sinless. In Catholicism a person comes to the Father through the Son, and to the Son through the Virgin Mary.

In the book *Understanding Catholicism*, written by Catholic theologians and endorsed by Catholic priests and theologians, it says:

Two other important roles that Mary plays for Catholics are as mother and as *queen of heaven*. She was given the title "queen of heaven" to show her power over death. Catholics believe she defied death to be taken up into heaven body and soul because her body did not deteriorate in the grave as a human body would, but instead was preserved. This belief has been defined as the "assumption of Mary into heaven." Catholics believe Mary rules over death as the queen of heaven. This role came out of the *Hellenistic mythology of Artemis* (later called Diana by the Romans). Artemis ruled over death as well.

Mary is "the mother of mercy, sweetness, and hope." Mary's role as *mediator* with her Son Jesus gives strength to the living, but her greatest function is in the Catholic understanding of death and redemption. According to Catholics, because Mary is human and has the closest connection to Christ, Jesus cannot refuse her requests...Mary gives God his human face in heaven as she did on earth. Mary has a way of touching God's heart. *Through her,* he becomes tangible as the God of mercy [106](emphasis added).

---

[106]ibid. *Understanding Catholicism*, Second Edition, p. 165.

These Catholic doctrines concerning Mary are not in the Bible. God's Word does not teach salvation through Mary! Jesus said that there is one way to the Father and that is through him! According to Catholicism, Mary was with God in the beginning. These are not minor doctrinal issues.

Is this hard to believe? In Catholic literature, available at most Catholic Churches or bookstores, you will find items such as a picture of the Father and the Son crowning Mary as "Queen of Heaven." Catholicism places Mary in a position of deity. In fact, they preach, teach, and believe that Mary did not die, but rather ascended up into the clouds physically in the same manner as Jesus.

> The council (the council of Ephesus–431 AD) decided on the doctrine that Jesus had one nature and was both true God and true man. It designated Mary as the mother of God, which elevated her to a central place of redemption. No longer was she simply a helper in God's plan, but her willingness to cooperate made *human redemption* possible.
>
> It was believed that Mary was taken up body and soul by God to reign in heaven. The church declared this belief to be true, and it has become an essential belief or Church doctrine...Mary is what is missing for many, the feminine face of God"[107] (emphasis added).

Luke 11:27-28 says, "And it happened, as he spoke these things, that a certain woman from the crowd raised her voice and said to him, 'Blessed is the womb that bore You, and the breasts which nursed You!' But He [Jesus] said, 'More than that, blessed are those who hear the word of God and keep it!'" Jesus did not place Mary on a higher level than any other believer.

---

[107]ibid. *Understanding Catholicism*, Second Edition, pg. 167

The Mother of Harlots

The Bible calls this city and governmental system a "whore." Why in the world would God call a city the Mother of Harlots? Roman Catholicism unashamedly proclaims that they are the "Mother Church." (Note: Rome and the Vatican City are synonymous with one another.) Do we see anywhere else in the Bible where God called a city a harlot? The answer is yes. In the Bible, when God begins to call a city or a nation a harlot it is because they have gone from worshipping the one true God to worshipping idols.

An excellent example of this is in Jeremiah 13:27: "I have seen thine adulteries and thy neighings, the lewdness of thy whoredom, and thine abominations on the hills in the fields. Woe unto thee, *O Jerusalem!* Wilt thou not be made clean? When shall it once be?" According to Jeremiah 3:9 she [Jerusalem] was committing whoredom with stones and with stocks (carved images or gods).

Interestingly, the "queen of heaven" is one of the false gods the Israelites worshipped (see Jeremiah 44:17-19). They insisted that things went well with them as long as they worshipped this queen of heaven.

The true church is the bride of Christ! The apostle Paul said "I have espoused you as a chaste virgin, to one husband, *Jesus Christ.*" In Ephesians chapter 5 Paul parallels the mystery of the husband and wife relationship with the mystery of Christ and his church. So we know that the Lord considers the true church a pure virgin, and the false church a harlot.

After 300 AD the Roman government basically followed ancient Babylonian customs and worship rituals. The Romans worshipped images of gods and even idols of Roman emperors. At the end of 300 AD they had many elements of Babylonian worship, then took on elements of Christian worship (in the time of Constantine) thus becoming a mixture of paganism and Christianity. Many of those Babylonian customs and worship rituals live on within the Catholic Church.

This brings us to another fascinating, but absolutely unscriptural, aspect of Catholicism, and that is sainthood. When a prominent Catholic dies, the Church allows individuals to petition the Vatican for that person to be placed in the running for sainthood. If the Vatican agrees that the person's works warrant consideration, they give the deceased Catholic the title of *venerable.*

When a person is placed in the running for sainthood, the Catholic Church allows churchgoers to create an idol or altar in order for them to pray to the deceased. If a notable miracle happens after praying to the idol, then the deceased is promoted to *blessed.*

Within the Vatican there is a council of bishops that meets regularly to examine claims of miracles in order to determine whether those proclaimed "blessed" have what it takes to become a saint. The Catholic Church even has to have the bones of the person that is considered blessed or a saint so that churchgoers may venerate (worship) them. Pope John Paul II has proclaimed over 400 saints! This is more than all the popes in the last century combined.[108]

Catholics have a saint and a prayer for every day and all occasions. Saints are friends of God who have proven their sincerity and reaped the rewards of their good lives. They are in heaven and have the power to help us. It never hurts to have friends in high places, and it is often smart to have someone speak on your behalf. *Saints offer intercession.*

Many Catholics will choose a particular saint as their patron because they feel a connection to this person. For example...You call on St. Anthony to help find lost objects; St. Jude is the saint for impossible cases. On February 3, Catholics have their throats blessed in honor of St. Blase, who was a philosopher and a physician"[109] (emphasis added).

---

[108]*National Geographic,* An Inside Look at the Vatican (on VHS home video).
[109]ibid. *Understanding Catholicism,* Second Edition, p. 11.

The bottom line is, that Catholics pray to the dead and worship idols! Praying to the dead is of no effect. You will *never* find the process of sainthood in the Bible. Not to mention, all throughout the Scriptures the Lord forbids us to make or worship any graven image (idol). Therefore, Catholicism is a revived form of idolatry.

Another aspect of Babylonian worship goes all the way back to Nimrod and the tower of Babel. In Babylonian worship a person had to confess everything they had done wrong; they had to pour out their heart to the priest in order to enter into the Babylonian style religion. This act of submission gave the priests a great amount of power over men and women's lives. How would you like it if your pastor knew about everything you have ever done?

The harlot possessed the souls of men.

Catholicism and its headquarters has possessed the souls of men for many centuries. Essentially, the Vatican says, "You just do what we tell you to do and you'll get to heaven. If you don't follow our rules we'll ex-communicate you." The Catholic Church has the power to take a person's salvation, and they have possessed the souls of men through fear and religious manipulation.

Our salvation is not through men or priests. Salvation is a work of the Holy Spirit, made possible by the shed blood of Jesus. The Bible says that there is *one* mediator between God and man (see 1 Timothy 2:5). That mediator is Jesus Christ, the Righteous One. We can go directly to God the Father and receive forgiveness (see Romans 10:9-10 and 1 John 1:9).

Yet, in the Catholic Church a person is encouraged to pray the rosary on a daily basis. The rosary is a prescribed prayer that is repeated while thumbing through beads. Along with prescribed prayers, a good Catholic must also confess his sins to a priest, then do penance in order to receive forgiveness.

In the Catholic Church, salvation is all about works! We find proof of this in a pamphlet called "How to Make a Good Confession" that gives nine steps to forgiveness including:

- Making the signs of the cross.
- Voicing prescribed words (i.e. "Bless me, father, for I have sinned...").
- Confessing sins to the priest.
- The priest assigning penance. This is required to "make satisfaction for your sins."[110]

The Catholic pamphlet offers no Scripture to substantiate these nine steps. Of course the reason for this is that these nine steps are not in the Bible! In addition, the sins that a good Catholic must confess are not just disobedience to God's Word, but also anything done with full knowledge and consent "against the Church's commandments."[111]

The more a person performs these Catholic rituals, the better chance they have of being saved, which means going to purgatory–another unscriptural teaching. In Catholicism the amount of money a person gives, the more often they partake of the sacraments, and the more works they do will ensure them a place in the kingdom of heaven.

What about the description of "Mystery"?

The Bible says of this woman who sat as a queen, that one of her names would be *Mystery*. One thing a person finds out quickly about the Catholic religion and its headquarters (the Vatican) is that everything is shrouded in mystery.

---

[110]Catholic pamphlet, *How to Make Good Confession*, by Rev. Kris Stubna, S.T.D.
[111]ibid. *How to Make Good Confession*, by Rev. Kris Stubna, S.T.D.

It was not until recent decades that the Catholic Church began holding masses (Catholic services) in English (or one's common language) instead of Latin. Less than fifty years ago when the average person went to mass they could not even understand what the priest was saying.

Furthermore, think about the following in reference to what Scripture calls Mystery, Babylon the Great: The first prayer a Catholic must pray is the "joyful *mystery*–the visitation." They also have the *mystery* of the annunciation, the *mystery* of the birth, the *mystery* of the presentation, the *mystery* of the finding of Jesus in the temple, the *mystery* of the crucifixion, the *mystery* of the carrying of the cross, and the *mystery* of the crown of thorns.[112]

Recently, Pope John Paul II introduced five new mysteries into the Catholic doctrine. He calls these the "Mysteries of Light," or "Luminous Mysteries." In his letter announcing these new mysteries, the pope described the rosary as an expression of the gospel in its entirety, stating, "It is a powerful way for us to participate in the 'contemplation of the Christian mystery.'"[113]

Interestingly, the word Mystery used in Revelation 17:5 is the Greek word *musterion* which comes from a derivative of *muo* (to shut the mouth); a secret or "mystery" through the idea of silence imposed by initiation into **religious rites**.[114] Mystery, Babylon the Great is obviously speaking of a religious organization.

Why does the Catholic Church cover itself in such mystery? The truth is if the Church shared all these spiritual secrets with the common person, then the common person would become like the spiritual elite. If this were to happen, the Church hierarchy would lose control. The leadership does not desire that the layperson become like them because then they would not be able to

---

[112]Excerpt from *Pray the Rosary*, Catholic pamphlet available at most Catholic Churches.

[113]Catholic pamphlet, *Pope John Paul II's New Mysteries of the Rosary*.

[114]*Strong's Greek and Hebrew Dictionary*, ref. #3466.

lead them blindly. Jesus said that the *truth* makes us free. Catholicism does not desire freedom in the ranks, but rather slaves held captive by fear of excommunication or hell.

Another mystery in the Catholic Church is very fascinating. When a Catholic takes communion, the priest holds up a wafer and speaks a prayer in Latin as he brings the wafer down and breaks it. As the priest recites this prayer, the Catholics believe that the wafer *literally* becomes the body of Jesus and the wine literally becomes his blood. They take literally the Scripture that says, "For my flesh is meat indeed, and my blood is drink indeed, and unless you eat of my flesh and drink of my blood..."

What Catholics need to understand is that Scripture interprets Scripture. In Matthew 26:28 Jesus gave communion to his disciples and said, "For this is my blood of the new covenant, which is shed for many for the remission of sins." If we were to stop there we would get the same impression—that the wine literally becomes the blood of Jesus. However, in Matthew 26:29 Jesus went on to say, "But I say to you, I will not drink of this *fruit of the vine* from now on until the day when I drink it new with you in my Father's kingdom." Jesus called what they were drinking the "fruit of the vine" which was simply symbolic of the blood of Jesus.

In the Catholic mass, after the priest gives the wafer, he takes the golden cup (one of the main symbols of the Catholic religion) in his hand, then holds the cup up to the parishioner's lips. During communion, or the Holy Eucharist, the parishioner cannot touch the cup because they believe that it contains the blood of Jesus and, like the Savior, it is considered holy. However, the priests can touch the cup because they are mediators—they are the only ones that can touch Jesus.

When a parishioner drinks from the cup, he cannot allow any to drop off his tongue. If he spills any, he has just spilled the blood of Jesus. To prevent spillage the priest puts a little net under the parishioner's mouth.

What is interesting is that if asked how the changing of the bread and wine occurs, they will reply, "It is a mystery." It is the same with the water the priest blesses which becomes "holy water." If you ask why or how the water becomes holy, they tell you, "it is a mystery."

The Word of God is the basis for all Christian belief. A person who says they believe in the God of the Bible should be able to back up his or her beliefs from Scripture. This means that the person sitting in the pew has the responsibility of digging into the Scriptures so they know what they believe and why they believe it (see Acts 17:11 and 2 Timothy 2:15).

The person in the pew should also be checking out what the pastor is preaching so that they may have assurance that it is biblically correct. Typically, in Catholicism, a parishioner is not encouraged to read or interpret their Bible. The pope and his hierarchy are the supreme authority, and the individual in the pew does not question their interpretation or decisions. Thus, Catholicism becomes a mystery.

The Catholic Church is shrouded in mystery! They do not offer explanations, nor can they back up these doctrines with solid Scripture. The sad part is that there are millions upon millions of good, well-meaning people who sincerely believe they are following God's will if they follow the teachings of the Catholic Church.

She had the voice of the bride and the bridegroom in her.

The phrase "the voice of the bride and the bridegroom in her" is a tough phrase to interpret. One possible interpretation is simply that this phrase helps us further identify this prophecy as speaking of a religious organization. In other words, this organization has the power to join a man and a woman together in marriage.

Another interpretation may rest upon the fact that Paul the apostle refers to the church as the *bride* of Christ and to Christ as the *Bridegroom*. This would indicate that there are born-again Christians within this worldwide religious organization. It also indicates that this worldwide religious organization has a form of godliness, but denies the power of the gospel and the Word of God. How do we know this? Because she joined herself to idols and, according to Revelation chapters 17 and 18, has become a harlot.

Are there born-again Catholics? Absolutely! An individual can read the Bible for himself or herself and become born again (based upon Scripture), yet still be stuck in the rut of tradition. The danger is, if they become stuck in the rut of tradition, their traditions will make the Word of God of no effect (see Matthew 15:6).

Still, if people were to follow only the strict doctrines of the Catholic Church, they would not hear the salvation message. Why? Because pure Catholicism teaches salvation through works. Ephesians 2:8-9 tells us, "For by *grace* you have been saved through *faith*, and that not of yourselves; it is the gift of God, not of *works*, lest anyone should boast."

Therefore, if there are born-again Christians within the Catholic Church (Mystery, Babylon the Great), then it would seem as though the Lord would strongly admonish them to come out. This is exactly what we see in Revelation 18:4: "And I heard another voice from heaven saying, 'Come out of her, *my people*, lest you share in her sins, and lest you receive of her plagues.'"

Once again, it is important to note that we are not coming against individuals, but rather a form of government and religious doctrine contrary to the Word of God.

Abominations of the Earth

Another name for the harlot given in Revelation 17:5 is the "Abominations of the Earth." This is a hard saying. In 1 Timothy 4:1-3 the apostle Paul said (speaking to the church), "Now the

Spirit speaketh expressly, that in the latter times some shall depart from the faith, giving heed to seducing spirits, and doctrines of devils; speaking lies in hypocrisy; having their own conscience seared with a hot iron; forbidding to marry, and commanding to abstain from meats."

As we have already learned, the "latter days" began on the Day of Pentecost and continue until the Second Coming of Christ. What prominent religion, a religion that has power over kings and nations, within the last 2,000 years has forbidden marriage for certain individuals and compels their followers to abstain from meats during certain times? The answer is clearly Catholicism! Paul plainly says that forbidding marriage and commanding to abstain from meats is a *doctrine of devils*.

To become a Catholic priest a person must take a vow of celibacy. As we have seen from Scripture, the apostle Paul called this teaching a doctrine of devils. History proves this to be true. This doctrine has cost the Catholic Church much in terms of money and reputation, and has also harmed the lives of countless individuals.

Newsweek (March 4, 2002) reported that since 1980 the Catholic Church has paid out $800 million to families to keep pedophilia a secret! We are not talking about affairs priests have had with women or homosexual affairs with other men. The cover-up *Newsweek* was speaking of is Catholic priests molesting children. The truly disgusting part is that the Catholic hierarchy has paid millions of dollars to keep it a secret!

It is estimated that within the next ten years the Catholic Church (this mysterious worldwide organization out of Rome—the Vatican), will pay *one billion dollars* to keep their congregations' mouths shut about their pedophilic priests.

The Catholic Church has used various types of rhetoric to account for these atrocities. Many of these people go into the priesthood with these existing problems, thinking that if they get close to God through religion that God will curb their perverse desires. Even if that excuse was true, it evidently is not working!

Within the history of the Catholic Church there are accounts of popes with illegitimate children, homosexual practices, and even pedophilia. To judge anyone by past history certainly seems unfair. We all have the ability to learn from our mistakes and change our ways. However, when we consider that the same practices are taking place in the Catholic Church today, it is inexcusable!

It all goes back to the fact that it's a secret society–a mystery. What they say is, "Remember, we keep secrets here." We are certainly not suggesting that all Catholic priests are this way. We are saying that historically this has been a problem because they have followed a doctrine of devils. Unscriptural teachings put people in bondage. Forbidding marriage has not only impacted the lives of Catholic priests, but also those they are supposed to be ministering to!

One abuse victim of the Catholic Church said, "I do not know what to do. First they did it to my body, but next they did it to my soul. How could I have faith again?" Another abuse victim started a support group called Recovering Catholics. Anytime a group gets off track in their doctrine they will get into a ditch. This is why we need to read our Bibles and understand these things.

When the Bible speaks of Mystery, Babylon the Great, the Mother of Harlots, and the Abominations of the Earth, can there be any greater abomination than the on-going abuse of innocent children? Jesus said it would be better to have a millstone hanged around a person's neck and be cast into the sea than to harm an innocent child.

Is it any coincidence that Revelation 18:21, which is speaking of the fall of this international religious organization, says, "Then a mighty angel took up a stone *like a great millstone* and threw it into the sea, saying, 'Thus with violence the great city Babylon shall be thrown down, and shall not be found anymore.'"

The woman is arrayed in purple and scarlet, and decked with gold, precious stones, and pearls.

We find another aspect of this worldwide religious organization in Revelation 17:4 where it says the "woman" is arrayed in purple and scarlet color, and decked with gold, precious stones, and pearls.

Although few may realize it, the Catholic Church is the wealthiest single organization on the face of the earth. No corporation has more members or money than the Catholic Church.

An article entitled "The Fabulous Treasure of Lourdes France" tells how the Catholic Church kept copious amounts of fabulous treasures a secret. Rumors had been circulating for decades of a priceless collection of gold chalices, diamond-studded crucifixes, silver, and precious stones, all donated by grateful pilgrims. The public learned of these treasures by accident after an indiscreet remark by a Catholic Church press spokesman.

Once the secret was out, Church authorities agreed to reveal part of the collection. They opened several floor-to-ceiling cases to reveal fifty-nine solid gold chalices, alongside rings, crucifixes, statues, and heavy gold brooches–many encrusted with precious stones. Almost hidden by the other treasures was the diamond-studded crown of the Notre Dame de Lourdes, made by a Paris goldsmith in 1876.

When asked of the value, Father Pierre-Marie Charriez, director of Patrimony of Sanctuaries, said, "I have no idea. It is of inestimable value." Catholic Church authorities also said they could not put a value on the collection. Across the road from the amazing find is a building housing hundreds of antique ecclesiastical garments, robes, mitres, and sashes–many in heavy gold thread.

Father Charriez had the audacity to say, "The Church itself is poor. The Vatican itself is poor." This is an institution vowed to poverty. Yet, truthfully, they are the richest institution in the world!

"And I saw the woman drunken with the blood of the saints, and with the blood of the martyrs of Jesus..."

Revelation also reveals that this woman has killed multitudes of Christians! In Revelation 17:4 we see that the woman has a golden cup in her hand, and her cup is full of abominations. Then, verse 6 says, "And I saw the woman drunken with the blood of the saints, and with the blood of the martyrs of Jesus..."

A refusal to attend mass 500 years ago meant a person was a blasphemer. Five hundred years ago if a person said that communion was not the actual blood and body of Jesus Christ, they would be subject to torture, or quite possibly even death.

Here are two testimonies of Christians whom the Catholic Church tortured and killed.

Constantia Bellone was a martyr of Roman Catholicism. Because she refused to go to mass, a priest ordered slices of flesh to be cut from various parts of her body. Finally he ordered a company of musketeers to fire upon her, and as they raised their muskets, the brave Protestant said: "I was brought up in a religion by which I was taught to renounce the devil, but should I comply with your desire and go to mass, I should be sure to meet him there in a variety of shapes. What horrid and lasting torments will you suffer in hell for the trifling and temporary pains which I now endure."

Anne Askew, because of her adherence to the Protestant faith, was driven from her home and two children by her husband who violently opposed her faith. Imprisoned because of her witness, an apostate by the name of Shaxton advised her to recant. Anne told him that it would have been good for him had he never been born. Much torture was heaped upon her. Placed on a cruel rack, her joints and bones were pulled out of place. Recovering from a swoon, she preached for two hours to her tormentors. On the day of her execution, she was carried to the stake in a chair, her bones being dislocated so that she could not walk. At the last moment she was offered the king's pardon if she would recant, but in suffering she was silent and died praying for her murderers in the midst of the flames. Her last words were: "I came not thither to deny my Lord and Master."[115]

At one point as Napoleon was going through Europe, he found priests barricaded in a monastery. As his men forced their way into the monastery, the priests said, "We don't have any slaves. We don't have any torture chambers." After Napoleon's men pulled the monks out of the cathedral and opened up the floors of the church, they found naked people the priests had beaten, starved, and tortured. The majority of the victims had gone insane.

As they were freeing the victims, and viewing this horrific scene, the majority of Napoleon's army became physically ill. These were hard-core soldiers, accustomed to killing in battle. However, when they saw these people and the torture they had endured, they could not take it!

Another example of horrible torture was when the Jesuit priests would dip resin-coated cloths in ground shards of glass. Then they would pour water in their victim's mouth while forcing him to swallow the cloth a little at a time. After the victim had swallowed the cloth containing shards of glass, the Jesuit priest would rip it out of the victim's mouth, pulling out their esophagus. This was punishment for blaspheming the church.

Priests would also judge blasphemers by fire. They would torture a person into submission, and as they were inflicting torture, they would ask the blasphemer to recant. If a person would not recant, the priests would continue to torture them. Many times they would torture them even if they did recant just

---

[115]*Last Words of Saints and Sinners*, Herbert Lockyer, (© 1969 Kregel Publications), pp. 140-141.

to make sure they never blasphemed the holy mother church again. In one six-year period the Catholic Church killed 6 million people! Most were killed by means of torture.

Most of this killing occurred during the Inquisition and the Crusades. During this time, history records some of the bloodiest and most horrible torture heaped upon those who would not bow to the pope. In the latter years of the Inquisition, no fewer than 900,000 Protestants were put to death in the pope's war to exterminate the Waldencians (1450-1570)–a movement begun by an educated businessman named Peter Waldo. The Waldencians were a group of Bible-believing Christians who would not take oaths and renounced the doctrine of purgatory. They also refused to celebrate the pope's festivals, and believed that the Bible was the source of all doctrine. In the Netherlands, over 100,000 Waldencians were massacred!

During the same period of time there was a group called the Huguenots (Protestants and followers of John Calvin). In St. Bartholomew's Massacre, lasting from August 24-29, 1572, approximately 50,000 Huguenots were killed. In the Huguenot Wars, 200,000 perished as martyrs, and another 500,000 fled for their lives. In Bohemia by the year 1600, a country with a population of 4 million (of which 3.2 million were Protestant), only 800,000 Catholics were left alive after the Jesuits went through.

By 1500, the Inquisition had extended to the New World, especially Peru and Mexico where countless lives were snuffed out. Catholic friars reportedly would baptize babies and children and throw them to starving dogs. The list of Catholic burnings and torture of Protestants is almost endless.[116]

In 1568, the Holy Office (the pope) condemned all of The Netherlands to death as heretics, not to mention the unspeakable torture that came before death.[117] Once again, the Catholic Church proved over and over that they wield a great amount of power over kings, nations, and tongues.

---

[116]*The Calvary Contender*, March 1, 1991.
[117]*The Rise of the Dutch Republic*, by John L. Motley, 1900 Edition, Volume 3, p. 9.

Think about it! Since her existence the Catholic Church has been responsible for the death of *68 million* Christians![118] Up until the turn of the century there were never more than one million killed in any one war. On the other hand, we have a religious organization that has sworn to bring peace to the earth, yet they have killed 68 million people that confessed to believe in Jesus Christ. Truly the Catholic Church is drunken with the blood of the saints and the martyrs of Jesus Christ.

The woman reigned over the kings of the earth.

In Revelation 17:18 we saw that the woman (Mystery, Babylon the Great, the Mother of Harlots) was a great city that reigned over the kings of the earth. There was a time during the dark ages (AD 500 to AD 1500) when Rome was so strong it ruled over every king in the known world.[119] At one point in history the Vatican had control over every king in Europe.

They exercised that amount of control by threatening a king with excommunication (eternal damnation) if he would not submit to Catholicism. The Vatican could oppose any king they desired to, and they could appoint any king they wanted. On top of that, any land that was undiscovered belonged to the Catholic Church.

In history we see the Spanish Armada take Central and South America. The fact is, Rome sent the Spaniards to conquer those lands in the name of the Catholic Church.

Ironically, in the end of the last days the Bible says that this woman (this city) will be destroyed in one day by the very ten kings that she was striving to control along with the Antichrist.

---

[118]J.B. Wilder, *The Other Side of Rome* (Grand Rapids, MI: Zondervan Publishing House) p. 153; and *Challenger, Mission to the Catholics*, February, 1994, pp. 1-2.
[119]ibid. *Encarta Encyclopedia*.

The Mother Church leads the world into a United Religion.

This system will lead the world into a global religion in which world leaders will try to force everyone to participate. This city and its leader have already spearheaded a one-world religion (the United Religions).

For many years now we have seen a kinder and gentler Catholic Church. For a long time Catholicism said, "If you are not part of our church you will die and go to hell." Recently it said, "The Mother church opens her arms for all her daughters to come back to her."

A few years ago one division of the Lutheran church began having services with the Catholics. Other churches also began establishing ties with the Catholic Church.

An article appeared in the *Indianapolis Star*, March 30, 1994, entitled, "Catholics, evangelicals affirm ties that bind." Another headline in the *Star*, June 17, 1994, read, "Southern Baptists embrace Catholics." In the *New York Times*, March 31, 1997, a headline read, "Baptists add Catholic rituals." And in the Associated Press, November 1, 1999, appeared, "Lutherans to end rift with Catholic Church."

In doing this, denominations are saying, "As long as you do not try to convert us, we will not try to convert you, and everything will be all right." As a result we see many Protestant churches saying that Catholicism is a Christian organization. However, you cannot be a Christian organization if you do not act in accordance with the Bible.

We cannot call an organization Christian that does not believe in being born again. Once again, Catholic doctrines and rituals do not lead a person into the born-again experience as taught in Mark 16:16, Romans 10:9-10, and Ephesians 2:8-9.

In Catholicism a person is sprinkled at birth, which makes them a member of the church. Next, a Catholic learns the catechism; the majority of which is *man-made doctrine* handed down by the Holy See (the governing body of the Catholic Church).

Then, as long as they are diligent to perform their Hail Marys (and other penance), partake of the sacraments, confess their sins to the priest, and receive the last rites before they die, they will be okay.

It seems evident that the Catholic Church will be part of the one-world government, and the pope will be the false prophet. *Time* magazine, January 2002, featured the greatest men of the world. In 1962 Pope John XXIII was the Man of the Year. Reflecting back the article stated:

> The 1960s were a decade of upheaval and renewal, and if Angelo Roncalli–the Italian farmer's son who had become pope at the age of seventy-six–had anything to say about it, the 900-million-member Roman Catholic Church would be no exception. Pope John convened the ecumenical council called Vatican II. Its purpose: to bring the Church into line with modern science, *economics, morals and politics* and to end the division that had dissipated the Christian message for centuries. In doing so, *Time* wrote, he "set in motion ideas and forces that will affect not merely Roman Catholics, not only Christians, but the whole world's ever-expanding population" (emphasis added).

In 1993 the Council of the Parliament of World Religions convened in Chicago, Illinois. During this meeting 8,000 people from all over the globe came together and celebrated the uniting of 125 of the world's religions. This gathering was called the United Religions Initiative.

This gathering of religions was far different from a group of born-again ministers from various Protestant churches getting together to pray and have an ecumenical meeting. The ecumenicalism the United Religions Initiative was promoting is all faiths–including those who do not believe the Bible–coming together for the purpose of a one-world religion–a common global ethic.

One very proud CPWR member is Covenant of the Goddess. On their website they speak very enthusiastically of the 1993 Chicago gathering of religions. They emphasize how "over 200 representatives of pagan religious groups attended the latest Parliament including: Covenant of the Goddess, Circle Sanctuary, EarthSpirit Community, and Fellowship of Isis."

At the 1993 CPWR meeting in Chicago they drafted a document called "Towards a Global Ethic: An Initial Declaration." The Global Ethic, along with the United Religions, is throwing out all they disagree with so that they can rally together around the things on which they do agree. Basically, they are writing a new Bible that is filled with paganism.

Here is an example of the ideology for the United Religions Global Ethic:

> We are women and men that have embraced the precepts and practices of the world's religions. We affirm that a common set of core values is found in the teachings of religions, and that these form the basis of a global ethic...There already exist ancient guidelines for human behavior which are found in the teachings of the religions of the world and which are the condition for a sustainable world order...We must sink our narrow differences for the cause of the world community, practicing a culture of solidarity and relatedness.[120]

In essence, the United Religions has reduced each of the world's religions down to the lowest common denominator. They say that we can all agree we should not commit murder, we should not steal, etc. As Christians, however, we cannot ignore the fact that Jesus said there is one way to the Father, and that is through him. That foundational truth is one of those "narrow differences" they have to "sink" in order to provide solidarity and relatedness.

---

[120]*Catholic Reporter*, August/September 1993. Also see the United Religions Website, World Wide Web.

The Parliament of World Religions does not mention the God of the Bible. Why? The reason is that the United Religions is a man-made religion! On the Council for the Parliament of World Religion's website they explain the key in promoting "interreligious harmony":

> The key to the conceptual framework of CPWR is the understanding that seeking unity among religions risks the loss of the unique and precious character of each individual religious and spiritual tradition.

Hans Kung is a Catholic theologian, and the president of The Global Ethic. He was asked how different religions, such as Catholicism and Islam, could come together if they believed that there are two different ways to heaven. Kung replied, "We don't believe in different ways to heaven."

In 1994 the Roman Catholic Church issued the first new catechism in approximately 400 years. One statement in Part One of this catechism is absolutely staggering:

> The plan of salvation also includes those who acknowledge the Creator, in the first place among whom are the *Muslims* that profess the faith of Abraham, *and together with us* adore the one merciful God, mankind's judge in the last days[121] (emphasis added).

The fact is, Muslims do not believe that Jesus Christ is Lord, and that he is one with the Father. They do not acknowledge Jesus as Savior, nor do they believe that Jesus died and rose from the dead, which is the cornerstone of a Christian's salvation.[122] To preach and believe in the killing of a prophet of Allah is heresy to the Muslims.

---

[121]*Catechism of the Catholic Church*, Section #841 under "Profession of Faith" / "The Church's Relationship with the Muslims."
[122]Quran, Surah 4:157.

Muslims also believe that a person commits the sin of *shirk*, or blasphemy, if they say that God became flesh and dwelt among us, which is exactly what the Bible teaches in John 1:14. To a Muslim, giving Allah an equal is the worst of all blasphemy. However, the Bible is clear that there is only one way to the Father and that is through Jesus. The new Catholic Catechism has made the blood of Jesus meaningless!

Today we have a Global Ethic and a Global Religion, both of which the Vatican was very influential in establishing. As the world's religions come together they are also denying the redemptive power of the blood of Jesus. The apostle Paul called this "a form of godliness, but denying its power."

Once again, Jesus said very clearly there is only one way to the Father, and it is through him. As we will see in the next section, this "United Religions" is nothing more than paganism on a global scale. Is it any wonder that the word Vatican literally means "hill of soothsayers and sorcerers"?

Obviously these are not fun things to discuss. No sincere Christian takes pleasure in exposing false doctrine. It breaks God's heart to see anyone caught up in doctrines of devils. Nevertheless, how can anyone be free of these things unless we reveal what the Scripture says about doctrines of devils and the city in which resides Mystery, Babylon the Great, the Mother of Harlots?

Mystery, Babylon the Great, has led the world into a one-world religion. This one-world religion looks good at first, but soon it will show its teeth. As Christians, we must be aware of these events, and we must stand up for Christ no matter what the cost. If we do not take a stand now we will be too weak to stand when the pressure is really on.

Let's Review

♦ The harlot rides on the beast (one-world government).

♦ This religious system looks like a lamb, but speaks like a dragon.

♦ The woman (the harlot) is a city on seven hills. Rome is a city on seven hills, and is the headquarters of an international religious system.

♦ The woman sits on many waters (peoples, tongues, and nations) and possesses the souls of men.

♦ The woman is arrayed in purple and scarlet.

♦ The woman has said of herself, "I sit as a queen."

♦ The woman is wealthy.

♦ The woman holds a cup in her hand full of abominations, and she is drunken with the blood of the saints and the martyrs of Jesus Christ.

♦ One of her names is Mystery, which speaks of initiation into religious rites as well as a religious organization that is full of mysteries.

♦ All of the characteristics of this woman point to the Catholic Church.

Interfaithism

We have looked at Mystery, Babylon the Great (Vatican City), the false prophet, and introduced something called the one-world religion. Up until Vatican II, the Catholic Church considered any non-Catholics heretics. Now, Catholicism has embraced other world religions.

Today we see multitudes of ecumenical services where very diverse religions–including ones who claim to believe that Jesus is Messiah, alongside those who do not–are worshipping together. God's Word says, "Unless two agree, how can they walk together?" (Amos 3:3). The reason these religions can get together and hold ecumenical meetings is that they do agree on one thing: they agree on a perversion of the gospel of Jesus Christ.

Catholicism has led the way to a one-world religion.

Catholicism has played a large role in promoting the one-world religion. As far back as 1986 in Assisi, Italy, Pope John Paul II joined in a circle to pray and meditate with snake handlers from Togo, shamans and tribal witchdoctors from West

Africa, Hindu gurus from India, Buddhist monks from Thailand, and liberal Protestant clergymen from Great Britain. Representatives from all these religions joined hands with the pope in "praying to their gods for 'peace'." The pope also announced in Assisi that there are "many paths to God."[123]

As you can imagine, the pope's message was well accepted. Yet, we do not have to look hard to see that it was simply humanism clothed in religious apparel. As we will see, this is the reason that interfaithism does not sit well with Bible believing fundamental Christians.

In 1994 we saw the first new Catholic catechism in 400 years. As we have already discovered, it embraces most world religions, especially the Muslim religion which is diametrically opposed to Christianity. This tells us that the Catholic Church is changing its doctrine in order to come in line with the new philosophy of this era–political correctness. The glaring problem with that idea is that the Word of God never changes! We cannot change the Bible to fit the world's philosophy or politics.

> And they *worshipped the dragon* which gave power unto the beast: and they worshipped the beast, saying, "Who is like unto the beast? Who is able to make war with him?" And there was given unto him a mouth speaking great things and blasphemies; and power was given unto him to continue forty and two months. *And he opened his mouth in blasphemy against God, to blaspheme his name, and his tabernacle,* and them that dwell in heaven. And it was given unto him to make war with the saints, and to overcome them: and power was given him over all kindreds, and tongues, and nations. *And all that dwell upon the earth shall worship him,* whose names are not written in the book of life of the Lamb slain from the foundation of the world.
>
> REVELATION 13:4-8

---

[123]Article, *Christian News* in a reprint of a 1993 article by Michael A. Hoffman in Researcher, Vol. 4, No. 3; and the April 1993, *Flashpoint*.

In this section we are going to look at one giant aspect of this passage: "And they *worshipped* the dragon which gave *power* unto the beast" (verse 4).

As we have seen in an earlier section, the beast is the one-world government. In the last section we saw that there is a powerful religious organization that is an accomplice with the beast. In the above passage we see the marriage between a global government and a world religion. As we study this it becomes apparent that this is happening right before our eyes. The political and the spiritual are quickly coming together on a worldwide scale!

Great Britain's prime minister Tony Blair, speaking at a special two-day international seminar at Lambeth Palace, in London, to attempt to break down barriers between their faiths called on faiths to unite. January 17, 2002, BBC News reported that Blair told a conference of Christians and Muslims that there is a renewed urgency for greater religious understanding in the wake of the September 11 terror attacks.

Dr. George Carry, the Archbishop of Canterbury, who was hosting the seminar, told reporters that the seminar was vital for building bridges between the faiths. The archbishop suggested that Christians should read the Quran, and the Muslims the New Testament to better understand each other's faiths.

The question is: What do Christians do when they read in the Quran that all those who do not bow down to Allah should be beheaded?[124] What do Muslims do when they read in the New Testament that Jesus proclaimed there is only one way to the Father and it is through Him?

---

[124]Found in the *Quran*: Surah 47:4, Surah 9:5, and Surah 9:29.

The United Religions Initiative

Since the formation of the United Nations, world leaders have been trying to bring the world's religious leaders together, but could never accomplish the task. An individual named Robert Muller (the same man we introduced in the section on one-world government) comes onto the scene.

Muller spent thirty-eight years working for the UN, and has been the assistant to three UN secretary generals (U Thant, Kurt Waldheim, and Javier Peres de Cuellar). As we have learned, Muller is called the "prophet of the UN," mainly due to his vision for the UN, which he has expressed in many of his writings.

Muller was born and raised a Catholic, and says the greatest influences in his life are the Buddhists. He calls himself a "Catholic Buddhist." With his books and proclamations, Muller has cast a vision for the United Religions.

Muller wrote a book called *The New Genesis: Shaping a Global Spirituality*. In this book he says, "The UN and the UR [United Religions] are the only hope for peace on this planet." He further said:

> The next stage will be our entry into a moral global age–the global age of love–*and a global spiritual age*–the cosmic age. We are now moving fast toward the fulfillment of the visions of the prophets who through *cosmic enlightenment* saw the world as one unit, the human race as one family, sentiment as the cement of that family, and the soul as our link with the universe, eternity, and God[125] (emphasis added).

That sounds like a bunch of dribble right out of the hippie era of the 1960s! We call that type of thinking humanism. Muller, along with the United Religions, is writing off the saving grace

---

[125]Robert Muller, *The New Genesis* (Garden City: Doubleday & Co., 1984), p. 100.

of the Lord Jesus and the life-changing power of God. The United Religions is substituting God's saving grace with man's religion, and man's best attempt at world peace.

Muller called on a man named William Swing, an Episcopalian bishop at Grace Cathedral in San Francisco. He asked the bishop to host an ecumenical service for many of the world's kings, dictators, and religious leaders.

In 1995, Muller and Bishop Swing gathered religious leaders from twelve different faiths (200 religious leaders in all) at Grace Cathedral in San Francisco for an ecumenical service. This meeting was held in conjunction with the celebration of the UN's fiftieth anniversary.[126]

When we picture a meeting like the ecumenical service in San Francisco, we might envision Jews, Muslims, Protestants, and Catholics attending. However, along with these prominent world religions, several other "religions" also participated, including druids [warlocks], wiccans, snake charmers [voodoo], and Lucis Trust.

You might be saying, "I have heard of druids and wiccans, but who is Lucis Trust?" At the turn of the last century [1900] Lucis Trust was a publishing company ran by numerous cult leaders and by its founder Alice Bailey. Bailey used her company to spread radical New Age ideas around the world.

Interestingly, in the early part of the 1900s, Lucis Trust started out with the name Lucifer's Publishing Company until negative press compelled them to change it. It is also interesting that for many years Lucis Trust had its headquarters at the location of the United Nations Plaza in New York before moving to Wall Street. The Rockefeller family owned the property, and later donated the land to the United Nations.

Another fascinating, and quite disturbing, aspect of the Bailey connection has to do with the *World Core Curriculum*, which Muller authored. The purpose of the curriculum is to provide

---

[126]United Religions Website, under the heading - "History and Organizational Design."

young people with a global education. Muller credits Bailey and Tibetan teacher Djwhal Khul for providing the basis for his curriculum. What is so conspicuous about that? Djwhal Khul never existed! Djwhal Khul was Alice Bailey's spirit guide![127]

All of these various world religions signed the United Religions Initiative at the 1995 ecumenical meeting. In June of 1999 the United Religions Conference completed their charter. Then, on June 26, 2000 (the 55th anniversary of the signing of the United Nations Charter), we see the ratification of the constitution for the United Religions Initiative.

At the 1999 Parliament of World Religions, Bishop Swing condemned Christian evangelism, saying, "Proselytizing, condemning, murdering, or dominating will not be tolerated in the Untied Religions zone–the whole world." In 1997, United Religions Initiative board member Paul Chafee said, "We can't afford fundamentalists in this small world."[128]

Along with many others who signed this Initiative we see a person named Juliet Hollister, who is in charge of the Temple of Understanding–a New Age organization with many political leaders as members.

The United Religions, and all those who endorsed it, professed their devotion to breaking down all the barriers of misunderstanding between the faiths. It now had a signed agreement for participation, but no bylaws.

Now we come to a person whom we introduced in the last section–Hans Kung. Not only is Kung an eminent Roman Catholic theologian, he is also a powerful globalist who was asked to draft the bylaws for the United Religions. The trouble is, how do you write bylaws for a religious organization in which everyone believes something different?

---

[127]ibid, *EndTime Magazine* May/June 2000.
[128]URI Forum at Grace Cathedral, held on 2/2/97.

Kung, along with Muller, drafted a document called *The Global Ethic*. Essentially, this document is the Bible for the one-world religion. Kung took things that each religion had in common and drafted it into an ethic. Amazingly, the word "God" does not appear once in *The Global Ethic*.

The Global Ethic proclaims that in the religions of the world there is a common thread of morality, respect for nature, respect for people, respect for families, and a common loyalty for government. A Christian might say, "What's wrong with that? It sounds pretty good."

Basically, the *Ethic* is an enormous pile of "feel good" philosophy. It is humanism at its highest. The Bible clearly says that there are none who are righteous, and that all have sinned and fallen short of the glory of God (see Romans 3:23-24). Christians understand that good works alone will not get a person into heaven. A Bible-believing Christian also understands that eternal life comes through believing and confessing that Jesus is Lord, and that God raised Him from the dead (see Romans 10:9-10). These fundamental Christian beliefs are in direct conflict with the United Religions.

Globalism expert Gary Kah reported in his book *The New World Religion*, "Mr. Kung makes clear that participation in this new 'ethic' will not be optional. He states, 'Any form of church conservatism is to be rejected. To put it bluntly: no regressive or repressive religion–whether Christian, Islamic, Jewish or of whatever provenance–has a long-term future.'"

In 1997 the conference for the charter writing process was held at Stanford University in California. At this meeting, the world's religions got together once again to conduct their first real church service. In this service there were pastors, teachers, witches, and warlocks–everybody worshipping at the same place.

A Christian leader by the name of Charles Gibbs, who is also the executive director for the United Religions Initiative, was one of the guest speakers. During the service, Gibbs wore a native headdress and danced on the stage with earth worshippers. He claims to be a Bible-believing, fundamental Christian.

A reporter asked Gibbs, "Reverend Gibbs, how is it that you can sit down and worship with druids, witchdoctors, New Agers, and witches?" Gibbs danced around the question. Reporters asked him again, "Mr. Gibbs, how in the world can you sit down and worship with witches knowing what the Bible says about witchcraft?" One reporter quoted a verse in 1 Samuel 28 where Saul broke his own law and consulted the witch of En Dor.

Gibbs replied, "I'm not going to get into a theological debate with you about this matter. I do not claim to have all the answers. But I will say about the Wiccans, I have sat with them, had many meetings and even ate with them and I know this for a fact–*they have good fruit*"[129] (emphasis added).

Essentially, Gibbs was saying, "They were nice to me. We had a good time over dinner. These are nice people." This is where interfaithism is heading. We will witness a barrage of rhetoric like this in the years to come. Then, it will not be long before people will become desensitized to interfaithism and the one-world religion.

Some will consider it shocking–and many already have –when they see the number of fundamental Christian leaders who will say, "Do whatever feels right in your own heart. The Bible doesn't have all the answers."

On June 26, 2000, these religious leaders all met in Pittsburgh at a meeting called "Building Bridges Forum," the purpose of which was to build bridges between religions–interfaithism. It was at this meeting that the United Religions Constitution was signed.

At the opening ceremony for the forum there was music and the warlike pounding of heavy drums. As the drums were pounding, the religious leaders were rubbing shoulder-to-shoulder, envisioning a global religious government where together they could stop all war.

---

[129]Excerpt from an interview Rev. Irvin Baxter Jr. had with Charles Gibbs (see www.endtime.org).

At the forum they asked a Hindu woman to open the meeting with prayer. She sat in the lotus position and began to pray. Suddenly, in the middle of her prayer she stopped and said, "Ahmmm" (a mantra type New Age hum). Simultaneously, every faith represented at the forum echoed her back. The Hindu woman repeated it and once again the religious masses echoed back. They continued doing this back and forth. One pastor at the meeting perceived that he was one of the only ones not humming. "This is weird!" the pastor thought to himself.

As this New Age hum continued, a big screen opened up showing the entire earth with set of hands coming out and grabbing the earth. As the hands reached out, the earth began to slip between the fingers of the hands. In the background the mantra intensified: "Ahmmm..." Every time the crowd would hum, the hands would grab the earth. This type of activity is called earth worship! Earth worship is pure paganism, and is one of the fundamental beliefs of the Council of the Parliament of World Religions.

At the Building Bridges Forum the CPWR had a webcaster–a person in charge of broadcasting the meeting over the World Wide Web. A pastor, who had his webcaster with him, visited the CPWR's sound booth where a woman was running the webcasting for the United Religions.

The UR's webcaster had on a black bandanna with a half moon and a pentagram on it. The pastor began talking with her about how they did their webcasting, and the fact that they were reaching an international audience. During the conversation the pastor asked, "By the way, what does the symbol on your headband mean? What religion are you with?" The UR's webcaster answered, "I am a Wiccan high priestess." The Wiccans were doing the webcasting for the United Religions!

At an earlier Parliament of World Religions meeting, held in Chicago in 1993, the keynote speaker was Gerald Barney, the lead author of the Global 2000 report for the Carter administration. Barney announced, "Five billion of us humans must prepare to die to the twentieth-century ways of thinking and being. Every person must learn to think like the earth, to act like the earth, *to be earth*"[130] (emphasis added).

Romans 1:21-23 says,

> Because that, when they knew God, they glorified him not as God, neither were thankful; but became vain in their imaginations, and their foolish heart was darkened. Professing themselves to be wise, they became fools, and changed the glory of the uncorruptible God into an image made like to corruptible man, and to birds, and four footed beasts, and creeping things.

This passage describes people who are their own saviors. Their religion (earth worship) is their only hope. The Global Ethic is all about saving the earth.

In August of 2000 the UN hosted a United Religions Forum. This time, however, it was not simply the UN asking the United Religions to put together a program, this time it was the UN paying for the entire show!

At this UN-hosted religious forum, the world's top religious leaders met at the organizations headquarters in New York. This was the first ever such meeting to take place at the UN. Sponsored by humanist billionaire Ted Turner, "interfaithism" and "global governance" were the themes of the event. Turner believes in the goals of the UN so much, that he donated *one billion dollars* to it.[131]

When Turner began to speak at this forum, he said, "I grew up as a Christian. I even thought of going into the ministry. But when I began to listen to the exclusiveness of the preacher that preached every Sunday morning, I began to look around and say,

---

[130]ibid. *One World,* Tal Brooke, (End Run Publishing, Berkeley, CA, 1989 & 2000), p. 72.

[131]*Ted Turner Speaks*, by Janet Lowe, (Canada: John Wiley & Sons, Inc. 1999), pp. 134, 211.

'Heaven's going to be a pretty empty place.'" (This is the same individual who said, "Christianity is a religion for losers," and that "anti-abortionists are bozos."[132])

Turner continued, "Now I believe there is possibly one God that manifests himself in many different ways to many different people on the face of the planet." That is the battle cry of interfaithism—that we all serve the same God, manifested in different ways to different people.

The United Religions headquarters is in the Presidio in San Francisco, which also happens to be the location of Mikhail Gorbachev's Green Cross International headquarters [U.S.].[133] There are many key players in this, and the same agenda links them together. Once again, what we are witnessing is the marriage of politics and religion on a global scale.

So we see that *The Global Ethic* is the Bible for the United Religions, and now globalists are pushing for the *Earth Charter* to be the Ten Commandments of the New World Order.

The Earth Charter

In 1987 we see the inception of the *Earth Charter*. Steven Rockefeller (Dean of Religion at Middlebury College, Vermont) and Mikhail Gorbachev authored the charter. Gorbachev affirmed his religion when he said, "The Cosmos is my God; Nature is my God."

Concerning the charter, Gorbachev said, "My hope is that this charter will be a kind of Ten Commandments, a 'Sermon on the Mount,' that provides a guide for human behavior toward the environment in the next century and beyond."

Canadian billionaire Socialist, Maurice Strong, who presided over the 1992 Earth Summit in Rio de Janeiro, is somewhat less tentative concerning the *Earth Charter*. "The real goal of the *Earth*

---

[132]Ibid. *Ted Turner Speaks*, by Janet Lowe, (Canada: John Wiley & Sons, Inc. 1999), pp. 143, 149.
[133]ibid. Article by Eddie Sax, *EndTime Magazine*, July/August 1999.

Charter," said Strong, "is that it will in fact become like the Ten Commandments." Strong not only works hand in hand with Mikhail Gorbachev, but also is good friends with former Vice President Al Gore who wrote the book *Earth in the Balance*. Strong has a 10,000-acre ranch in Colorado in the middle of which he has a New Age temple.[134]

The Global Ethic and the *Earth Charter* are glaring examples of man's best efforts to save the planet. Both of these documents are void of God, and they elevate humankind as the savior of the world.

If a Christian says they believe the United Religions motto, then they have to admit that they do not believe in anything whatsoever. The reason for this is, if the United Religions creed is correct, then the God of the Bible (the Christian's God) contradicts himself and his Word is no longer truth.

Robert Muller said, "My religion and my nationality must be abandoned in this planetary age."[135] Within the United Nations there is brewing a force that will back up Muller's ideas. Here is another quote from him:

> If Jesus were to come back to earth, his first visit would be to the United Nations to see if His vision of human oneness and brotherhood had come true. Truly He would make the United Nations the body of Christ.[136]

That is not only demented, but it is also very disturbing that anyone in a position of such power would make that kind of statement.

Sri Chimnoy, a Hindu guru and a chaplain at the United Nations, said:

> No human force will ever be able to destroy the United Nations. For the United Nations is not a human building or a mere idea. It is not a man-made creation. The United

---

[134]Article, "The New World Religion," by William F. Jasper.
[135]ibid. *The New Genesis: Shaping a Global Spirituality*.
[136]ibid. *EndTime Magazine*.

Nations is the "vision light" of the Absolute Supreme, which is slowly, steadily, and unerringly illuminating the ignorance, the night of our human life. The divine success in the Supreme progress of the United Nations is bound to become reality. At his choice hour, the Absolute Supreme will ring in his victory bell on the earth through a loving and serving heart of the United Nations.[137]

This UN guru is basically saying that the UN is the body of Christ. This is the same Hindu guru that claims to be in a perpetual state of cosmic consciousness. (They used to call that a "trip" on LSD.) Once again, global religious leaders see the UN as the savior of the world.

The Council for a Parliament of the World Religions [CPWR] promotes peace, world disarmament, world courts, poverty control, control of natural resources, and fair economic laws. That is a whole lot more than religion. If they succeed in disarming the world, the only people who have arms will be the UN.

Right now the Geneva Convention can try a person in International Court for "religious exclusiveness," which is defined as a hate crime. According to the United Religions charter, the UR endorses the International Court system of the United Nations, along with International Law.[138]

The United Religions even dabbles in economics. The UR believes we must change the distribution of wealth in the world, to narrow the gap between the rich and poor because 17 percent of the world's population controls 75 percent of the wealth. The UN and United Religions are saying that we need to disperse the wealth.

This idea raises several very important questions:

1. Who is qualified to disperse the wealth, and under what criteria?

2. Why should any individual have wealth taken away that they have earned?

---

[137]Article by Eddie Sax, *EndTime Magazine*, July/August 1999.
[138]ibid *EndTime Magazine*.

3. Who gave the UN, the United Religions, or the International Court the idea that they can control an individual's finances, or better yet the finances of an entire nation?

We call this type of governmental policy Communism. Sure, we would love to eliminate poverty. However, the most effective way to do this is through teaching others how to better themselves, thus giving them the tools they need to lift themselves. It is like the old saying, "Give a person a fish, and you'll feed him for a day. Teach a person to fish and you'll feed him for a lifetime."

The United Religions even has a position on environmentalism, proclaiming, "The UR is leading the way in solving aggressive opposition to nature. Deforestation, loss of wild lands..." One of the first things the UR will probably pursue is to protect wild lands. Essentially, this means control of land.

Many Americans do not realize that the UN has already exerted control over many areas of the United States. For instance it lists Yellowstone National Park as a "World Heritage Site." The UN declared the park "in danger" (a ruling used by the Clinton Administration to close down a proposed gold mine owned by Crown Butte Mining Company). Independence Hall, where America's founding fathers proclaimed independence from Great Britain, is also a World Heritage Site.[139] Is it any wonder that it was President Clinton who said, "We can't be so fixated on our desire to preserve the rights of ordinary Americans."[140]

Another item on the United Religion's agenda is population control. Jesus called the Pharisees hypocrites because they were doing the very things they preached against. The United Religions claims that they are concerned with human rights, and yet they desire to decrease the human population through abortion. The question is, how long will it be before genocide and euthanasia will also be accepted as a form of population control?

---

[139]*The New American*, article by William F. Jasper, October, 22 2001, p. 30.
[140]*USA Today*, March 11, 1993, p. 2A.

The United Religions claims it will do something about the "loss of production of agriculture, loss of lands, degradation of resources, water, renewable energy, extinction of species to save the sacred and connective world community." The United Religions, alongside the UN, believes it is the savior of the world. The United Religions sees the UN as their partner and vehicle to propagate their agenda, and vice versa.

Archbishop Desmond Tutu (who wrote the foreword to the book *The Coming World Religions*) said, "Our home is heaven, where God is. On earth we learn how to discover home, and each faith leads its inherits homeward."

Of course Christians would agree that heaven is our home. We would also agree that the magnificence of the earth should point its inhabitants to the Creator. We understand this because we see God's powerful hand in creation. In the same breath, however, Archbishop Tutu says *all faiths* point their inherits homeward. That is not true!

Matthew 7:13-15 says,

> Enter ye in at the strait gate: for wide is the gate, and broad is the way, that leadeth to destruction, and *many there be* which go in thereat: Because strait is the gate, and narrow is the way, which leadeth unto life, and *few there be* that find it. Beware of false prophets, which come to you in sheep's clothing, but inwardly they are ravening wolves.

Scripture declares that if anybody tries to enter into heaven any other way than through Jesus Christ they are the same as a thief. There is no other way by which a man can be saved but through the name of Jesus. The Bible is clear that unless a person believes Jesus is the Messiah they will die in their sins. That is pretty exclusive.

Right now we see interfaithism being promoted in many facets of the federal government as well as our local communities. Two examples are the prison systems and military. In order to be a chaplain in most prisons and to be a chaplain in the U.S. military, a person must embrace interfaithism.

Interfaithism is blatantly being promoted in our cities and towns. A pastor noticed a billboard in his community that depicted people from many different religions praying together. The caption read, "A World at Prayer is a World at Peace." The pastor called the 800-number (800-299-pray) and said, "I saw your sign. Are you interfaith?" The woman on the other end said proudly, "Why yes we are! Isn't it wonderful!"

When a person first sees billboards like these they might think, "That's not all bad." But if a Christian really begins to search their heart and recognize interfaithism for what it is, they realize it cannot work for those who believe that Jesus is the Messiah, and the only way to the Father.

The UN and the United Religions are now sister organizations which work hand in hand with one another. Soon, conforming to the beliefs of the United Religions will not be an option. A day is coming when they will not ask us–they will tell us.

The ethics of the United Religions flies in the face of the Great Commission Jesus gave to those who believe in him. Sharing the good news of the gospel is one of a Christian's primary responsibilities.

We are living in a new era; an era where fundamental Christians will be viewed as narrow-minded bigots. We must stay informed and not be caught with our guard down. At the same time, we must continue to walk in love, and speak the truth of God's word with boldness.

This is not a time to shrink back, but rather to aggressively move forward in the strength and power of God!

Let's Review

- The one-world government will be partnered with a religious organization, which will cause people to worship the beast.
- The United Religions is a sister organization to the United Nations, and has the influential support of many powerful global leaders.
- The United Religions *is not* a Christian organization.
- The United Religions is earth worship on a global scale.
- The United Religions agenda goes way beyond holding ecumenical meetings. It seeks to control land, resources, population control, global education, gun control, and redistribution of the world's wealth.
- It goes against the word of God for a Christian to support the ethic and agenda of the United Religions.

Part
IV

The Seven Trumpets

It is very difficult to line out all of the minor events that occur in the world today. Many of those minor events may, or may not, be interwoven into the fulfillment of major prophetic events. What we are saying is, if the prime minister of Israel sneezes it is not automatically a fulfillment of Bible prophecy. This is an area in which we can easily get off track if we are not careful.

At the same time, on our prophetic road toward the Second Coming of Christ, God has given us many enormous road signs that help clue us in as to our location in prophecy. It is true that we may not be able to forecast or accurately assess all of the minor events taking place in the world today–that is, wars and rumors of wars. However, we can recognize and analyze major world events that clearly line up with prophecy. Those events give us an indication, foundation, and location in the prophetic timeline. As we will see, the seven trumpets in Revelation are clearly those types of major prophetic events.

We recognize that some may argue that our analogies, interesting as they may be, are simply speculation. Fair enough. That is why we are presenting these ideas as merely strong possibilities. The key is, we must acknowledge the possibility that the majority of these trumpets may have already sounded simply because we have been in the last days for nearly 2,000 years. That is a scriptural truth.

The Seven Trumpets are the Backbone of Revelation

The seven trumpets are the backbone of the book of Revelation. There are three sevens spoken of in Revelation we need to know about—the seven seals, the seven trumpets, and the seven vials.

The seven seals are:

1. A white horse, the description of which aligns itself with the spiritual system of *Catholicism*. The one who sat on the white horse had a bow, and crown was given to him and he went forth conquering and to conquer (Revelation 6:2).

2. A red horse whose description depicts the earthly system of *Communism*. Power was given to him that sat on the red horse that he might take peace from the earth, and they should kill one another, and there was given to him a great sword (Revelation 6:4).

3. A black horse whose description speaks of *capitalism*. He that sat on the black horse had a pair of balances in his hand, and he bought and sold (Revelation 6:5-6).

4. A pale horse that describes the effects and spiritual system of *occultism*. His name who sat on him was Death, and hell followed with him. Power was given unto them over the fourth part of the earth, to kill with the sword, and with hunger, death, and the beasts of the earth.

5. The fifth seal describes the impact and effects of the *abomination of desolation*. In this seal we see the souls of those slain for the word of God, and for the testimony they held. This event

happens at the beginning of the last three-and-a-half years of Daniel's seventieth week. As we will see in a later lesson, this is the time of Satan's wrath.

6 & 7. These seals are clearly the *wrath of God*. When they are opened we see the same thing we will see at the seventh trumpet, and the same thing we see in Matthew 24:29 and Revelation chapter 16. As we will learn in a later lesson, the wrath of God is poured out *after* the Great Tribulation.

An overlapping takes place in many of these prophetic events. If we learn about all the separate pieces of the puzzle, it becomes easier to put the whole picture together.

In Revelation we also see seven vials (or bowls in the New King James Version). We will explore these later because, as we will discover, all of the vials have to do with the wrath of God.

We see yet another seven in Revelation–the seven thunders. However, in Revelation 10:4 God says, "Seal up those things which the seven thunders uttered, and write them not." He does not reveal the understanding of the seven thunders.

As we explore the prophecy of the seven trumpets we must acknowledge that though there are many things that appear to fit from a historic standpoint, it is still not conclusive evidence. The seven trumpets, as do other events in prophecy, involve a great deal of symbolism, which admittedly calls for some speculation. Nevertheless, we will see that the possibilities put forth are not only very intriguing, but also very possible.

On the other hand, if these historical and prophetic possibilities put forth (concerning what the seven trumpets represent) turn out to be true, the vast majority of the church (as well as the world) is in for a rude awakening! Once again, time will give us a more accurate picture.

The turn of the last century brought enormous change!

In the last 2,000 years many things have remained the same. However, at the turn of this last century [1900] everything seemed to increase. The world's population drastically increased while technology began to speed up at an alarming rate.

In the early 1900s there was a noticeable transformation in industry and technology that affected individuals, and even had an impact on nations. Daniel 12:4 speaks of this when it says, "But thou, O Daniel, shut up the words, and seal the book, even to the time of the end: *many shall run to and fro, and knowledge shall be increased.*"

This increase in technology has allowed people to run to and fro like never before. It has been said that we travel more in one year than our great-grandparents traveled in their entire lifetime. Who could have imagined that in less than 100 years we would go from horse and buggy to the moon?

Right now it is almost impossible to keep up with the knowledge we have at our fingertips! It is estimated that military technology is at least eight years ahead of the average individual. Few would argue that a paradigm shift occurred at the dawn of this last century. When this type of drastic change occurs in the world, there is a good chance we will see it spoken of in Bible prophecy.

While this has been one of the most progressive centuries in the history of mankind, it has also been one of the most brutal. One would think that along with the radical advances in technology, travel, and culture that man's civility would increase as well. The truth is, technology and culture may change, but man's unrenewed heart still requires the saving grace of the Lord Jesus Christ.

Possibilities of the Seven Trumpets

We will begin with the seventh trumpet, and then go back to the first.

> And the seventh angel sounded; and there were great voices in heaven, saying, "The kingdoms of this world are become the kingdoms of our Lord, and of his Christ; and He shall reign for ever and ever"
> REVELATION 11:15

The seventh trumpet is very clear and simple. It is the pouring out of the wrath of God, and the Second Coming of Christ. Revelation 11:18 says, "The nations were angry, and your wrath has come..."

When do the kingdoms of the earth become the kingdoms of our Lord? This event occurs at the seventh trumpet. When does the outpouring of God's wrath occur? Also at the seventh trumpet, which is the last prophetic trumpet. Jesus subdues the nations at His return. We will discuss in a later section the wrath of God being poured out.

The First Trumpet

> And the seven angels which had the seven trumpets prepared themselves to sound. The first angel sounded, and there followed hail and fire mingled with blood, and they were cast upon the earth: and the third part of the trees was burnt up, and all green grass was burnt up.
> REVELATION 8:6-7

Keep in mind that the apostle John is viewing these events almost 2,000 years before they take place. Thus, he is describing modern events, wars, and technology in the best way he knows how. Like Daniel, John had not seen anything like this before.

It is also important to remember that these trumpets are major events, which affect the entire world. That fact alone makes these events easier to recognize within world history and current events.

In the first trumpet John saw fire, brimstone, blood, smoke, and the destruction of many people during this great world event. What might the first trumpet be as we consider the enormous shift in world events at the turn of the last century?

We have already learned, before this time the most people who ever died in a war numbered 1,000,000. World War I brought more killing and destruction than any previous war, killing 8,000,000! It is reported that among all who participated in World War I (32 nations) there were over 37,000,000 casualties of war (civilian and military). This was because for the first time nations had artillery and bombs that could cause large numbers of casualties. The total monetary cost of World War I was approximately 186 billion dollars.[141] Without a doubt this was a major world event!

In World War I we saw many advancements in weaponry as compared to previous wars. However, the battlefield remained much the same. During all the years of fighting in Europe the battlefield only progressed about ten miles. Warfare in World War I consisted primarily of trench warfare, which was like a meat grinder.

In World War I a military tactic was implemented called the "scorched earth policy." This tactic was the way opposing armies created a battlefield. During this major world event described in Revelation 8:7 it says, "And the third part of trees was burnt up, and all green grass was burnt up." In World War I the opposing armies basically set Europe on fire. After World War I Europe was scorched!

It is very possible that John saw a vision of the First World War in which he saw fire mixed with blood, and trees and grass being burned. The smoke, fire, and brimstone he saw could easily be attributed to the scorched earth tactic along with the modern artillery used in World War I.

---

[141]ibid. *Encarta Encyclopedia.*

The Second Trumpet

And the second angel sounded, and as it were a great mountain burning with fire was cast in to the sea: and the third part of the sea became blood; And the third part of the creatures which were in the sea, and had life, died; and the third part of the ships were destroyed.

REVELATION 8:8-9

The second trumpet consists of several things:
1. A war.
2. One-third of the creatures in the sea (that had life) died.
3. One-third of the ships destroyed.
4. A mountain cast in the middle of the sea on fire.

We learned in a previous section that the carnage increased from over 30,000,000 casualties in the First World War to 61,000,000 casualties in World War II. The estimated cost of WW II was more than 1 trillion dollars, which is more than all previous wars combined![142]

The Second World War ended after America dropped atomic bombs on the Japanese cities of Hiroshima and Nagasaki. It is very possible that the apostle John saw a vision of the island of Japan (a mountain cast in the middle of the sea) brimming with smoke and fire from two atomic bombs.

Another interesting statistic from World War II is that one-third of the merchant and military vessels in the oceans sank. Jane's Intelligence Digest reported, "Military and merchant ships that participated in World War II were 105,127 of which 36,387 sank." This amounted to 34.6 percent of all the ships!

Are these things just coincidence, or a fulfillment of Bible prophecy? How many times in the history of humankind can we view a major world event where an island is burning with fire

---

[142]ibid. *Encarta Encyclopedia.*

and one-third of the ships in the ocean sink? Could God do it again? Of course! However, what are the odds of both of these catastrophic events occurring within the same major world event?

The Third Trumpet

> And the third angel sounded, and there fell a great star from heaven, burning as it were a lamp, and it fell upon the third part of the rivers, and upon the fountains of water; And the name of the star is called Wormwood: and the third part of the waters became wormwood; and many men died of the waters, because they were bitter.
>
> REVELATION 8:10-11

The third trumpet is a peculiar prophecy. In the Ukraine, on April 26, 1986, a nuclear power plant called Chernobyl was conducting some unauthorized testing. While conducting these tests, engineers noticed heat rising in the reactors. About thirty-five seconds later, at 1:23 AM, an explosion in the Chernobyl No. 4 reactor blew a 1,000 metric ton steel lid and concrete containment into the air.[143] This explosion (plus two prior explosions) exposed the Ukraine and the surrounding countries to a full nuclear fire that took three weeks to extinguish![144]

A toxic radioactive cloud soared a mile into the sky. This toxic cloud sent radioactive particles into Germany, Sweden, Italy, and most of Europe. The impact of Chernobyl hit nearly every country in Europe.

The firefighters who rushed into this intense radioactive situation had no idea what they were about to encounter–that their skin would begin falling off in ribbons. More firefighters were called until they were finally able to put out the fire. (Read testimonies from Chernobyl at www.endtime.com.)

---

[143]*Terre Haute Tribune Star*, 2002.
[144]ibid. Grolier's *Encyclopedia.*

After the fire was out, the government had to kill thousands of caribou, rabbits, and other wild animals that had become radioactive. The radioactivity was so strong that even after the fire was out, bulldozers were brought in to bury the fire trucks. Then, they had to bury the bulldozers that buried the fire trucks.

More than 3 million acres of farmland–an area about the size of Connecticut–is *considered lost for a century*. To date, over 100,000 people have died, and hundreds of thousands more have been affected by the radioactive fallout from Chernobyl. As of 1990, authorities acknowledged that several million people were still living on contaminated ground.[145]

This nuclear accident released 1,000 times more radiation than the atomic bombs at Hiroshima and Nagasaki. That makes Chernobyl the worst nuclear explosion in history.

After the Chernobyl nuclear disaster, a cloud blew radioactive waste all over Europe. A government film documentary about Chernobyl states that the worst part about the accident was not the explosion or the radioactive cloud. Scientists say the worst part was the radioactive particles in the rain. Radiation literally rained down into the rivers of Europe!

The Bible says, "The waters became bitter." The result of this radiation-laced rain was that it filled Europe's water system with Cesium 137 (radioactive fallout), which has a half-life of thirty years. Some experts predict that in the years to come the death toll will be no less than two million![146]

What is even more fascinating is that the name Chernobyl in Ukrainian means *Wormwood*. Once again, consider the odds of this prophecy fitting the Chernobyl nuclear accident even down to the name in the prophecy–Wormwood.

---

[145]ibid. Grolier's *Encyclopedia*.
[146]ibid. *Encarta Encyclopedia*.

The Fourth Trumpet

> And the fourth angel sounded, and the third part of the sun was smitten, and the third part of the moon, and the third part of the stars; so the third part of them was darkened, and the day shone not for a third part of it, and the night likewise. And I beheld, and heard an angel flying through the midst of heaven, saying with a loud voice, "Woe, woe, woe, to the inhabitants of the earth by reason of the other voices of the trumpet of the three angels, which are yet to sound!".
>
> REVELATION 8:12-13

In the first three trumpets we see physical or earthly events happening (grass being burned up, ships sinking, etc.). The first three trumpets are happening in the physical realm.

The fourth trumpet is very vague. In this trumpet we see the elimination of one-third of the sun, moon, and stars. How is that possible? If we lost one-third of the sun, this planet and all those on it would quickly die. Therefore, we have to ask ourselves if this is a literal cutting out or something else.

The sun, the moon, and the stars are the primary ways that human beings calculate and set the standards for time as we know it (e.g., days, months, years). Consequently, is it possible this trumpet is dealing with the reduction of time?

We are not going to get real deep into physics. Nonetheless, physicists have conducted many studies that prove time is a physical property, including physicists at Harvard who have sped up and slowed down time by using heat and cold.[147] These studies have also revealed that at the speed of light (186,000 miles per second) time stops.

---

[147]*Scientific News*, June 9, 1984 p. 359.

When considering the possibilities of the fourth trumpet, think about Matthew 24:22: "And except those days should be shortened, there should no flesh be saved; but for the elect's sake those days shall be shortened."

Scientists admit that altering time is possible. Nevertheless, they have not discovered how to accomplish the manipulation of time. This speaks of the fact that individuals might be able to gain understanding of such things, but will never be able to manipulate time. When considering that, can God speed up or slow down time? Of course he can. God created time, as we know it, for the benefit of humanity. Therefore, because he is the creator of time, he can certainly manipulate time as he sees fit.

Almost daily we hear someone say, "Isn't time flying by? There's not enough hours in the day!" We know from our study in Daniel (Daniel's seventy weeks) that God has a specific time frame for fulfilling all prophecy. He has even revealed the number of days in which the Antichrist will have power on the earth.

We know that God cannot lie. Therefore, we can confidently say that each hour, each day, and each year will come to pass just as his Word prophesies. Unless God sped up time, and shortened days, he would be a liar. Why? Once again, in Matthew 24:22 Jesus said, "For the sake of the elect the days *will be* shortened."

This could be that of which the fourth trumpet speaks. We know that God cannot lie, and that he has the capability to speed up time. If He were to literally change time, we would not realize it because we live within time.

As interesting as all this may be, it is still too difficult to come up with any outstanding possibilities concerning the fourth trumpet.

The Fifth Trumpet

And the fifth angel sounded, and I saw a star fall from heaven unto the earth: and to him was given the key of the bottomless pit. And he opened the bottomless pit; and there arose a smoke out of the pit, as the smoke

265

of a great furnace; and the sun and the air were darkened by reason of the smoke of the pit. And there came out of the smoke locusts upon the earth: and unto them was given power, as the scorpions of the earth have power. And it was commanded them that they should not hurt the grass of the earth, neither any green thing, neither any tree; but only those men which have not the seal of God in their foreheads. And to them it was given that they should not kill them, but that they should be tormented five months: and their torment was as the torment of a scorpion, when he striketh a man. And in those days shall men seek death, and shall not find it; and shall desire to die, and death shall flee from them. And the shapes of the locusts were like unto horses prepared unto battle; and on their heads were as it were crowns like gold, and their faces were as the faces of men. And they had hair as the hair of women, and their teeth were as the teeth of lions. And they had breastplates, as it were breastplates of iron; and the sound of their wings was as the sound of chariots of many horses running to battle. And they had tails like unto scorpions, and there were stings in their tails: and their power was to hurt men five months. And they had a king over them, which is the angel of the bottomless pit, whose name in the Hebrew tongue is Abaddon, but in the Greek tongue hath his name Apollyon [destroyer]. One woe is past; and, behold, there come two woes more hereafter.

REVELATION 9:1-12

Many things about the fifth trumpet seem to relate very well to a particular current event.

In the fifth trumpet we see:

1. The bottomless pit opened up.
2. Smoke coming up out of the pit while the sun and the air were darkened.
3. The creatures were given power to hurt men for five months.
4. Men seeking death, but not finding it.

5. The king over these creatures was Abaddon, and in the Greek tongue Apollyon, which means the destroyer.

In 1990 an Iraqi dictator named Saddam Hussein rose up and decided to seize hundreds of oil wells in Kuwait. The UN told Hussein to get out; however, he continued to occupy Kuwait for *five months* (from August through December of 1990).

At the beginning of January [1991], after numerous warnings, the United States and the UN gave an ultimatum to Hussein. After giving an ultimatum to Iraq, the U.S. and the UN formulated a plan to force Iraq out of Kuwait. The Persian Gulf War began on January 16, 1991. President George H.W. Bush stated that the Iraq crisis was the first big test for the New World Order.[148]

Hussein's armies left Kuwait in a mad tirade while setting 730 of the world's richest oil wells on fire. It was the worst fire in history! Those dealing with the fires said that without modern technology it would have taken 1,000 years for the oil wells to burn out. That's how severe this situation was.[149] One person witnessing the oil well fires said that it was a hellish sight. At any moment this witness expected little demons to come running out of the fires.[150]

In the prophecy of the fifth trumpet we see that the sky was dark because of the smoke. In Kuwait, while over 700 oil wells burned, the sky was as dark as nighttime for three solid months.

Hussein had sent his helicopters into Kuwait to set the oil wells on fire. It is possible that the locusts with the tails of a scorpion, the face of a man, iron breastplates, and the sound of many chariots were helicopters. Remember we must keep in mind that the apostle John was viewing modern events nearly 2,000 years before they occurred.

---

[148]Excerpt from President George H.W. Bush's speech to Congress on March 6, 1991.
[149]ibid. *Grolier's Encyclopedia.*
[150]Government Documentary, "The Fires of Kuwait."

Prophecy also reveals that the king over these creatures was Abaddon, and in the Greek tongue Apollyon, which means *the destroyer*. On December 13, 1997, an interesting article appeared in the *Jerusalem Post Weekly* International Edition. The article was about one of the last Israelis to escape out of Baghdad in Iraq before the first Gulf War. The Jewish individual interviewed described how horrible it was to live under the cruel hand of Hussein.

During the interview this Israeli related a peculiar story that Hussein's mother had a horrible time giving birth to him. The Arab doctors advised her to have an abortion because they did not believe she would survive giving birth. She went to the Jewish sector to consult with Jewish physicians as they had a reputation of being more competent than the Iraqi doctors. The Jewish doctors nursed Saddam's mother through the pregnancy. After finally giving birth to her baby, she named him Saddam because he had given her so much trouble. The article in the *Jerusalem Post* said that the name Saddam means "the destroyer."

In Europe many times Saddam Hussein was referred to as Saddam "the destroyer" Hussein.[151] It is not just a nickname—it is what his name literally means. (Saddam also enjoyed being called "the anointed one," and he used to tell his people that he was a direct descendant of the prophet Mohammad.)

Several things in this prophecy are difficult to interpret, yet simple answers might be found within the events of the first Gulf War. One of these difficulties is "the teeth of a lion." One possibility might lie within the testimony of an eyewitness who reported that Saddam's helicopters have lion's teeth painted on them.

Another mystery is "they had hair as the hair of women." One possibility might be cultural. In many Arab countries men have long black hair that they braid up under their turban.

---

[151]*The Observer U.K.*, Sunday July 4, 2004, and *Iraq News*, 13 January 1999.

It is hard to ignore the many items in the fifth trumpet prophecy that parallel the first Persian Gulf War, and the actions of a madman named Saddam "the destroyer" Hussein. Once again, consider the odds of so many things spoken of in this prophecy lining up with a major world event.

The fact that America was still dealing with Saddam Hussein until the end of the second Gulf War might help reveal the full time period of the fifth trumpet. As we will see, it is also possible that the second Gulf War came after the sounding of the sixth trumpet, which also may have sparked America's war on terrorism.

The Sixth Trumpet

And the sixth angel sounded, and I heard a voice from the four horns of the golden altar which is before God, saying to the sixth angel which had the trumpet, "Loose the four angels which are bound in the great river Euphrates." And the four angels were loosed, which were prepared for an hour, and a day, and a month, and a year, for to slay the third part of men. And the number of the army of the horsemen were two hundred thousand thousand: and I heard the number of them. And thus I saw the horses in the vision, and them that sat on them, having breastplates of fire, and of jacinth, and brimstone: and the heads of the horses were as the heads of lions; and out of their mouths issued fire and smoke and brimstone. By these three was the third part of men killed, by the fire, and by the smoke, and by the brimstone, which issued out of their mouths. For their power is in their mouth, and in their tails: for their tails were like unto serpents, and had heads, and with them they do hurt. And the rest of the men which were not killed by these plagues yet repented not of the works of their hands, that they should not worship devils, and idols of gold, and silver, and brass, and stone, and of wood: which neither

can see, nor hear, nor walk: Neither repented they of
their murders, nor of their sorceries, nor of their fornication, nor of their thefts.

REVELATION 9:13-21

The sixth trumpet describes a war started by a 200-million-
man army (200 thousand thousand). This is clearly the most
dreadful world war. Within this war we see the destruction of
one-third of humankind. The sixth trumpet is where we
are heading.

As of the year 2000, there were approximately six billion
people in the world. This prophecy—which describes at least two
billion people being killed by war (by fire, smoke, and brimstone—has obviously not occurred, and until this century could
not have occurred. Why? During the writing of the Revelation of
Jesus, the world's population (according to the population curve)
was only around 250 million.[152] The point being, up until this
century there has never been a country that could field a 200-
million man army.

Prophecy tells us that this army is prepared for an hour, and
a day, and a month, and a year to slay the third part of men (Revelation 9:15). In this prophecy we see that this army has been
prepared over a period of time, and for a specific time.

In the middle of the twentieth century a Communist revolution broke out in China. As the revolution was coming to a close
in 1949, a Communist leader named Mao Tse-tung forced Chinese emperor Chiang Kai-shek out of China. Kai-shek fled to
what now is modern-day Taiwan.

Kai-shek planned to use Taiwan as a base to build an army in
order to go back and recapture China. Even though he never succeeded in this, he did succeed in building what is now the modern
nation of Taiwan.

---

[152]*Age of the Earth* (VHS Home Video & DVD), Creation Science Evangelism
(Part 1), Dr. Kent Hovind 2002, also see www.drdino.com.

270

Today Taiwan has the twelfth largest economy in the world, and the second largest gold reserve. They are also the second largest producer of computer chips.[153]

After the Communist revolution Mao Tse-tung was not strong enough (after expending resources to take over China) to go into Taiwan and overthrow Chiang Kai-shek. Even so, China has sworn that they will take Taiwan one day in order to reunite the Chinese people.

Recently a 150-year lease ran out between Great Britain and Hong Kong, and Communist China swallowed up Hong Kong in one giant gulp. A few years later China swallowed up another small province called Macao. After they took Macao they began to say, "Taiwan next!" Taiwan is the only democratic China there has ever been. Years ago the U.S. signed an accord with Taiwan stating that we would never allow anyone to overtake them.

A real wakeup call came when the *New York Times* reported that a high Chinese official had said to Charles Freeman of the U.S. State Department, "We don't think you will intervene when we invade Taiwan because we don't think you're willing to trade Los Angeles for Taiwan." Freeman noted that it was a "not-so-veiled threat to hit downtown L.A. with a nuclear attack."[154]

Right now the U.S. has an 80 billion-dollar trade surplus with China. If a nation's economy rises 3 percent in one year it is considered good. For the last twenty years the Chinese economy has grown 10 percent per year. During that period China has dumped massive amounts of money into their military. It has not only beefed up their army, but has also purchased nuclear submarines from Russia that could sink a U.S. aircraft carrier!

---

[153]ibid. *Encarta Encyclopedia.*
[154]Policy Statement on Missile Defense—U.S. House of Representatives Policy Committee, issued May 9, 1996. Information is also available at www.endtime.com.

Once again, it was not until the middle of this last century that there has been a country who could come close to fielding a 200-million-man army. Before Mao Tse-tung died, he boasted in his diary of having that capability. Today China is considered a world superpower with great nuclear capability.

In the last couple of decades we have witnessed a dangerous game of cat and mouse between the U.S. and China. One example happened a few years ago when the Clinton Administration was accused of accepting funds from China. Around that same time a Chinese spy was captured stealing military secrets from Los Alamos (one of America's top secret research and development facilities).

It was also during that same time we were fighting in conjunction with the UN peacekeeping force in Kosovo against an army funded by the Chinese. The next thing that happened was that one of our spy planes (that was supposed to be undetectable) was shot down.

Following that incident the Americans *accidentally* bombed the Chinese embassy in Kosovo. We blamed the bombing on old maps. Eight-hundred-and-seventy Chinese were polled. All of them were asked, "Do you think the bombing of the Chinese embassy was an accident?" All 870 of the Chinese people polled said they did not believe the bombing was an accident.

After the bombing, Chinese people rioted at the American embassy in China throwing blood on the embassy grounds. The Chinese demonstrators shouted, "War now!" and "Take Taiwan now!" The Chinese say that they are going to take back Taiwan so quickly that America with either have to send troops to Taiwan, or let China have it.

Another example of the political pushing and shoving that took place occurred in 1996 when Taiwan had their first democratic election. To send a message to Taiwan concerning this election China fired two missiles into the ocean near Taiwan. In response, President Clinton sent 100,000 men and two aircraft carriers to the Straits of Formosa.

In the past, politicians have been very weak in their dealing with China. President Nixon sold out Taiwan because it was a whole lot safer to build a relationship with a country that has one billion people than one with twenty-five million. President Carter laid down trade with Taiwan. His policy was set in place so that the U.S. might trade with Communist China.

To the contrary, President George W. Bush has stated publicly that we will do whatever it takes to defend Taiwan. The Chinese government responded by saying that the U.S. was right on the edge of the point of no return.[155]

Currently, China has over twenty-four nuclear warheads aimed at major military installations and cities in the United States. They have boasted that they *will* take back Taiwan, and they do not believe Americans are willing to lose millions of people in order to stop them.[156]

In *Time* magazine, a headline read "Threat of China Impending." In the article Chinese generals stated that there will be an all-out war with China by the year 2015. Currently the U.S. does not have a nuclear defense system that will guard against a full Chinese nuclear attack.

Early in his administration President Bush set up a "shadow government," and he has asked for the authority to use nuclear weapons. He also asked the military to develop smaller nuclear weapons that will destroy only part of a city. Supposedly, this is for America's war on terrorism. Nevertheless, according to Scripture what is truly looming over the world is a major nuclear war.

Right now India and Pakistan also have nuclear weapons, and several times in recent years they have been very close to war. Keep in mind that India has over one billion people. North Korea has also said that they are developing nuclear weapons.

---

[155]*Reuters Asia* (periodical), article by John Ruwich, "China Slams U.S., Vows to Defeat Taiwan."
[156]*London Times*, February 27, 1999, "China prepares to use nukes against U.S., according to German intelligence."

North Korea has over 23 million people; China has over one billion. If China was pulled into a nuclear war in that region, it could easily account for a large portion of the world's population.

Clearly all of these trumpets are events that affect the entire world. With that in mind, at the sounding of the sixth trumpet we see four angels being loosed that are bound at the river Euphrates which runs right down the middle of Muslim territory.

On September 11, 2001, four airplanes were highjacked by Muslim extremists in the United States. All of those airplanes were used as missiles to attack specific targets. Three of the four hit their targets, but all four led to the loss of American lives.

Consider how the events of September 11 changed the world! President Bush declared that we are at war. This war on terrorism will have many fronts, it will affect many people, and it will be a long one. Is it possible that the sixth trumpet has already sounded?

Did the Chinese have anything to do with the terrorists' attacks on America? The fact is, not only did the Chinese help fund these Muslim terrorists, but many people when fleeing Afghanistan were allowed to enter China. China is not a friend to the United States.

The fulfillment of the sixth trumpet (the worst world war in history) will usher in a powerful United Nations that for the first time will be given authority to rule over the sovereignty of nations. This one-world government will be the platform for the Antichrist and the one-world religion.

The Seventh Trumpet

As we have already seen, the seventh trumpet is simple. It is the wrath of God being poured out, and the Second Coming of Christ (which is the biggest world event). The seventh trumpet is also the time at which saints are judged and given rewards (see Revelation 11:18).

The last trumpet is the culmination of all things concerning man's government (the times of the Gentiles). It is a time when the Lord deals with the beast by pouring out his wrath, then afterward setting up his government on the earth.

Once again, we must be careful not to fit every modern-day event into Bible prophecy. God has not described every little war and rumor of war. On the other hand, he has given us several prophecies concerning major world events that we can clearly see the fulfillment of as we view world history. These events are gigantic mile-markers on the highway of Bible prophecy.

It is also noteworthy that—as far as we can tell—all of the trumpets except the fourth have somehow played a role in the momentum of a one-world government. After WW I and WW II there was a proposal of a one-world government. Then, after WW II we see the formation of the UN.

Many articles suggest that the Chernobyl nuclear accident aided in the collapse of the iron curtain, which in turn set Communism loose and forced Russia to be a team player in a global environment. The first Gulf War (the fifth trumpet) was the first real test of the UN peacekeeping force in the New World Order. The sixth trumpet will most likely give immediate power and global dominion to the UN. Of course, the seventh trumpet will be the downfall of the one-world government as Jesus sets up his global government.

As we examine the possibilities of the trumpets, we can easily see that we are very close to a difficult, but powerful, time for Christians on this earth. Most importantly we come to the realization that we are very near to the Second Coming of Christ. The question is, *are you ready?*

Let's Review

- The seven trumpets occur within the last days.
- The seven trumpets are major world events.
- The first trumpet is possibly WW I.
- The second trumpet is possibly WW II.
- The third trumpet is possibly the Chernobyl nuclear accident.
- The fourth trumpet is very vague, but might be the speeding up of time.
- The fifth trumpet is possibly the first Gulf War.
- The sixth trumpet is a major World War in which one-third of the earth's population is killed.
- The seventh [last] trumpet is the wrath of God being poured out, the saints judged and given rewards, and the kingdoms of this world becoming the kingdoms of our God.
- All of the trumpets (except the fourth) have played a role in the suggestion, formation, or propagation of the one-world government.

Satan's Wrath

And there appeared a great wonder in heaven; a woman clothed with the sun, and the moon under her feet, and upon her head a crown of twelve stars: And she being with child cried, travailing in birth, and pained to be delivered. And there appeared another wonder in heaven; and behold a great red dragon, having seven heads and ten horns, and seven crowns upon his heads. And his tail drew the third part of the stars of heaven, and did cast them to the earth: and the dragon stood before the woman which was ready to be delivered, for to devour her child as soon as it was born. And she brought forth a man-child, who was to rule all nations with a rod of iron: and her child was caught up unto God, and to his throne. And the woman fled into the wilderness, where she hath a place prepared of God, that they should feed her there a thousand two hundred and threescore days

REVELATION 12:1-6

The woman clothed with the sun.

In Revelation 12:1-6 we see some interesting events. There has been a lot of speculation concerning the woman clothed with the sun, and the moon and twelve stars around her head. Many times when God reveals a symbol in one part of the Bible we will also find it somewhere else in Scripture. And when we find it, it will reveal more about the symbol.

In Genesis chapter 37 an individual by the name of Joseph had a dream. In his dream he looked out and saw a sun, a moon, and eleven stars. Sound familiar? In this dream the sun, moon, and eleven stars bowed down and worshipped him.

Joseph's father, Jacob, asked him (paraphrase), "What do you think, that I am the sun, your mother Rachel is the moon, your brothers are the eleven stars, and that we are going to bow down and worship you?" Joseph replied, "I don't know! I just had the dream!" We know as the story concluded that this is exactly what happened.

In Revelation we see twelve stars, and in Genesis we only see eleven. How can we account for this discrepancy? The reason there were only eleven stars is because Joseph was the twelfth. The twelve stars in Revelation chapter 12 are representative of the twelve tribes of Israel (Jacob's twelve sons), thus representing Israel itself.

The Great Tribulation is also called the time of Jacob's trouble. Think about it! Jacob literally gave life to the twelve tribes of Israel (the twelve stars). We see in Scripture that during the Great Tribulation the devil will persecute Israel like never before, and this will be the time of Jacob's trouble.

As we read on in Revelation 12:1-6 we see that the woman gave birth to *a child*. Then, another sign in heaven appeared, and the dragon (having seven heads, ten horns, and seven diadems on his heads) drew a third of the stars of heaven with his tail. Who is the dragon? Revelation 12:9 tells us clearly that the dragon is the devil.

What are the seven heads and ten horns? These are the same symbols we see illustrating nations within the one-world government out of which rises the Antichrist. When the devil fell from heaven, he became the god of this world's system. For several millennia Satan has exercised influence and power through worldly government.

The dragon in Revelation chapter 12 draws a third part of the stars from heaven with his tail. Verse 4 goes all the way back to when Satan fell and drew a third of the angels in heaven with him. Then, he waited as the woman travailed to give birth to the man-child so he could devour the child as soon as it was born. Who is the man-child? The child the devil tried to devour was Jesus. He tried to devour Jesus through the use of earthly government (specifically through the Roman governor Herod).

When Jesus was born, wise men came and asked Herod about the birth of a king. Herod asked, "Why don't you tell me where this child is so that I can worship him also."

The wise men–knowing that Herod did not wish to worship Jesus, but to kill him–got wise to Herod's scheme and left by a different route than they came. Herod was furious! As a result, he killed all the children two years old and under. The devil was waiting to devour the child and used earthly government as his pawn to accomplish the task. Joseph and Mary had to flee to Egypt in order to protect Jesus. In the last days the devil has used, and will continue to use, earthly government to try to destroy Israel and her offspring (the Church).

In Revelation 12:4-5 we see that the devil tries to devour the child (who was to rule the nations), but the child is caught up to the throne of God. Amazingly, we see the first advent of Jesus summed up in only these two verses. The woman [Israel] gave birth to the child [Jesus] who will rule all nations. Then, the devil tried to destroy him, but was unsuccessful. After this the woman fled into the wilderness where God had prepared a place to feed her for 1,260 days (3 ½ years).

A war in heaven!

All this leads us to Revelation 12:7-17:

And there was war in heaven: Michael and his angels fought against the dragon; and the dragon fought and his angels, and prevailed not; neither was their place found any more in heaven. And the great dragon was cast out, that old serpent, called the devil, and Satan, which deceiveth the whole world: *he was cast out into the earth,* and his angels were cast out with him. And I heard a loud voice saying in heaven, "Now is come salvation, and strength, and the kingdom of our God, and the power of his Christ; for the accuser of our brethren is cast down, which accused them before our God day and night. And they overcame him by the blood of the Lamb, and by the word of their testimony; and they loved not their lives unto death. Therefore rejoice, ye heavens, and ye that dwell in them. Woe to the inhabitants of the earth and of the sea! For the devil is come down unto you, having great wrath, because he knoweth that he hath *but a short time."* And when the dragon saw that he was cast unto the earth, he persecuted the woman which brought forth the man-child. And to the woman were given two wings of a great eagle, that she might fly into the wilderness, into her place, where she is nourished for a time, and times, and half a time [3 ½ years], from the face of the serpent. So the serpent spewed water out of his mouth like a flood after the woman, that he might cause her to be carried away by the flood. But the earth helped the woman, and the earth opened its mouth and swallowed up the flood which the dragon had spewed out of his mouth. And the dragon was enraged with the woman, and he went to make war with the rest of her offspring, who keep the commandments of God *and have the testimony of Jesus Christ*

REVELATION 12:7-17

We see some fascinating things happening in this portion of Scripture. All of a sudden there is a war in heaven. In Revelation 12:7-17 we see a fight break out between the dragon (the old serpent, the devil) and Michael the Archangel. It also tells us that day and night Satan has been accusing the brethren before the throne of God. Finally, God gives Michael the authority to cast the devil to the earth. A scriptural reality is that whatever happens in the spiritual realm manifests itself in the natural realm. The worldly realm is Satan's kingdom, and he is going to stay on top of it for as long as he can.

As we have already learned, for the first three-and-a-half years of the final seven-year period (Daniel's seventieth week) the Antichrist is a peacemaker. He accomplishes this task with great persuasion and swelling words while compelling many nations to follow. In verse 12 the devil is cast to the earth, and he comes to the earth having great wrath, because he knows he has a short time.

Once again, the first three-and-a-half years of Daniel's seventieth week consists of a peace agreement. Logically, a viable peace agreement (more than likely one enforced by the UN) is what allows the Jews to rebuild their third temple. As we will see in this and the next two sections, the church is still here during Daniel's seventieth week. Halfway through Daniel's seventieth week the Antichrist has a change of heart.

Why does the Antichrist have a change of heart?

Three-and-a-half years into the last seven-year period there will be a very noticeable shift in the way the Antichrist will deal with the Jews and the saints. What causes this noticeable shift? As we will see, the abomination of desolation (the Antichrist cutting off the Jewish sacrifices and the persecution of the Jewish people) coincides perfectly with the devil being cast to the earth. At that time the devil will begin to exhibit great wrath through the Antichrist, and we see from Scripture that he also targets the saints.

In Revelation 12:7 we see a war in heaven where Michael and his angels fight against the dragon. The great dragon is cast out and his angels with him. At this point in time (the last 3 ½ years) there is a mass slaughter of believers, "Those who loved not their lives unto the death." The good news is that these believers do not lose! Verse 11 says, "They overcame him by the blood of the Lamb and the word of their testimony." They receive a crown of life because they loved not their lives even unto death. For the Christian, even death is not defeat!

As Christians we need not be afraid of dying. God's Word tells us, "To live is Christ...to die is gain." When we have a relationship with Jesus Christ, we know that no matter what happens we will live forever with the Lord. Jesus said, "Anybody who wishes to save their life will lose it, but anybody who loses their life for my sake will surely find it" (Matthew 16:25).

The Scriptural Time Period of the Great Tribulation

Now we come to Revelation 12:12, which reveals the true time period of the Great Tribulation. "Woe to the inhabitants of the earth and of the sea! For the devil is come down unto you, having great wrath, because he knoweth that he hath but a *short time*." This is the beginning of the abomination of desolation.

It is in the middle of the final seven-year period that the abomination of desolation spoken of in Daniel 9:27 occurs. At that point the Antichrist begins to persecute Israel and the saints. This is the same time period Revelation 12:12-17 speaks of as we see the devil being cast to the earth. He comes down having great wrath.

We also see in this passage that the devil persecutes Israel. As this happens, Israel is carried away by the Lord (via the wings of eagles) and nourished for three-and-a-half years (time, times, and half a time). Therefore, we can see that at the beginning of the last three-and-a-half years the Antichrist has a change of heart. We can also identify in Scripture what transpires to cause this change (Satan being cast to the earth).

These passages we have looked at perfectly parallel Jesus' words in Matthew 24:15-21:

> Therefore when you see the "abomination of desolation," spoken of by Daniel the prophet, standing in the holy place (whoever reads let him understand), then let those who are in Judea flee to the mountains. Let him who is on the housetop not go down to take anything out of his house. And let him who is in the field not go back to get his clothes. But woe to those who are pregnant and to those who are nursing babies in those days! And pray that your flight may not be in winter or on the Sabbath. For then there will be great tribulation, such as has not been since the beginning of the world until this time, no, nor ever shall be.

In Matthew chapter 24 Jesus warned that when we see the abomination of desolation spoken of by the prophet Daniel standing in the holy place (the temple), let those in Judea flee. He went on to explain that in that day there will be great tribulation as there has not been since the beginning of time, nor shall there ever be. Jesus also mentions the specific target of the Antichrist's aggression—Judea.

From Scripture we see that the Great Tribulation begins at the middle mark of Daniel's seventieth week. This is when the Antichrist comes into the holy place and sets himself up as God. The Bible warns that those in Judea (which is modern-day Hebron, and the Golan Heights–the West Bank) should not go back for their coats; they should not go into the city; women will be raped; children will be murdered; and it will be a holocaust like they have never known before. All of this in the name of peace!

So we see that the Great Tribulation begins at the abomination of desolation, and is a time of Satan's wrath. Therefore, a biblically accurate term for the last three-and-a-half years of Daniel's seventieth week would be the Great Tribulation, or Satan's wrath. Also, during this time it is not only Jews that are being persecuted and killed, but also Christians. Revelation 13:7 speaks of the same hour when it says, "And it was given unto him to make war with the *saints*, and to overcome them: and power was given him over all kindreds, and tongues, and nations."

Power being given to the Antichrist over all kindreds, tongues, and nations leads us to believe that he will be the leader of the United Nations (one-world government). The UN and the United Religions are the most likely vehicles the Antichrist will use to persecute the saints.

In Revelation chapter 12 we see that the dragon (Satan) gives the Antichrist his power. Daniel 9:27 tells us,

> And he [the Antichrist] shall confirm a covenant with many for one week [seven years]. *And in the midst of the week* he shall cause the sacrifice and the oblation to cease. And for the overspreading of abominations he shall make it desolate, even until the consummation [the coming of the Lord]. And that determined shall be poured out upon the desolate.

And in Daniel 8:23-25 we see,

> In the latter time of their kingdom when the transgressors are come to the full, a king of fierce countenance and understanding dark sentences shall stand up. And his power shall be mighty, but not in his own power. He shall destroy wonderfully and shall prosper and practice and shall destroy the mighty and the holy people and through his policy, also, he shall cause craft to prosper in his hand and he shall magnify himself in his heart. *And by peace he shall destroy many.* He shall also stand up against the Prince of princes *but he shall be broken without hand.*

The Prince of princes is Jesus who will destroy "without hand."

Interestingly, all UN actions are called "peacekeeping" actions. When the armies march against Israel at the Battle of Armageddon it will simply be the UN peacekeeping forces coming together to bring Israel into submission so that they may rule over them.

What makes the Antichrist have a change of heart so quickly? We know that the Great Tribulation begins in the middle of the week (at the abomination of desolation), and it will last for three-and-a-half years. In Daniel 7:25 we see that the Great Tribulation will last for time, times, and the dividing of times (3 ½ years). Revelation 13:5 tells us that the Great Tribulation will last for 42 months (3 ½ years). Then, in Revelation 12:6 it says the Great Tribulation lasts 1,260 days (3 ½ years).

Also in Revelation chapter 12 we see that Satan comes down to the earth having great wrath knowing he has only a short time to do the last of his evil deeds. At that point the Antichrist (the world leader who brought peace through politics) begins to have a change of heart.

All of a sudden the Antichrist goes from being a person who is demonically *influenced* to a person who is literally *possessed* by the devil. The Bible describes the Antichrist as the "son of perdition," which basically means "Satan's son."

A fallen spirit (in this case the devil himself) desires to have a body as a host (preferably human). A perfect example from the Scriptures is Matthew 8:28-32 when the demons who possessed the Gadarene man pleaded with Jesus to cast them into a herd of swine. Clearly they desired to inhabit a body. On the other hand, the Bible says born-again believers are temples of the Holy Ghost.

For the first three-and-a-half years the Antichrist is a smooth talker, but in Daniel 7:25 we see that he is no longer speaking of peace. Daniel 7:25 tells us, "He shall speak great words against the most high, and shall wear out the *saints* of the most high, and think to change times and laws: and they [the saints] shall be given into his hand until a time and times and the dividing of time [3 ½ years]."

In Revelation 13:5-7 we see:

> And there was given unto him a mouth speaking great things and blasphemies; and power was given unto him to continue *forty and two months*. And he opened his mouth in *blasphemy against God*, to blaspheme his name, and his tabernacle, and them that dwell in heaven. And it was given unto him to make war with the *saints*, and to overcome them: and power was given him over all kindreds, and tongues, and nations.

Suddenly this peacemaker begins to curse God, his temple, and all those who dwell in heaven including the angels. Why is this information important? Whenever we see time frames mentioned—forty-two months, along with very specific actions—it becomes a benchmark in prophecy.

As we begin to line these things up, we see this specific event (the abomination of desolation) revealed in the midst of Daniel's seventieth week. We also see that Satan being cast down to the earth energizes this event.

Therefore, in the following parallel passages we see the specific time frame of the Great Tribulation, which begins at the abomination of desolation, and is the time of Satan's wrath.

In review:

- In Revelation 12:7-17 the devil persecutes Israel for the last three-and-a-half years of Daniel's seventieth week.
- In Revelation chapter 13 power is given to the Antichrist to persecute the saints for forty-two months.
- In Matthew 24:15 we see the "abomination of desolation spoken of by Daniel the prophet" standing in the holy place. This is when the persecution of Israel begins (see Matthew 24:15 and Daniel 9:27).
- Matthew 24:21 tells us at that point (the abomination of desolation) that there will be great tribulation, such as has not been since the beginning of the world.

♦ Matthew 24:29 says, "Immediately after the tribulation of those days..." The Great Tribulation begins at the abomination of desolation and continues for three-and-a-half years.

Again, the first half of the last seven-year period is a peace agreement with Israel. Then the devil is cast to the earth and he personally begins to persecute Israel and the saints via the Antichrist. The last three-and-a-half-years of Daniel's seventieth week is Satan's wrath–the same thing Daniel called "the time of the over spreading of abominations that they shall make desolate."

The Abomination that Makes Desolate

This brings us to an interesting question: What is the abomination that makes desolate? We read about what happens in heaven, but what happens on earth at that time? There will be a world leader who has been deceiving the nations. When this world leader becomes a dictator, "He opposes and exalteth himself above all that is called God's."

The Antichrist enters the temple of God, and professes that he is God. Concerning this event the Scriptures say, "Showing as many as would believe that he was God." Keep in mind, at this point most people in the world will think that the UN and its leader are the greatest thing since sliced bread! The UN will have brought peace to the world and to one of the most turbulent places in the world–the Middle East.

Remember the *Earth Charter* we spoke of in a previous section? Remember how Mikhail Gorbachev said that he wants the *Earth Charter* to be the Ten Commandments of the New World Order? In 2002 they placed the *Earth Charter* in a special box and transported it to the UN's Earth Summit II in Johannesburg, South Africa.

An article by William F. Jasper, entitled "The New World Religion," has a picture of the box containing the *Earth Charter*. Underneath the picture a caption reads:

The venerated Earth Charter is housed and transported in the Ark of Hope, a blasphemous mimicry of the biblical Ark of the Covenant, which held the two tablets containing the Ten Commandments that God gave to Moses.

Painted on the outside of the Ark of Hope are the inscriptions and symbols of Wicca! How blatant can the United Religions be? Now Gorbachev has an Ark to house his "Ten Commandments" of the New World Order!

This same article went on to say:

Also within the Ark of Hope are the Temenos Books, containing aboriginal Earth Masks and "visual prayers and affirmations for global healing, peace, and gratitude." These items were created by three thousand artists, teachers, students, and mystics. According to the Temenos project, a Temenos is a "magical sacred circle where special rules apply and extraordinary events inevitably occur."

The Ark, *Earth Charter*, and Temenos Books were placed on display at the UN Summit site and then put to work building a new global ethic.[157] (Copies of "The New World Religion" article can be obtained by calling 920-749-3784, or online at www.thenewamerican.com.)

With all that in mind, picture the Jews having completed their third temple and re-establishing Old Testament animal sacrifices. Once the world realizes what Jewish worship involves (the cutting of animals' throats and burning them on an altar) the United Religions and animal rights activists will go berserk! This could be an explanation for the Antichrist bringing the Jewish sacrifices to an end (see Daniel 9:27b).

---

[157]Artical by William F. Jasper, first appeared in the *New American*, September 23, 2002.

What would be the next logical step after the Antichrist puts a halt to Israel's sacrificial worship? Imagine the United Religions (along with the world leader) taking the Jewish Ark of the Covenant out of God's temple and replacing it with the Ark of Hope! This would amount to an enormous abomination! Why? If this action were to occur, it would mean that God's covenant would be taken out of his temple and replaced with a covenant of pagan worship.

We realize this is speculation. However, if this scenario played out, the UN and the UR would be setting themselves up as gods of this world. Unfortunately, most people in the world would cheer. The world will view Christians and Jews as radicals who must be silenced because they see a great abomination taking place in the Jewish temple.

In the middle of Daniel's seventieth week we see the Antichrist causing the oblation and the sacrifices to cease. The Jewish worship and sacrifices become desolate. The Antichrist walks into the temple of God and right into the Holy of Holies!

At some point in time it appears as though he will have an image of himself, the one-world government, or the United Religions erected in the temple of God. Obviously, this is an abomination to God. The Antichrist will insist that people worship this image. The Bible says, "And as many as would not worship the beast, *they should be killed.*" This image of the beast (one-world government) might be, or might include, the image of the UN and United Religions. The UN's symbol is the earth with a laurel around it (a laurel is symbolic of honor, or victory).

At the UN's Earth Summit II in South Africa the opening ceremony involved children holding hands and singing around an enormous model of the earth. We have already established that the heartbeat of the United Religions is earth worship, and the heartbeat of the UN is saving the planet.

Think about the parallel between God pouring out his wrath on the beast and the false prophet, and pouring out his wrath on Egypt. When he poured out his wrath on Egypt, he was attacking each of the Egyptian's gods (see Exodus 12:12). What did the Egyptians worship? They worshipped the sun, the river, and the earth. They were earth worshippers! (We will go more in-depth concerning God's wrath in a later section.)

When we see the abomination of desolation happen, this is when 666 (the mark of the beast) comes into effect. Up to this time, it was a person's choice whether or not to take the mark, but it will become mandatory after the abomination of desolation. If a person refuses to take the mark of the beast, they will not be able to buy or sell, and they will experience great persecution.

There will be many within the grip of the one-world government who will be beheaded for refusing to take the mark. Beheaded! Oh, come on...no one does that in this modern age! On the contrary, up until a few decades ago, France used the guillotine as their method of execution. More recently, consider all the beheadings taking place after kidnappings in Iraq by extremist Muslims (preceding the transfer of power after the second Gulf war).

In the midst of Daniel's seventieth week, the Antichrist enters the third Jewish temple. Then, the Antichrist will cause the sacrifices and the oblations to cease as he sits down in the temple of God. At this point he begins to boast and blaspheme by saying, "I am God!" These acts, along with the persecution of the Jewish people, constitute the abomination of desolation.

Computerized gods?

There are strange happenings in India right now. In New Delhi, the Hare Krishnas have built a high-tech temple. When building this temple, they consulted with a special effects company in Los Angeles, California. The Krishnas had them make nine high-tech, computerized gods for their temple in New Delhi. They call this temple in New Delhi "The Glory of India."[158]

---

[158]BBC News, April 5, 1998, "Robot Gods at Temple."

When a person walks into the Hare Krishna temple, they experience nine huge electronic gods speaking and reading Hindu Scriptures. These high-tech gods also do various motions while demanding worship. This could very well be a prototype for what the Antichrist will do.

Devout Jews will not be able to submit to the desires of the Antichrist because the abomination of desolation is breaking the Ten Commandments. When the Jews are faced with this horrible reality, they instantly realize that the Antichrist is not their Messiah.

Great Persecution

The actions of the Antichrist parallel the persecution that Daniel, Shadrach, Meshach, and Abednego went through in Nebuchadnezzar's day. Nebuchadnezzar ordered these four men to bow down and worship an image. Daniel's response was, "I will not!" Soon there will be an entire nation of Shadrach, Meshach, and Abednegos who say they will not worship an image or take a mark.

Jesus warned Israel that when they see these things happen, those who are in Judea and Samaria better flee for the mountains! The Bible warns that even if they are on their roof they should not go back for their wallet. They should hit the ground running and not look back! There is coming a persecution of the Jews like never before. The worst holocaust the Jews have ever seen is on the horizon. This is the work of the Antichrist.

We learned that the woman clothed with the sun and moon having twelve stars around her head is Israel. We also know the dragon goes out to make war against her offspring (the church). At the time of the abomination of desolation there is clearly a multitude of saints because it says, "power was given to the dragon that he might wage war on the *saints*, and he might overcome them." Evidently this is not an easy task. Daniel 7:25 confirms this when it says, "He will *wear out* the saints."

We know the Antichrist wages war against the nation of Israel. The only thing that saves Israel at this appointed time is the fact that the Antichrist hears rumors of some kings coming against him. Nevertheless, it is a rough season for Israel. There are two military campaigns during the last three-and-a-half year period, one in which Israel is mortally wounded.

When the fifth seal is opened in Revelation 6:9-11 we see a group of people slain for the word of God and their witness. These are Christians! These saints, dressed in white robes, are saying, "How long, O Lord, until you avenge our blood on the earth?" It is apparent in Scripture that this influx of martyrs happens during or after the abomination of desolation.

This is not only the greatest persecution that will have ever hit the Jews, but there will also be a great persecution of Bible-believing, fundamental Christians who love God more than their own lives. Jesus said that if anyone seeks to save his life they are going to lose it, but for anyone that loses their life for his sake, they shall surely find it. That's what being a Christian is all about. We must love Christ more than our job, more than our money, more than our car, and more than our entertainment. We must love Him! We must adore Him! He is life! He is everything!

The good news is—we do not lose. When we read Revelation chapter 20, we discover that we win! We also see in Revelation 12:11, "And they overcame him by the blood of the Lamb and by the word of their testimony, and they did not love their lives to the death."

The 144,000 Jews

In Revelation chapter 7 we see a unique group of people the Antichrist persecutes during this three-and-a-half year period. We're going to read about 144,000 Jews. These people are very different. There has been a lot of speculation about this group of people. Who are they?

> And after these things I saw four angels standing on the four corners of the earth, holding the four winds of the earth, that the wind should not blow on the earth, nor on the sea, nor on any tree. And I saw another angel ascending from the east, having the seal of the living God; and he cried with a loud voice to the four angels, to whom it was given to hurt the earth and the sea, saying, "Hurt not the earth, neither the sea, nor the trees, till we have sealed the servants of our God in their foreheads." And I heard the number of them which were sealed: and there were sealed *an hundred and forty and four thousand* of all the tribes of the children of Israel.
>
> REVELATION 7:1-4

God seals his children on their foreheads. As we know, the devil also seals *his* children on their foreheads. We may think the devil comes up with new ideas, yet he does not create anything. The devil has never had an original idea. For instance, satanism is set up much like Old Testament temple worship. The difference is that satanism is a *perversion* of Old Testament worship.

Scripture says, "And I heard the number of them that were sealed: and there were sealed an hundred and forty and four thousand of all the tribes of the children of Israel." The Lord seals 12,000 from each tribe of Israel. Scripture goes on to name all the tribes of Israel–Judah, Benjamin, etc.

Does a Jewish person know from which tribe their ancestors originate? Some would say yes, and some would say no. It does not matter, however, if they know which tribe they are from because God knows. It stands to reason that if the Lord numbers all the hairs on our head, then he also knows of which tribe each Jew is a descendant. He knows their lineage perfectly.

In Revelation 14:1-4 we see some interesting facts about this 144,000:

> And I looked, and, lo, a Lamb stood on the mount Sion, and with him an hundred forty and four thousand, having his Father's name written in their foreheads. And I heard a voice from heaven, as the voice of a great thunder: and I heard the voice of harpers harping with their harps: and they sung as it were a new song before the throne, and before the four beasts, and the elders: and no man could learn that song but the hundred and forty and four thousand, which were redeemed from the earth. These are they which were not defiled with women: for they are *virgins*. These are they which follow the Lamb withersoever He goeth. These were redeemed from among men, being the *firstfruits* unto God and to the Lamb.

This is a peculiar passage for many reasons. We know that during this tribulation period (Satan's wrath) a vast amount of Jews are being persecuted. We also know that God takes a group of Jews and seals them in their foreheads. In addition he keeps them for time, times, and the dividing of time. The question is; who are they?

There are a couple of clues that might help identify the 144,000. Two specific things separate them from everyone else. Scripture explains that they do not defile themselves with women–for they are *virgins*. They also follow the Lamb wherever he goes, and they were the *first fruits* unto God and to the Lamb. Scripture reveals that they are: 1. virgins, and 2. They are born-again Jews.

They must be born again because a person does not follow the Lamb wherever he goes unless they know that Jesus is the Messiah. The Bible says that these 144,000 are the "firstfruits" of the Lamb. This is the first mass of people who become born again out of the Jewish nation during this last three-and-a-half year period.

The regathering of the Jewish people and the reviving of the Jewish nation was a magnificent time for the Jews. Most of those Jews were Orthodox Jews. Of course we know that there are born-again Jews. However, as a whole the nation of Israel today consists of Orthodox Jews who do not believe that Jesus is the Messiah. (By the way, the *Jerusalem Post* sells a tape series on how *not* to become a Christian.)

This being the case, what is the firstfruit? Somehow a group of 144,000 Jewish people all of a sudden become believers. We are going to talk about how that might happen, but the strange thing is that they are virgins (meaning they are pure).

In biblical terms this is a contradiction. When the Bible speaks of a man who has not been with a woman, it uses the term "eunuch." A virgin is a woman who has not been with a man, and a eunuch is a man who has not been with a woman. So to what is Revelation 14:1-4 referring?

Remember when we examined Babylon the Great? She was a harlot! God referred to a city, and the actions of those who partook of her religion as harlotry.

God always called an apostate, or compromising, church a harlot and a pure Bible-believing church a virgin. The apostle Paul said, "I pray that I could present you a *chaste virgin* unto the Lord." So we see that this passage is not talking about *physical*, but rather *spiritual* virgins who are pure before the Lord.

More than likely, this passage is referring to a group of Jews who do not fornicate with, or take part in, the United Religions or other religions. They are pure in their hearts before the Lord. Therefore, spiritually speaking they are virgins.

Why would God seal 144,000 born-again Jews? A parallel passage in the Old Testament gives more information about this group of people whom the Lord seals with a mark.

Ezekiel chapter 9 says:

> He cried also in mine ears with a loud voice saying, "Cause them that have charge over the city to draw near, even every man with his destroying weapon in his hand." And behold six men came from the way of

the higher gate, which lieth toward the north, and every man a slaughter weapon in his hand; and one man
among them was clothed with linen, with a writer's
inkhorn by his side: and they went in, and stood be-
side the brazen altar. And the glory of the God of Israel
was gone up from the cherub, whereupon he was, to
the threshold of the house. And he called to the man
clothed with linen, which had the writer's inkhorn by
his side; and the Lord said unto him, "Go through the
midst of the city, through the midst of Jerusalem, *and
set a mark upon the foreheads of the men that sigh and
that cry for all the abominations that be done in the midst
thereof.*"

EZEKIEL 9:1-4

What a fascinating parallel passage! In Ezekiel we see that
they sigh and cry over the abominations that are going on in
Israel. The sealing is complete in the seventh chapter of Revelation, which takes place at the end of the last days. Therefore, it
is possible that these 144,000 are alive right now! Most of them
are probably not born again at this point; however, they will be.

Speculation about the 144,000 Orthodox Jews.

In recent years much of the Jewish nation has been agnostic,
or very liberal in their belief about God. When Yitzhak Rabin
and Shimon Peres were running for office in Israel, the Jews
wanted peace at any cost. (By the way, the name Peres means "to
divide," and that is exactly what these people were good for–
dividing the land of Israel.)

It is during this time that we see the Oslo Peace Accords
which Peres and Rabin helped draft. The Oslo Peace Accord
traded land for peace with the Palestinians.

Keep in mind that the Palestinians do not really want peace.
What the Palestinians truly want is Israel piece by piece! They
want to push the Israelis into the Mediterranean Sea. As the Bible
says, Jerusalem is a burdensome stone.

The ultraOrthodox Jews (who know that God has given them every bit of Israel to possess and to occupy) understand they must take *all* of Israel. They also understand that if they do not take the whole land, the Gentiles will be thorns in their sides and thistles in their eyes.

Thousands of years ago God promised, and established, the land of Israel. What happened when Rabin began to trade land for peace? As we have already learned, the first city they gave away was a place called Jericho. Consider the irony! Jericho was the first city God had given the Israelites in the Promised Land. Next they give up Bethlehem (the birthplace of Christ), and then they give up a place called Hebron to the Palestinians.

Peres and Rabin gave away all of Hebron, except the portion containing the burial sites of Abraham, Isaac, and Jacob. After this startling event, a large group of Orthodox Jews showed up in Hebron and began to tear their clothes and weep which they also did in the Old Testament whenever an abomination occurred. As Hebron is being given away to the Palestinians, ultraOrthodox Jews began tearing their clothes in shreds, throwing dirt on their heads, and sighing and crying.

Many of these Jews (who are completely sold out to the Old Covenant) began to move into Hebron and settle. Some ultraOrthodox Jews even rented office space next to Rabin's office in Jerusalem and devoted twenty-four hours a day to fasting, prayer, sighing, and crying. The majority of these people were from a place called the West Bank.

We have learned how God fought for Israel in the 1967 War of Redemption (the Six-Day War). The Israelis ended up taking land all the way to the Jordan River, an area known as the West Bank.

On May 11, 1997, the Associated Press reported:
[Moshe] Dayan said he granted permission (after the Six-Day War) to settler leader Moshe Levinger to enter Hebron on the condition that the American-born rabbi and his family would stay only for the weeklong Jewish holiday

of Passover. Levinger never left Hebron, and became the father of the Jewish settler movement that today includes 144,000 Israelis living throughout the West Bank.

Concerning these West Bank settlements, the Associated Press also reported, "Palestinians have insisted that the settlements occupied by the Jews must be evacuated when returned to Palestinian control, but hard core settlers say they will never leave their home."

Right now there are Orthodox Jewish settlers in the West Bank and it is constantly in the news because of ongoing clashes between the Israelis and the Palestinians. These West Bank Jews are ultraOrthodox, Old Testament-thumping, Messiah-is-on-his-way Jews.

Could the West Bank Jews be the ones who sigh and cry over the abominations in the land? Could they be the ones who are sealed on their foreheads–later becoming the firstfruits of Israel?

Matthew 24:15 says when you see the abomination of desolation spoken by the prophet Daniel standing in the holy place, let those that are in Judea flee into the mountains.

Here is the amazing thing: *The West Bank is historically Judea.* When the Antichrist shows up at the abomination of desolation, the first place he is going to turn his wrath is the West Bank settlements. What justification will the Antichrist have? The International Criminal Court will consider the West Bank Jews criminals according to the Oslo Peace Accord because they are living on land which (according to the World Court) belongs to the Palestinians.

On July 9, 2004, the International Criminal Court ruled 14 to 1 that the barrier Israel has erected to keep the Palestinians out of the West Bank is a violation of International law.[159] According to the UN's Criminal Court these Jews are occupying the West Bank illegally. We know that God has sealed them. Yet the

---

[159]The News Hour with Jim Lehrer, July 9, 2004.

international community (via the UN) will justify their future actions against Israel and the West Bank Jews through International Criminal Court rulings, which are already in existence.

The Two Witnesses

In Revelation chapter 11 we see two witnesses come on the scene. These two witnesses might possibly be the tools God uses to get the 144,000 born again. The two walk into the middle of Jerusalem and fight against the Antichrist in the middle of all this turmoil.

As we look at these two witnesses it says:
1. They have power to shut up the sky that it does not rain.
2. They have power to send plagues on the Antichrist.
3. They have power to turn the water into blood.
4. They have power that when something comes against them, fire comes out of their mouths.

The two that God sends to witness become a thorn in the Antichrist's side. The Bible tells us that at the end of Satan's wrath the two witnesses are killed in the view of peoples, tribes, tongues, and nations (see Revelation 11:9).

These two witnesses are reminiscent of Moses and Aaron walking into Pharaoh's court and casting down the staff that became a snake. Pharaoh's magicians did the same thing, but Aaron's rod swallowed up all of the magician's rods (see Exodus 7:8-13).

It is amazing when God does things like that! He gives the devil a little power only to reveal that he has greater power. When God began pouring out his plagues upon Pharaoh's land, as he poured out lice upon Egypt, Pharaoh's crazy magicians said, "That's nothing, we can make more lice." Then God said through Moses, "I will bring frogs upon you." Again Pharaoh's magicians said, "That's nothing we can make more frogs." This is a giant indication of how ignorant the devil and his followers are. Why would *anyone* bring plagues upon themselves?

God proved he was more powerful than the Egyptian's frog god, fly god, river god, etc. He proved himself to be the One who is sovereign over life and death as he took the lives of all the firstborn of the Egyptians. We serve the same God today!

In Scripture we see that power is given to the dragon (the devil) and he goes out with great wrath knowing that he has a short time. He wastes the last bit of his power killing the two witnesses. Now, he is out of bullets.

After the Antichrist kills the two witnesses, they lie in the street for three-and-a-half days. After this time the witnesses come to life, and immediately they begin to ascend into heaven. In Revelation 11:13 we see that in the same hour there was a great earthquake that kills 7,000 people. Then, the seventh angel (trumpet) sounded. The seventh (last) trumpet is the Second Coming of Christ and the pouring out of the wrath of God.

Therefore, when we speak of the two witnesses, it helps give us another clue as to the time frame of the Great Tribulation. Revelation 11:3 says that they prophesy for 1,260 days. The two witnesses arrive on the scene during Satan's wrath, and then they are caught up to heaven at the last trumpet.

Who are the two witnesses?

Some people speculate that one of the witnesses might be Moses. This idea comes from the fact that the plagues the two witnesses bring resemble the ones brought through Moses. Others say that Elijah must be one of the witnesses because Elijah called fire down from heaven.

More than likely Moses is not one of the witnesses as the Bible says it is appointed for man *once to die* and then the judgment (Hebrews 9:27). This, by the way, also means that technically we die when we are raptured.

How is it possible that we die during the rapture? The Bible says that this mortal must put on immortality, and this corruption must put on incorruption. We know that our physical bodies (flesh and blood) cannot inherit the kingdom of God (see 1

Corinthians 15:50). This means we must be changed from mortal to immortal. According to Scripture this happens in a moment, in the twinkling of an eye. (According to General Electric the twinkling of an eye is ten-thousandths of a second.)

Being changed from mortality to immortality in the twinkling of an eye–that is the way to go! You cannot hurt too much during that sort of transformation. According to Scripture our mortal bodies have to die. First Corinthians 15:36 says, "Foolish one, what you sow is not made alive *unless* it dies." We also know that people can die twice; consider Lazarus. At the same time, we do know that each of us has to die at least once.

If we follow that line of thinking, there are two people in the Bible who did not die. Enoch walked with the Lord and he was no more for the Lord took him, and Elijah was caught up in a chariot of fire. Hebrews 11:5 tells us that Enoch was taken away "so that he did not see death." So where in the world have these two guys been since they did not die?

Could it be possible that God has reserved Enoch and Elijah in heaven for a specific time and season? His Word is true, therefore Elijah and Enoch have to die once because it is appointed unto every man once to die and then the judgment. Please understand this is *speculation*.

Review of the time of the Great Tribulation (Satan's wrath).

- ◆ Daniel 7:25 tells us that saints shall be given into the Antichrist's hand for time, times, and half a time (3 ½ years).
- ◆ Daniel 12:1-7 tells us that the power of the holy people shall be shattered for time, times, and half a time (3 ½ years).
- ◆ Revelation 11:2 tells us that the holy city shall be trodden down for forty-two months (3 ½ years).

- In Revelation chapter 12 the woman (Israel) flees into the wilderness and is nourished for 1,260 days (3 ½ years).
- Revelation 13:5 says the beast is given authority for forty-two months (3 ½ years).
- And as we just saw, the two witnesses stand in the middle of Jerusalem prophesying for 1,260 days (3 ½ years).

The Great Tribulation is a three-and-a-half-year period, and it is the time of Satan's wrath. In comparison, God's wrath and Satan's wrath are two totally different events. As we will see, when Satan is done doing his best, it is time for God to show his stuff. However, something important happens in between God's wrath and Satan's wrath. We will cover that next.

Let's Review

- The first three-and-a-half years of Daniel's seventieth week consists of a peace agreement.

- Satan gets kicked out of heaven and persecutes Israel and the saints for three-and-a-half years. This is the time of Satan's wrath.

- The last three-and-a-half years of Daniel's seventieth week (Satan's wrath) coincides with the abomination of desolation spoken of in Daniel 9:27. The abomination of desolation is the beginning of the last three-and-a-half years of Daniel's seventieth week.

- The abomination of desolation spoken of by Daniel parallels what Jesus spoke of in Matthew 24:15. Jesus said that this event is the beginning of the Great Tribulation.

- We also saw that the Antichrist wages war against the *saints* for three-and-a-half years.

- The two witnesses also witness for the last three-and-a-half years and are caught up as the last trumpet sounds.

- All of these times and events are parallel passages and give us the prophetic time frame of Satan's wrath–three-and-a-half years.

The Resurrection of the Saints

This topic is one of the most debated topics in the Christian Church. In order to fully understand it we must examine many Scriptures, remembering that the Word of God interprets itself. In other words, we must employ the proper rules of Bible interpretation.

1. Five contexts we must consider when interpreting the Bible:
   a) The context of the passage. (What do the verses before and after say?)
   b) Context of the entire book.
   c) Other books by the same author.
   d) The entire Testament (Old or New).
   e) The entire Bible.

2. The Bible is a progressive revelation. A good example is in the book of Daniel where we see prophecy being sealed up, while in the book of Revelation the seal is taken off. This is another reason parallel passages are a necessary tool in Bible interpretation.

3. The Bible is to be interpreted literally. This is done in light of the writer's style, grammar, and setting. The Bible contains three different styles of literature:

    a) Prose: Includes all history and teaching.

    b) Poetry: Includes one-third of the Old Testament.

    c) Apocalyptic: Prophetic; the meaning is hidden in symbolism.

4. The Bible must be interpreted in light of history and culture.

5. The Bible is interpreted in light of who is doing the talking and to whom.

Some Christians get very upset when others use the word *rapture* as it is not in the Bible. However, the word "rapture" simply means "a catching away," and we do see a catching away spoken of in the Bible. Therefore, it is not heresy to refer to the catching away of the saints as the rapture.

As we continue in this teaching, we must determine in our hearts to accept what the Word of God says concerning this subject, even if it goes against the traditions of men. What we are about to dive into is not "splitting hairs," or just a matter of semantics. We will draw our conclusions from the truth of God's Word. We should all seek truth above tradition and facts over fiction, even if it is not what our flesh desires.

The average Christian does not desire to be present on the earth during the mark of the beast, or Satan's wrath. In light of those events–many of which we have already learned about–a pre-tribulation rapture sounds awfully good! Nevertheless, we should all desire the truth so that we may stand in faith and be ready for His coming. In order for Christians to be a mighty part of what God desires to do in these last days, we must have truth and understanding. Fables and false doctrines that tickle our ears do nothing to prepare the church for the days ahead.

A large part of our study has been an assessment of Bible prophecy in light of the Bible itself, and of history and current world events. History reveals that a proposal for a one-world government came after the last two major world wars. After the next world war the one-world government (the United Nations) will easily assume power. This occurs in conjunction with the rise of a charismatic political leader the Bible calls the Antichrist.

We have also learned that the sixth trumpet alludes to a major world war as we see a 200-million-man army rising up and one-third of the world's population being killed. Now that we have examined the seven trumpets, we can speculate as to the time of the Great Tribulation (in reference to the seven trumpets). The Great Tribulation will most likely occur between the sixth and seventh trumpet. This reasoning is due to the fact that the seventh trumpet is God's wrath being poured out, and the return of Christ as the "kingdoms of this world become the kingdoms of our God."

Another very important aspect of our study has been the seventy weeks of Daniel. We learned that at the beginning of Daniel's seventieth week there will be a peace agreement made between the Antichrist and Israel. Three-and-a-half years into the peace agreement we see the devil being cast to the earth and persecuting Israel because he knows he has a short time (see Revelation 12:12). At that time power is given to the Antichrist for forty-two months so that he may also wage war against *the saints* in order that he may overcome them (see Revelation 13:5-7).

In the last section we took a close look at the wrath of Satan, which occurs during the last three-and-a-half years of Daniel's seventieth week. We also learned that the last three-and-a-half years is what Jesus referred to as "a time of great tribulation." We will take a closer look at the wrath of God in the next section after we have examined the catching away of the saints.

Dispelling False Teaching

Before we get to the specifics of what the Bible teaches concerning the rapture of the church, we will attempt to address many questions concerning pre-tribulation versus post-tribulation rapture doctrine.

The rapture of the Church is such an important part of our study on end-time prophecy that we feel the need to address some misconceptions and false teachings. The vast majority of Christian teaching on end-time prophecy (cross-denomination-ally) involves pre-tribulation rapture doctrine. This is the teaching that the church will be caught away before the final seven-year period.

Pre-tribulation rapture doctrine has been the most popular end-time teaching for many decades. This is very evident on Christian TV, in Christian movies, and in Christian bookstores across the country. The largest selling Christian books (fiction and non-fiction) concerning the rapture of the saints espouse pre-tribulation rapture doctrine. Therefore, the odds are that most Christians have heard, or read about, a pre-tribulation rapture.

The aforementioned being the case, we should address various aspects of this teaching point-for-point. Much of this section will be dispelling the false teaching of a pre-tribulation rapture. If you are not familiar with these misconceptions, then going through this section will help you learn a few of the major differences. Conversely, if you have been taught pre-tribulation rapture doctrine, then consider the arguments put forth in this section.

Even though this is the only time within this book that we will present this argument, obviously we cannot address every aspect of the doctrine, only the most common.

Does the last seven-year period concern only the Jews?

For many decades the majority of fundamental Christians have taught that the catching away of the saints occurs *before* Daniel's seventieth week. One of the cornerstones of this theology is the idea that the last seven-year period does not concern the church, but rather "thy people"–referring only to the Jews (see Daniel

9:24-27). Therefore, pre-tribulation rapture doctrine assumes that because this passage is speaking of events taking place in Israel that the church must have already been raptured.

While it is true that these verses are speaking of events taking place in Israel, it is also true that they supply the Church with a measuring rod for prophetic events. As we will see (and have already learned), there are no solid parallel passages to support the idea that the Church is not on the earth as these prophetic events take place in Israel. In fact, many Scripture references tell us the Church will be here during Daniel's seventieth week.

Matthew chapter 24 is another passage misunderstood to say that the Great Tribulation concerns only the Jews. We must make several points concerning this passage:

1. We have already learned that the Great Tribulation begins at the three-and-a-half year mark of the last seven-year period (Daniel's seventieth week). We have learned that much of the Antichrist's attention will be on Israel and the persecution of the Israeli people.

2. We have learned that many, many Scriptures show the saints are still here during the last three-and-a-half years.

3. Even though Matthew 24:15-21 speaks of horrific events taking place in Israel, it does not prove that the saints are not on the earth at that time.

4. Who was it that asked the question concerning the last days? It was the disciples who asked Jesus about the events of his coming, and the end of the age (see Matthew 24:3). What were the disciples (who later became apostles)? The apostles of the Lamb (as they are referred to) were *born-again Jews*. The apostles became the foundation of the New Testament Church. Therefore, it is reasonable to assume that Jesus was speaking to the Church, as well as revealing events taking place in Israel.

5. Consider the fact that the Church has existed alongside the nation of Israel for the last 2,000 years as God continues to deal with the Jewish people. Christians have already witnessed the fulfillment of many prophecies concerning Israel, and we will continue to witness fulfillment of prophetic events.

6. In Matthew chapter 24 Jesus speaks of events from the Early Church all the way to the rapture of the saints. Within this chapter the rapture of the saints is referred to only once. As we will see, it occurs "immediately after the tribulation of those days." Some would argue that "the elect" spoken of in Matthew 24:31 are the Jews. However, Romans 11:7 and Titus 1:1 also refer to Christians as the elect.

In addition, we do not see a rapture of the Jews in Scripture. Subsequently, Matthew 24:31 must be talking about the catching away of believers, which happens *after* the tribulation of those days. According to the apostle Paul, the Jews have been blinded for a period of time. Paul and the apostle John both tell us the Jews will see their Messiah, but this occurs at Jesus' Second Coming (see Romans 11:25-27 and Revelation 1:7). We will cover the time frame of the rapture more in-depth later in this section.

Is the church keeping the Antichrist from being revealed?

Another doctrine that presumably supports a pre-tribulation rapture is that the removal of the Church must occur before the revealing of the Antichrist. Teachers have echoed this doctrine for over a century.

The reasoning behind this doctrine is that the Church as a whole is holding back the full power of the devil being loosed into the earth. This teaching is primarily based upon a passage in 2 Thessalonians 2:1-10.

Let us examine this teaching in context of the passage.

> Now we beseech you, brethren, concerning the coming of our Lord Jesus Christ, and by our gathering together unto him, that ye be not soon shaken in mind, or be troubled, neither by spirit, nor by word, nor by letter as from us, as that the day of Christ is at hand. Let no man deceive you by any means: for that day shall not come, *except* there come a falling away first, and that man of sin be revealed, the son of perdition;

who opposeth and exalteth himself above all that is called God, or that is worshipped; so that he as God sitteth in the temple of God, shewing himself that he is God. Remember ye not, that, when I was yet with you, I told you these things? And now ye know what withholdeth that he might be revealed *in his time,* for the mystery of iniquity doth already work: only he who now letteth will let, until he be taken out of the way. And then shall that wicked be revealed, whom the Lord shall consume with the spirit of his mouth, and shall destroy with the brightness of his coming: even him, whose coming is after the working of Satan with all power and signs and lying wonders, and with all deceivableness of unrighteousness in them that perish because they received not the love of the truth, that they might be saved.

The doctrine of the church restraining the Antichrist comes from 2 Thessalonians 2:6-7. Those who teach this doctrine say that the Church (the one that "withholdeth") must be taken out of the way in order for the Antichrist to be revealed.

It is obvious that something is restraining the Antichrist from being revealed. However, in order to interpret the Bible correctly, we must examine the verses before and after. We cannot pull one Scripture out of context and make a doctrine out of it.

Paul begins by telling us not to be deceived into thinking that the day of the Lord (the coming of Christ and our gathering together with him) had already occurred. He goes on to explain that that day (the coming of the Lord and our gathering together with him) will not come except: 1. A falling away comes first, and 2. The revealing of the man of sin, the son of perdition (the Antichrist).

How ironic! This is the same passage that is used to promote the doctrine that the Church must be taken out of the way in order for the Antichrist to be revealed. As we can see, the rapture (our gathering together to him) will not happen until *after* the Antichrist is revealed!

Is the "falling away" mentioned in 2 Thessalonians 2:3 the rapture of the church?

In order to get around what this passage plainly reveals, classical pre-tribulation rapture theology teaches that the phrase "falling away" used in 2 Thessalonians 2:3 means "the departure of the church." This is the only way that this passage will fit into pre-tribulation rapture doctrine.

Those who teach this theology use the following reasoning: The Greek word translated "falling away" is *apostasia*. The root word for *apostasia* is *aphistemi*, which is generally translated "departed," or "departing from." It is this type of interpretation that pre-tribulation rapture teachers use to explain that the great falling away is the departing of the Church from the earth.

The fact is that even the root word for *apostasia* still does not help the case for pre-tribulation rapture theology. The word "apostasia" is used twice in the New Testament. Its other use is in the book of Acts where it means to "depart from the truth."[160] It means the same thing in 2 Thessalonians 2:3.

Remember this: A person does not have to be a Greek and Hebrew scholar to understand the Bible. In addition, if we have to go to the root word of a Greek word to prove a point, then our case is very weak.

It also makes no sense in light of how the Scripture would read if we were to insert this theology. If we insert the aforementioned line of thinking into 2 Thessalonians 2:3, it would read like this: "Let no one deceive you by any means; *for the gathering together to him will not come unless the gathering together to him comes first.*" Once again, that does not make any sense in light of the passage as a whole.

We must also consider that if there was a strong case for this theology, we would see parallel passages to back it up, and it would be in agreement with the context of the passage.

---

[160]James Strong's Greek and Hebrew Lexicon, Strong's # 646.

When does the revealing of the Antichrist occur? As we have already learned, Satan does not enter the Antichrist until the middle of Daniel's seventieth week. It is logical to assume that the Antichrist is on the scene at the beginning of Daniel's seventieth week; however, Satan does not enter him until the middle of the week. (Refer to the Seventy Weeks of Daniel, The Antichrist, and Satan's Wrath.)

What about tribulation saints?

Something is holding Satan back from being revealed through the Antichrist. Most traditional teaching claims that it is the Church that is restraining the Antichrist through exercising authority over the devil and his forces. These same folks also teach that people will be born again *after* the church is raptured. Pre-tribulation rapture theology calls these people "tribulation saints."

One puzzling aspect of pre-tribulation theology is the idea that the 144,000 born-again Jews go about witnessing for Christ. The fact is, we see just the opposite in Scripture. Yes, the 144,000 are the firstfruits of Israel, but it is also prophesied that they must *flee* from the Antichrist. These Jews are not witnessing; they are busy escaping the wrath of Satan. (See the lesson on Satan's Wrath.)

If the Church must be raptured in order for the Antichrist to rise to power, then this raises some interesting questions. What about others who get born again during the last seven-year period? Jesus said, "Where two or three are gathered in my name, I am in the midst of them." That being the case, every time two or three people get born again (after the rapture), what would they have? A church! Therefore, the Church could pray and continue to hold back the Antichrist causing him not to be revealed, or simply thwart his plans and purposes.

One basic rule of Bible interpretation is that Scripture interprets Scripture. Where else in the Bible can we find the Church keeping Satan from being revealed during Daniel's seventieth week? If the Church is holding Satan back, then the Antichrist (and Satan within him) could easily have risen during the Dark Ages when the Word of God was hidden. Churchgoers during the Dark Ages learned about everything but the Word of God. The Church is not holding Satan back from being revealed. If that were the case, the Church could have also held back Adolph Hitler.

Is the Holy Spirit restraining the Antichrist?

Others have taught that the Holy Spirit is restraining the Antichrist from being revealed. Once again, this is circular reasoning. Scripture reveals that the Holy Spirit never leaves the earth, therefore the restraining of the Antichrist would continue even after the rapture of the saints. In John 14:16 Jesus said, "I will pray the Father, and he will give you another Helper, that he may abide with you forever–the Spirit of truth."

Of course, the pre-tribulation rapture argument is that the Holy Spirit will never leave us, but Christians leave the earth taking the Holy Spirit with them. Again, the same teachers who teach this also say that people are getting born again during the Great Tribulation.

If people are getting born again after the rapture of the Church, then the Holy Spirit must still be on the earth drawing people to Christ. Jesus said that unless one is born of water and the Spirit, he cannot enter the kingdom of God (see John 3:5). Since we see in Scripture that the Holy Spirit is not taken from the earth, that means He would always be restraining the Antichrist, never allowing him to be revealed.

Here is another point to consider: In Revelation 12:17 we see that the Antichrist wages war against the woman and "the rest of her offspring, who keep the commandments of God and have the testimony of Jesus Christ." Daniel 7:21 tells us, "I beheld, and the same horn [the little horn is the Antichrist; see lessons on the Modern Nations, and the Antichrist] made war with the *saints*, and prevailed against them." Also, in Revelation 13:7: "And it was given unto him [the Antichrist] to make war with the *saints*, and to overcome them."

If we have no Scripture to back up a pre-tribulation rapture, then we must assume that the saints mentioned in the previous verses are those of the Church. The fact is, we see that the saints are still here during the last three-and-a-half years of Daniel's seventieth week. Therefore, the Holy Spirit is also here on the earth.

In 2 Thessalonians chapter 2 we can see that the Antichrist will be revealed in his time. Then, in Revelation chapter 12 we see that Michael the Archangel is the one who executes God's will when he casts Satan to the earth. Second Thessalonians 2:6 says, "And now ye know what withholdeth that he might be revealed *in his time*." Satan rising within the lawless one will not happen until the proper time.

How can time be something that restricts or restrains? Consider this scenario: Your child has the money to buy a new Christian music CD. However, you tell him that he cannot buy the CD for three days. What is keeping your child from buying the CD? Is money, or the capability to purchase, keeping him from it? No. Time is restraining him. When time has passed, and the proper time has come, he will be able to buy the CD.

What held back Jesus from coming into the earth? Satan did not hold Jesus back. Herod could not hold him back. Nor could the iniquity of the Jews hold him back. Galatians 4:4 tells us, "But when the fullness of the *time* was come, God sent forth his Son..." God does things in his time. Once again we see the marvelous truth that God is in control of times and seasons.

As we have seen in Scripture, God has a prophetic time clock. Nowhere in the Bible do we see the church holding Satan back from coming into the earth. Prophetic events will unfold no matter how hard the Church prays to stop them. Why? Because God has foreordained these prophetic events; therefore, they will happen in their proper time. God cannot lie! The amazing thing is, God has revealed these events and their prophetic timeline in his word!

The truth dispels the notion that the rapture of the church could happen at any moment. As we have already learned, our gathering together unto him will not occur until after the Antichrist is revealed. This scriptural truth presents us with a specific time frame for the rapture of the Church. As we will also see, the Church is not caught away until the last trumpet. Once again, this presents us with a specific time frame and much prophecy that is yet to be fulfilled before this important event.

"Wait a minute!" you say. I thought Matthew 24:36 said no man knows the day or the hour that he will come." Jesus told his disciples that it was not for them to know times or the seasons "which the Father has put into his hands" (see Acts 1:7).

What event was Jesus speaking about that only the Father knows the time and season thereof? Acts 1:6 reveals the answer when the disciples asked, "Lord, wilt thou at this time restore again the kingdom to Israel?" The restoration of the kingdom of Israel is indicative of Jesus setting up his earthly reign. This event occurs at his second coming. That *day* and the *hour* are in the Father's hands. Therefore, we cannot know the exact day and hour that Jesus will return. However, in 1 Thessalonians 5:4 the apostle Paul said, "But ye, brethren, are not in darkness, that that day should overtake you as a thief."

So we understand that we will not know the day and the hour, but we can also see that God has given us benchmarks and road signs in prophecy. It is not God's desire that we be in the dark concerning the events leading up to Christ's second coming.

The Lord has marvelously explained many events and a specific timeline in which prophecy will be fulfilled. We have learned that those who understand will instruct many, and do great exploits. Thus, we can conclude that the events we see in the Word of God (i.e. Daniel's seventy weeks, the period of Satan's wrath, the time of God's wrath, etc.) have been revealed for us to understand so that "that day will not overtake us as a thief."

Is the devil chomping at the bit to enter the Antichrist?

Traditional pre-tribulation theology gives the impression that Satan cannot wait for the Church to be removed so that he may enter the Antichrist. Is this the picture we see in Scripture?

Revelation 12:7-12 reveals that Michael the Archangel battles with Satan in order to cast him to the earth. Why would Satan fight so furiously with Michael? Verse 12 reveals the main reason: "Because he knoweth that he hath but *a short time.*" As we learned in the lesson on Satan's Wrath, the short time is forty-two months; time, times, and dividing of times; or 1,260 days. This event, just like everything else God has foreordained, will occur in its proper time.

Satan does not want to be cast to the earth because at that point he knows he has a short time. That is why he comes down having great wrath. Therefore, the true picture Revelation 12:7-12 leaves us with is that Satan does not relish the idea of being cast to the earth.

As Satan is cast to the earth Scripture says: "Now is come salvation, and strength, and the kingdom of our God, and the power of his Christ: for the accuser of our brethren is cast down which accused them before our God day and night. And they overcame him by the blood of the Lamb, and by the word of their testimony; and they loved not their lives unto the death."

The time of Satan's wrath sounds scary. In reality it is a very powerful time for the saints! Even though there will be heavy persecution, we also see that there is salvation, strength, and the power of Christ. This resembles the time of the Early Church with its fervor, passion for evangelism, and continual evidence of the miracle-working power of God.

If Christians are not appointed unto the wrath of God, then how can we possibly be here during the final seven-year period?

The fact that believers are not appointed unto God's wrath is one of the most passionate arguments of those who believe in a pre-tribulation rapture. They will argue that if the Church is still on the earth during the final seven years, then we will suffer the wrath of God along with nonbelievers. Therefore, the church must be caught away first before the final seven-year period.

The Bible does tell us that the children of God are not appointed unto his wrath. First Thessalonians 5:9-10 says, "For God hath not appointed us to wrath, but to obtain salvation by our Lord Jesus Christ, who died for us, that, whether we wake or sleep, we should live together with him."

In order to understand that this is not a valid pre-tribulation rapture argument, we must understand that in Bible prophecy there are two wraths poured out:

1. The wrath of Satan. As we have already seen, Satan's wrath occurs during the last three-and-a-half years of the final seven-year period. He accomplishes this through deception. In Revelation 12:9 we see that Satan "deceives the whole world," and in Revelation 20:8 we see that Satan "deceives the nations." The wrath of Satan is *man-to-man*. He works through people which, in turn, cause violence, hatred, and wars. Among other things, the wrath of Satan involves the mark of the beast, believers being beheaded for their witness, persecution upon Israel, and the one-world government coming against nations.

2. The wrath of God. The wrath of God is very distinctive in nature. Once we understand what the wrath of God looks like in Scripture, there will be no confusing it with the wrath of Satan. In the next lesson we will see that God's wrath is not poured out until the last trumpet at the end of the final seven-year period.

So the truth is, we are *not* appointed unto God's wrath. However, when we understand the time at which his wrath is poured out, then we also understand that 1 Thessalonians 5:9-10 does not prove a pre-tribulation rapture.

Even though, as we will see, God's wrath is not poured out until the end of the last seven-year period (at the last, or seventh trumpet), that does not mean that it will be a cakewalk for Christians. We know from Scripture that the Antichrist will persecute the saints along with Israel. Even Christians who live in America may have a tough time living out their faith.

At this point in our study it should be clear that, according to Revelation 12:12-17, what Israel and the Christians will suffer during the last three-and-a-half year period is Satan's wrath.

Do types and shadows prove a pre-tribulation rapture?

Another item we must discuss is types and shadows–two of the theological items that classical pre-tribulation rapture theology refers to in order to back up its doctrine.

Types and shadows are past biblical events that foreshadowed future biblical events with a parallel meaning. One example might be the sacrificing of a lamb (for remission of sins) in the Old Testament, foreshadowing Jesus who became the perfect Lamb sacrificed for the sins of the world.

Classical pre-tribulation rapture doctrine will use an event such as Noah being shut up in the ark as an illustration of how Christians will be raptured before the wrath of God is poured out (meaning before the final seven-year period).

There are several problems with using types and shadows to build a case for a pre-tribulation rapture.

1. The same types and shadows can be used to teach *post*-tribulation rapture theology. Consider Noah within the safety of the ark during the flood. We see that God protected Noah and his family from his wrath (the worldwide flood). However:

a) Noah still endured the wrath of Satan (figuratively speaking) working through man while he was building the ark.

b) Noah certainly received protection from the wrath of God. However, he was delivered from God's wrath as it was being poured out (at the last trumpet–figuratively speaking).

Noah witnessed the beginning of the wrath of God as well as the effects of the wrath of God, yet he was delivered from its destructive power. We can use the same line of reasoning with Lot being delivered from Sodom and Gomorrah, and with the children of Israel being delivered from Egypt.

2. Pre-tribulation theology teaches that the Great Tribulation is a time of God's wrath being poured out upon the earth. As we have already learned, and will continue to learn, this is simply not the case. Therefore, types and shadows do not help prove anything against post-tribulation rapture teaching. Why? The reason is, *we agree* that Christians are not appointed unto God's wrath. However, as we will see in the next lesson it is clear in Scripture that the pouring out of God's wrath does not occur until after the Great Tribulation.

3. Types and shadows may aid in supporting a doctrine. Nevertheless, solid doctrine comes from Scripture interpreting Scripture, the context of the passage, the context of the entire Bible, and the other basic rules of Bible interpretation. Therefore, as fascinating and awe-inspiring as types and shadows can be, we simply cannot make doctrine out of them.

Jesus did say, "But as the days of Noah were, so also will the coming of the Son of man be" (Matthew 24:37). At the time of the flood, all the earth was wicked except one family that found grace in the eyes of the Lord. Thank God that before the Second Coming of Christ there will also be one family that finds grace in the eyes of the Lord–the family of God!

What about the very popular "Left Behind" scenario?

Pre-tribulation doctrine also teaches that there are many saints who become born again as a result of the realization that they have been "left behind." These saints are mercilessly persecuted as they attempt to avoid the mark of the beast, or keep from becoming martyrs.

There are many problems with this scenario.

1. We have already addressed one of the major problems with this teaching; the fact that when two or three become born again we now have a church. Therefore, those two or three can pray and continue to hold back, or "restrain" the Antichrist. In other words, the Church never truly leaves the earth, and neither does the Holy Spirit.

2. Pre-tribulation rapture theologists will quote 1 Thessalonians 5:2 to try and substantiate the "imminence" of the rapture. This verse says that the day of the Lord comes as a thief in the night. However, when we keep this Scripture in context we see that it is not addressing Christians, but rather un-believers. When we read verse 4 in context we see, "But ye, brethren, are not in darkness, that that day should overtake you as a thief." This lets us know that we can recognize the signs and the season of his return. Who does the Lord overtake as a thief? The answer is, those who are in darkness.

Therefore, in Scripture we not only see that nonbelievers are not looking for the return of Christ, but we also see that his return is hidden from those who do not believe. This truth leads us to the next problem with the "Left Behind" scenario.

3. What would happen if millions of born-again believers suddenly disappeared? Within the "Left Behind" scenario we see planes crashing, cars driving off the road, etc. The truth is it would be the greatest wake-up call the world has ever experienced! We would not be talking about a few people who are simply searching for answers, and then remember what aunt Edna used to preach. What we would witness is millions of people whom all of a sudden begin to take the Bible very seriously.

The greatest revival, or wake-up call, the world has ever witnessed is not the idea conveyed in Scripture when it speaks of "those in darkness." "Those in darkness" conveys the idea that they do not know God or care about his teachings, and that this event is hidden from unbelievers.

Is the Church raptured in Revelation 4:1?

One other portion of Scripture used for pre-tribulation rapture theology is Revelation 4:1. In this verse the Lord says to the apostle John "come up hither." Pre-tribulation rapture theologists will argue that after that verse we do not see the Church talked about anymore.

As a result, those who believe in a pre-tribulation rapture say that this must be when the rapture occurs. According to that theology, believers will escape all the "bad stuff" that happens further on in the book of Revelation.

We must make several points in order to clearly understand this event in Revelation 4:1 and how it relates to the entire book.

1. As we have already pointed out, the book of Revelation is not in chronological order.

2. The trumpet John heard was a voice. The voice in Revelation 4:1 should not be confused with the angelic trumpets that sound later in the book. Nor is it the equivalent of the great sound of a trumpet in Matthew 24:31, or the last trumpet in 1 Corinthians 15:52 when God gathers his elect.

3. In Revelation 1:10 we see the same scenario when it says, "I was in the Spirit on the Lord's day, and heard behind me a great voice, as a trumpet." So, we see a voice *like a trumpet* in Revelation 4:1 and also in Revelation 1:10. Which one is the rapture of the Church? The key is that this is a voice *like* a trumpet, not a trumpet.

4. It is also important to understand the layout of the book of Revelation. In Revelation 1:19 the Lord instructed John to, "Write the things which thou hast *seen*, and the things which *are*, and the things which shall be *hereafter*."

John followed the Lord's instructions to the letter, and first described the things he had seen. He saw Jesus in the midst of the seven candlesticks, "one like unto the Son of man..." Then, he goes on to describe Jesus standing in the midst of the seven candlesticks. This is what John had seen.

John continues to follow the Lord's instructions, and in Revelation chapters 2-3 he writes the things "which are." These involve the seven churches to which the Lord had given instructions–seven literal churches that were in operation in John's day.

Then, at the beginning of Revelation chapter 4 the Lord begins showing John the things "which shall be hereafter." What is the time frame of these things? The events spoken of from this verse on are events taking place *after* John received his vision (from around AD 95 forward).

As we have already learned, the saints are talked about after Revelation 4:1. Once again, these are not just "tribulation saints." That argument is built upon a faulty foundation. We see the church described as martyrs, saints, and those who "keep the commandments of God, and have the testimony of Jesus Christ."

Some have even taught that John himself was raptured. Keep in mind that the Revelation of John was given in a vision. History records that the apostle John died here on the earth. Revelation 4:1 is not the rapture of the church, but simply the apostle John being caught up in the spirit and the Lord showing him "the things which shall be hereafter." (The "hereafter" obviously means within the time period of the last days.)

Biblical Truths Concerning the Resurrection of the Saints

What does the Bible reveal concerning the method of the resurrection? What does it say concerning this great gathering together of the saints?

> Behold, I show you a mystery; we shall not all sleep,
> but we shall all be changed, in a moment, in the twin-
> kling of an eye, *at the last trump:* for the trumpet shall
> sound, and the dead shall be raised incorruptible, and
> we shall be changed.
>   1 CORINTHIANS 15:51-52

In this verse we see that the rapture occurs at the last trumpet. In a previous lesson we learned that there are seven trumpets
spoken of in the book of Revelation. The phrase "last trumpet"
leads to several obvious conclusions:

1. There is a *series* of trumpets.

2. The trumpet spoken of in 1 Corinthians 15:52 is the *last* in
the series.

3. There are no more trumpets *after* the gathering together of
the saints.

As we allow Scripture to interpret Scripture we ask ourselves
where else in the Bible do we find a series of trumpets. Of course
the answer (as we have already learned) lies within the seven
trumpets of the book of Revelation. Therefore, in the context of
the Bible itself we understand that the gathering together of the
saints occurs at the last trumpet spoken of in the book of Revelation. As we will see, this fits perfectly with other parallel passages
concerning the rapture.

We can see in Scripture that Jesus comes for his saints at the
last trumpet. Understanding this will give us a definite time frame,
or mile-marker within prophetic events.

In verse 52 we see that we are *changed* in a moment, in the
twinkling of an eye. In a moment our mortality puts on immortality. When we read this passage, it might cause us to assume
that the phrase "changed in a moment" means we are raptured in
a moment. However, Scripture does not say that we are raptured,
or gathered together, in a moment.

First Thessalonians 4:17 tells us that we shall be "caught up
together...to meet the Lord in the air." When we put 1
Thessalonians 4:16-17 together with 1 Corinthians 15:52 we see

that our physical bodies are changed in a moment, then we are caught up to meet the Lord in the air. These are two separate happenings within the same event. We are not told how much time elapses between being changed in a moment, and then being caught up to meet Jesus in the air. We have only assumed that they happen simultaneously. They may occur at the same time…but they may not.

With that in mind, it is very possible (we stress that this is simply a scriptural possibility) that our last days here on the earth will parallel Jesus' final days on the earth after his resurrection. It is apparent in Scripture that Jesus had a glorified body after his resurrection from the dead. He even walked the earth in a glorified body for forty days after his resurrection (see Mark 16:12-19; Luke 24:51; John 20:17-19; and Acts 1:1-11). After this, he ascended (meaning to float or rise upward) into heaven. The apostles watched Jesus ascend out of their sight. Not only did he walk the earth in a glorified body for many days, but we also see that his ascension was not instantaneous.

Matthew 27:52-53 says, "And the graves were opened; and many bodies of the saints who had fallen asleep were raised; and coming out of the graves after His resurrection, they went into the holy city and appeared to many" (NKJV). In this passage we see dead saints rising during Jesus' first coming, and actually walking around appearing to many people. It is possible (again, emphasis on the word *possible*) that many events of Jesus' second coming will parallel his first coming.

If we are changed from mortal to immortal, and then walk the earth as Jesus did for many days before we are gathered to him, this would explain and refute a couple of things:

1. It explains how it would be possible for the pouring out of the wrath of God to begin at or around the same time that Jesus sends his angels to gather his elect. If the saints were in glorified bodies on the earth as the wrath of God is beginning, then God's wrath will not harm the saints.

2. This scriptural possibility also throws an enormous wrench in the "Left Behind" teaching–the idea that planes will crash, millions of cars will drive off the road, and millions will be killed as Christians simply disappear.

In Scripture we see believers being changed in a moment, but not raptured in the twinkling of an eye. As we have said previously, the "Left Behind" scenario would no doubt cause a major revival, or turning to God. Why? Imagine how you would feel if suddenly millions of people disappeared and millions were killed all over the globe. It makes no sense to think that it would cause people to turn *from* God, but instead it would cause people to turn to God.

Imagine the darkness people would be in if world events were "business as usual," then suddenly the wrath of God begins. Biblically speaking, that would be a more accurate portrayal of the state of people's hearts and world events just before the outpouring of God's wrath. Matthew 24:38-39 backs this up:

> For as in the days before the flood, they were eating and drinking, marrying and giving in marriage, until the day that Noah entered the ark, *and did not know until the flood came* and took them all away, so also will the coming of the Son of Man be.

Within our study it is very important to understand that in Scripture we only see two comings spoken of: the Bible refers to Jesus' return as his Second Coming.

> But now is Christ risen from the dead, and become the firstfruits of them that slept. For since by man came death, by man came also the resurrection of the dead. For as in Adam all die, even so in Christ shall all be made alive. But every man in his own order: *Christ the firstfruits; afterward they that are Christ's at His coming. Then cometh the end,* when He shall have delivered up the kingdom to God, even the Father; when He shall have put down all rule and all authority and power. For He must reign, till He hath put all enemies under His feet. The last enemy that shall be destroyed is

death. For he hath put all things under His feet. But when He saith all things are put under Him, it is manifest that He is excepted, which did put all things under Him. And when all things shall be subdued unto Him, then shall the Son also Himself be subject unto Him that put all things under Him, that God may be all in all.

1 Corinthians 15:20-28

First Corinthians 15:23 gives the order of the resurrection:

1. Christ–the firstfruits (this is indicative of his first coming).

2. They that are Christ's at his coming. The Greek word used for "coming" in 1 Corinthians 15:23 is *parousia*. This is the technical term signifying the second advent of Jesus.[161]

There are only two comings of Christ spoken of in the Bible—his first coming and his second coming. How do we know that the coming of Christ spoken of in 1 Corinthians 15:23 is his second coming just before the end of this age, which is also known as the times of the Gentiles? This verse goes on to say that directly after the dead in Christ are raised at his coming, "Then cometh the end." So when we parallel Matthew 24:29-31, 1 Corinthians 15:22-54, and 1 Thessalonians 4:16-17 in context, we view the whole sequence:

1. Christ was resurrected and became the firstfruits during his first coming.

2. After the tribulation of those days (at the last trumpet), the Lord himself descends from heaven with the voice of an archangel and the trumpet of God.

3. The dead in Christ will be raised incorruptible.

4. Christians who are alive are changed in a moment (from mortality to immortality), in the twinkling of an eye.

5. We will be caught up together to meet him in the air (as he sends his angels to gather his elect from the four winds).

---

[161]James Strong's Greek and Hebrew Lexicon, Strong's # 3952.

6. Then comes the end when the kingdoms of this world become the kingdoms of our Lord. God's wrath is poured out, and Jesus returns at the battle of Armageddon with his saints.

7. Then the millennial reign of Christ begins. ("He must reign until he puts all enemies under his feet"–the last enemy being death. As we will see, the last enemy is destroyed after the millennial reign of Christ.)

There is an interesting passage in the Old Testament that speaks of the "Day of the Lord" and the "Day of his wrath" as the day of the trumpet.

> The great day of the Lord is near, it is near, and hasteth greatly, even the voice of the day of the Lord: the mighty man shall cry there bitterly. *That day is a day of wrath,* a day of trouble and distress, a day of wasteness and desolation, a day of darkness and gloominess, a day of clouds and thick darkness, *a day of the trumpet* and alarm against the fenced cities, and against high towers.
>
> ZEPHANIAH 1:14-16

Then, in Revelation chapter 11 we see a description of the witnesses being raptured (just before the last trumpet sounds), and a description of the last trumpet.

> And they of the people and kindreds and tongues and nations shall see their dead bodies three days and an half, and shall not suffer their dead bodies to be put in graves. And they that dwell upon the earth shall rejoice over them, and make merry, and shall send gifts one to another; because these two prophets tormented them that dwelt on the earth. And after three days and an half the Spirit of life from God entered into them, and they stood upon their feet; and great fear fell upon them which saw them. And they heard a great voice from heaven saying unto them, "Come up hither." And they ascended up to heaven in a cloud; and their enemies beheld them. And the same hour was there a great earthquake, and the tenth part of the city fell, and in the earthquake were slain of men seven thou-

sand; and the remnant were affrighted, and gave glory to the God of heaven. The second woe is past; and, behold, the third woe cometh quickly. And the seventh angel sounded; and there were great voices in heaven, saying, "The kingdoms of this world are become the kingdoms of our Lord, and of his Christ; and he shall reign for ever and ever." And the four and twenty elders, which sat before God on their seats, fell upon their faces, and worshipped God, saying, "We give thee thanks, O Lord God Almighty, which are, and wast, and art to come; because thou hast taken to thee thy great power and has reigned. And the nations were angry, *and thy wrath is come,* and the time of the dead, *that thou shouldest give reward unto thy servants the prophets, and to the saints,* and them that fear thy name, small and great; and shouldest destroy them which destroy the earth." And the temple of God was opened in heaven, and there was seen in his temple the ark of his testament: *and there were lightnings, and voices, and thunderings, and an earthquake, and great hail.*

REVELATION 11:9-19

In this passage we see that the Antichrist kills the two witnesses, then the two witnesses rise from the dead and a voice from heaven says, "Come up hither." That same hour there is a great earthquake. What is happening at that point? This Scripture describes the outpouring of God's wrath. At that time the seventh angel sounds (the last trumpet), and God begins to pour out His wrath.

It is also at this time that the saints, the prophets, and those that fear his name are judged and given rewards. The phrase "the time of the dead" indicates that the dead are raised along with the gathering of the saints, and then given rewards.

Revelation chapter 11 and 1 Corinthians chapter 15 reveal that the gathering together of the saints and the resurrection of the dead occur at the last trumpet (at the beginning of God's wrath).

Scripture is clear that we are not appointed unto God's wrath. However, we do see that God gathers His children as He begins to pour out His wrath. What we have seen in Scripture is that the church will be here until the last trumpet.

Another Scripture we have alluded to that parallels (confirming that the rapture occurs at the last trumpet) is Matthew 24:29-31:

> Immediately *after the tribulation of those days* shall the sun be darkened, and the moon not give her light, and the stars shall fall from heaven, and the powers of the heavens shall be shaken: And then shall appear the sign of the Son of man in heaven: and then shall all the tribes of the earth mourn, and they shall see the Son of man coming in the clouds of heaven with power and great glory. *And He shall send His angels with a great sound of a trumpet, and they shall gather His elect* from the four winds, from one end of heaven to the other.

What a fantastic parallel passage. Within this passage we see that the gathering together of his elect (the saints) takes place after the tribulation of those days (Satan's wrath). We also see that the rapture occurs in conjunction with the commencement of God's wrath (we will study that in-depth in the next lesson). As the wrath of God is poured out, the Lord sends his angels, with the great sound of a trumpet, to gather the saints.

The Method by Which the Lord Gathers His Elect

Something else we can see in Scripture is the method by which Jesus gathers his elect.

> "The kingdom of heaven is likened unto a man which sowed good seed in his field: But while men slept, his enemy came and sowed tares among the wheat, and went his way. But when the blade was sprung up, and brought forth fruit, then appeared the tares also. So the servants of the householder came and said unto

him, 'Sir, didst not thou sow good seed in thy field? From whence then hath it tares?' He said unto them, 'An enemy hath done this.' The servants said unto him, 'Wilt thou then that we go and gather them up?' But he said, 'Nay; lest while ye gather up the tares, ye root up also the wheat with them. Let them grow together until the harvest: and in the time of harvest *I will say to the reapers, gather ye together first the tares, and bind them in bundles to burn them: but gather the wheat into my barn.*'"

MATTHEW 13:24-30

Once again in Matthew 24:29-31:

Immediately *after the tribulation of those days* shall the sun be darkened, and the moon shall not give her light, and the stars shall fall from heaven, and the powers of the heavens shall be shaken: And then shall appear the sign of the Son of man in heaven: and then shall all the tribes of the earth mourn, and they shall see the Son of man coming in the clouds of heaven with power and great glory. *And he shall send his angels* with a great sound of a trumpet, and they shall gather together his elect from the four winds, from one end of heaven to the other.

Then, in Revelation 14:14-20 we see:

And I looked, and behold a white cloud, and upon the cloud one sat like unto the Son of man, having on His head a golden crown, and in His hand a sharp sickle. And another angel came out of the temple, crying with a loud voice to Him that sat on the cloud, "Thrust in thy sickle, and reap: for the time is come for thee to reap: for the harvest of the earth is ripe." And He that sat on the cloud thrust in His sickle on the earth; and the earth was reaped. And another angel came out of the temple which is in heaven, he also having a sharp sickle. And another angel came out from the altar, which had power over fire; and cried with a loud cry to Him that had the sharp sickle, saying, "Thrust in thy sharp sickle, and gather the clusters of the vine of the earth; for her grapes are fully ripe." *And the angel thrust in his sickle into the earth*, and gathered the vine of the earth, and cast it into the great winepress of the wrath of God. And the winepress was trodden without the city, and blood came out of the winepress, even unto the horse bridles, by the space of a thousand and six hundred furlongs.

As we view all these Scriptures concerning the Lord "putting in the sickle" and gathering his elect we see several distinct things:

1. We see the wheat (God's people) separated from the tares, or unbelievers.

2. We see a parallel of the parable of the wheat and the tares in Revelation 14:15 where the harvest of the earth (believers) is gathered. Then, in Revelation 14:17-20 we see the clusters of the vine (unbelievers) gathered, and the vine of the earth thrown into the winepress of the wrath of God (the battle of Armageddon).

3. It is apparent that Jesus descends and orders the gathering, but the angels are the ones who do the work of gathering the elect.

4. This event happens just before, or in conjunction with, the pouring out of God's wrath. How do we know this? The measurement given in Revelation 14:20 is the measurement of the Valley of Megiddo–the site of the battle of Armageddon.

5. All of these Scriptures together show clearly that the gathering of the saints occurs just before, or at the same time as, the wrath of God is being poured out on the earth. Matthew 24:29-31 is explicit as it shows God's wrath being poured out immediately after the tribulation of those days (Satan's wrath). Then, God sends his angels with the sound of a trumpet to gather his elect from the four corners of the earth.

Now we have a biblically accurate view of the gathering to-gether of the saints. The rapture occurs at the last trumpet, and immediately after the tribulation of those days (Satan's wrath). We also see that the rapture occurs as the wrath of God is poured out, just before the battle of Armageddon.

> And at that time shall Michael stand up, the great prince which standeth for the children of thy people: and there shall be a time of trouble, such as never was since there was a nation even to that same time: and at the time thy people shall be delivered, every one that shall be found written in the book. And many of them that sleep in the dust of the earth shall awake, some to everlasting life, and some to shame and ever-lasting contempt.
>
> DANIEL 12:1-2

In Daniel 12:1-2 we see a very brief version of the sequence of events:

1. Michael the Archangel stands up (parallel passage: Satan is cast to the earth having great wrath–Revelation 12:7-12)

2. There is a time of great trouble such as there never was (the last 3 ½ years of Daniel's seventieth week–Satan's wrath)

3. At that time (after Satan's wrath) "thy people shall be de-livered, everyone found written in the book" (the gathering of his elect–born-again Christians).

4. "Many of them that sleep in the dust of the earth shall awake, some to everlasting life, and some to shame and everlast-ing contempt" (the final judgment).

At the last day...

The resurrection of the dead and the gathering together of his elect happens at the "last day." In John 11:20-24 Martha told Jesus that if he had only arrived earlier, her brother Lazarus would not have died. Jesus replied, "Your brother will rise again." Then Martha said to Jesus, "I know that he will rise again in the resurrection at the *last day.*" In Job 19:25 Job said, "For I know that my redeemer liveth, and that he shall stand at the *latter day* upon the earth."

Jesus spoke several times of raising up his own in the last day:

> For I came down from heaven, not to do mine own will, but the will of him that sent me. And this is the Father's will which hath sent me, that of all which he hath given me I should lose nothing, but should raise it up again at the *last day*.
>
> JOHN 6:38-39

> No man can come to me, except the Father which hath sent me draw him: and I will raise him up at the *last day*.
>
> JOHN 6:44

> Whoso eateth my flesh, and drinketh my blood, hath eternal life; and I will raise him up at the *last day*.
>
> JOHN 6:54

All of these Scriptures speak of believers being raised at the "last day." This is the last day of human government, and the first day of God's government on the earth. This is why in Revelation 11:15–as God's wrath is being poured out–great voices in heaven shout "the kingdoms of this world are become the kingdoms of our Lord, and of his Christ; and he shall reign forever and ever." This occurs at the last day.

When we read the book of Revelation we have to understand that *it is not* in chronological order. It is similar to all four Gospels being combined into one book. In the Gospels we see similar events, but if we were to combine them they would not match up chronologically. However, when we view the same events in different Gospels we gain a more accurate picture of the details of each event.

The book of Revelation describes the same events in several different chapters:

1. God's wrath (6, 11, 16)
2. Babylon falling (14, 16, 17, 18)
3. Satan's wrath is also spoken of in several different chapters, and through those parallel passages we easily determine that Satan's wrath is poured out for a specific time period (3 ½ years).

As we will see in the next section the wrath of God *is not* poured out several different times. His wrath is poured out at a specific time, which is at the seventh trumpet, or "the last day." Therefore, just because God's wrath is spoken of many times in the book of Revelation, we conclude that all the passages are speaking of the same event (parallel passages). Thus we see that these Scriptures are not a continuation of these events, but rather a repeating of the same story wherein we find more details concerning a particular event.

There are two specific resurrections spoken of in the book of Revelation:

1. The first resurrection.
2. The resurrection at the Great White Throne Judgment. This resurrection occurs after the Millennium. (We will discuss this more in-depth in a later section.)

> And I saw thrones, and they sat upon them, and judgment was given unto them: and I saw the souls of them that were beheaded for the witness of Jesus, and for the word of God, and which had not worshipped the beast, neither his image, neither had received his mark upon their foreheads, or in their hands; and they lived and reigned with Christ a thousand years. But the rest of the dead lived not again until the thousand years were finished. *This is the first resurrection.*
> REVELATION 20:4-5

Scripture tells us that the ones who make the "first resurrection" are:

1. Those who were beheaded for the witness of Christ. (This does not mean that every Christian will be beheaded.)

2. Those who did not love their lives unto death.

3. Those who did not receive the mark of the beast.

4. Those who did not worship the beast.

This description given is clearly saints who endured, or were martyred, during the Great Tribulation. In other words, the first resurrection occurs after Satan's wrath, which includes the mark of the beast. This lines-up perfectly with all the Scriptures we have studied thus far.

Those who make the first resurrection are the ones who rule and reign with Christ 1,000 years. The rest of the dead do not rise until after the 1,000-year reign of Christ is fulfilled. At the end of the 1,000 years we see the Great White Throne Judgment. At that time if a person's name is not found in the book of life they are cast into the lake of fire. (We will cover the period of time beyond the Millennium in a later section.)

Consider this: If the rapture took place before the Antichrist is revealed, then Revelation 20:4-5 would not make any sense. In other words, it would have to call it the *second* resurrection.

What we have learned from Scripture is that the rapture occurs at the last trumpet, which is after the "tribulation of those days." We have also learned that there are only two resurrections spoken of in the Bible, and that the gathering together of the saints occurs after the Antichrist is revealed. In order to make any other case from Scripture, we would have to take scriptures out of context.

We realize this is not popular teaching. Yes, we would all love for the rapture to occur before Satan's wrath. However, we must accept what Scripture tells us and not what our flesh desires.

One of the great challenges we have before us in the body of Christ today is that the majority of the Church already has its bags packed. This is due to the fact that the most popular end-time teaching has told us that we are going to be gone from the earth before anything really bad begins to happen. Unfortunately, that theology has aided in producing a great amount of apathy in the body of Christ.

Furthermore, imagine the great disappointment when Christians realize that we are still here as events in the world grow worse and worse. It would be like telling your family to pack their bags for a vacation because difficult times are coming, but we are going to escape. Then, after having their bags packed, they discover they are not going to escape after all.

God will give his children strength in these times the same as he did in the Early Church. We have the same Holy Spirit that allowed the apostles and early disciples to operate in wisdom and power as they lived under an oppressive Roman government.

Remember, God has not given us a spirit of fear. At the same time, he has not sugarcoated what lies ahead on the world's stage. He reveals these events for a reason—so we can be ready to do his will and have an impact in this last day's harvest of souls.

Let us make up our minds to be people who live by faith, and not by sight. Let us draw closer to God than ever before so that we may be those who do great exploits and instruct many in these last days.

Let's Review

- The gathering together of the saints occurs after the Antichrist is revealed.
- The phrase "falling away" means a departure from the truth, not the rapture of the church.
- Michael the Archangel is the means God uses to cast Satan to the earth.
- The saints are raptured at the last trumpet.
- There are only two resurrections spoken of in the Bible. After the resurrection of the saints comes the end.
- Believers are not appointed unto God's wrath.
- Jesus sends his angels to reap the harvest of the earth as the wrath of God is being poured out.
- God does not desire that his children be in darkness concerning these events.

God's Wrath

In the last two lessons we looked at the wrath of Satan and the resurrection. Now we must look at the other "wrath" spoken of in the book of Revelation, and that is the wrath of God.

The wrath of God comes in its fullness in one day. However, we will see the pouring out of certain plagues over a *length* of days. In comparison, the time of God's wrath is much shorter than the time of Satan's wrath. In terms of intensity, we will see that God's wrath is very powerful.

Now that we recognize many of the pieces of God's prophetic time clock, we should also be able to recognize when the wrath of God is on the horizon. When we see the events of the last portion of Satan's wrath unfolding, we can look up "for our redemption draweth nigh." We will not know the exact day or hour of Christ's return, but we can know the signs of the season— simply because we are not children of darkness, but rather children of light. That day will not overtake us as a thief as it will those who do not know the Lord.

Biblical Terms for the Wrath of God

Many different terms are used in Scripture for the wrath of God. We need to identify these terms and what this event looks like so we can identify the wrath of God in Scripture.

The first term is simple, "The wrath of God." When we see this term, we know that this is a specific event that happens (as we will see) in a very short time. We can find this term and others in Joel 2:10-31, Zephaniah 1:10-15, Matthew 24:29-31, 2 Peter 3:10, and Revelation 11:15-19.

- ◆ In Joel we see this day spoken of as: "the day of the Lord," and "the great and terrible day of the Lord."
- ◆ In Zephaniah we see the day of God's wrath spoken of as: "the great day of the Lord," "the day of wrath," "a day of the trumpet," and "the day of the Lord's wrath."
- ◆ Second Peter 3:10 also calls this "the day of the Lord."
- ◆ In Revelation chapter 11 we see the seventh angel sound and the four and twenty elders say, "Thy wrath has come."

So we understand that the "day of the Lord" and "God's wrath" is the same event. First Corinthians 1:6-8, 1 Thessalonians 5:2, and 2 Thessalonians 2:1-2 also speak of the day of the Lord, the day in which God pours out his wrath. Second Peter 3:10 begins by saying, "But the day of the Lord will come as a thief in the night; in which the heavens shall pass away with a great noise."

Now when we read about the Lord "coming as a thief," we understand that this event occurs directly after Satan's wrath, and just before the wrath of God. So we know that this term also coincides with the wrath of God. We see this event ("the Lord coming as a thief") spoken of in Matthew 24:42-43, 1 Thessalonians 5:2, and in 2 Peter 3:10.

Another phrase used to describe the time of the pouring out of God's wrath is "the coming of the Lord." We see this phrase used in Matthew 24:29-31, 42-43, 1 Corinthians 1:6-8, and 2 Thessalonians 2:1-2.

God's wrath, the day of the Lord, the coming as a thief, and the coming of the Lord all speak of God's judgment upon those in iniquity. When we read these terms in Scripture, we can identify the time frame in which they are happening.

What does God's wrath look like?

As we view God's wrath being poured out in Scripture, we see that it looks the same (or very similar) each time. We can read about the wrath of God in Ezekiel 38:18-23, Joel 2:28-32, Zephaniah 1:10-15, Matthew 24:29, Revelation 6:12-17; 11:18-19; 16:17-21.

In these passages we see:
1. Great shaking in the earth (earthquakes)
2. Mountains thrown down
3. Pestilence and blood
4. Great hailstones
5. Fire
6. Brimstone
7. Wonders in the heaven and in the earth
8. The sun darkened
9. The moon turned into blood
10. The powers of heaven shaken
11. Lightnings and thunderings

What we find in Scripture is that the wrath of God is easy to identify because it always looks the same. We see the same types of signs on the day of Jesus' crucifixion: The sun was darkened, the earth quaked, rocks split, graves opened, and many of the bodies of the saints who had fallen asleep rose from the dead. Those descriptors are a foreshadowing of what will occur the next time that Jesus comes and God pours out his wrath.

At Jesus' second coming the earth will quake, the sun becomes dark, and saints will rise up out of their graves. On the cross Jesus said, "It is finished." Even Jesus' words foreshadow the resurrection of the saints and the wrath of God (at his second coming) as God brings to an end earthly government and

Jesus begins his 1,000-year reign. Revelation 10:7 says, "But in the days of the sounding of *the seventh angel,* when he is about to sound, the mystery of God would be finished, as he declared to his servants the prophets." Then in Revelation 16:17 we see (as the wrath of God is poured out) a loud voice coming from heaven saying, "It is done!" (NKJV).

Ezekiel chapter 38 talks specifically about the wrath of God. Verse 18 speaks of the time when Gog will come against Israel, which is at the battle of Armageddon. Then, verse 19 speaks of "the fire of God's wrath." Revelation 6:16 also speaks of the wrath of the Lamb and the great day of his wrath.

The sixth seal, the seventh trumpet, and the seven vials are all the same thing–the wrath of God. God does in a very short time period what the devil does not come close to in three-and-a-half years!

The Bible reveals that there is such a great earthquake coming that islands will pass away and mountains will be moved! This environmental change will impact the whole earth and take us right into the Millennium.

Where is God's wrath poured out?

Revelation 15:1-8 through 16:1-21 describes the outpouring of God's wrath. These passages tell us the specifics of where the wrath of God is poured out. According to Revelation 15 verse 1 and 7, and Revelation 16:1 all the vials (bowls in the NKJV) are the wrath of God. That point is very clear.

The seven vials contain:
1. Noisome and grievous sores
2. Sea turning to blood
3. Rivers and fountains of water becoming blood
4. Men scorched with fire
5. Darkness
6. Euphrates dried up
7. Voices, thunderings, lightnings, great earthquake, islands fleeing away, mountains not being found, and great hailstones

Do we see the wrath of God poured out on the entire earth? According to Scripture the pouring out of the wrath of God is upon:

1. The men that had the mark of the beast, and upon them that worship his image (Revelation 16:2).

2. The sea, which becomes blood. (It says "sea" singular. It appears as though this is a specific place rather than the entire ocean. More than likely it is in the region in which the beast–the one-world government–operates–Revelation 16:3.)

3. It is poured out upon the rivers and the fountains of waters. It appears as though God's wrath affects drinking water. The angel of the waters explains that these plagues are poured out upon those who shed the blood of the saints and the prophets. Because they shed the blood of God's children, they get blood to drink.

In Revelation 6:10 we see those martyred during the Great Tribulation crying out, "How long, O Lord, holy and true, until you judge and avenge our blood on those who dwell on the earth?" We see the answer in Revelation 16:5-6 as an angel says, "Thou art righteous, O Lord, which art, and wast, and shalt be, because thou hast judged thus. For they [the beast and Antichrist] have shed the blood of saints and prophets." So we see that this plague is poured out on those who [for the previous three-and-a-half years] have shed the blood of saints and prophets.

4. Upon those who blasphemed the name of God and would not repent or give him glory (Revelation 16:9).

5. God's wrath is poured out upon the seat of the beast. This plague certainly seems to indicate that darkness comes to a specific place–the seat of the beast (the one-world government). This does not appear to be a *global* plague (see Revelation 16:10).

It is interesting that many of the vials parallel the plagues that God poured out on Egypt as he delivered the Israelites from Pharaoh. When God pours out his wrath again, he will deliver the Israelites from the Antichrist. However, it is important to note that he pours out His wrath on specific groups of people.

When is the pouring out of God's wrath?

The sixth and seventh seal, a portion of the seventh trumpet, and all seven vials are the wrath of God. This happens after the wrath of Satan. Again, Revelation 10:7 says, "But in the days of the voice of the *seventh angel*, when he shall begin to sound, the mystery of God *should be finished*, as He hath declared to His servants the prophets."

In Zechariah 12:1-11 we see the coming deliverance of Israel and several keys that identify the time period:

1. All the nations come against Israel.

2. They look upon him whom they pierced (indicating post-cross time frame).

3. The plain of Megiddo that is the valley of Armageddon.

This passage in Zechariah speaks of the day of God's wrath and judgment at Armageddon in the Valley of Megiddo. It also reveals whom God pours his wrath upon. Zechariah 12:9 tells us, "And it shall come to pass in that day, that I will seek to destroy all the nations that come against Jerusalem."

Upon whom is the outpouring of God's wrath? Those who blaspheme him, those who have killed his saints and his prophets, and those who attack Israel at Armageddon.

Revelation 16:15 says:

> Behold, I come as a thief. Blessed is he that watcheth, and keepeth his garments, lest he walk naked, and they see his shame.

What does that Scripture remind us of? It parallels the gathering together of the elect (the rapture) as we see in Matthew chapter 24:29-44. As we learned in the last section, it is possible that Christians have already been changed from mortal to immortal as the outpouring of God's wrath begins.

It also appears as though just after Satan's wrath (possibly as Christians are witnessing the outpouring of God's wrath, but not being touched by this wrath) is when Jesus comes and gathers his elect as a thief in the night. It is at that point that we meet the Lord in the air. It is possible that the world will be so focused on the events of God's wrath that they will not even notice millions of Christians being gone. This would back up the reality of Jesus coming "as a thief in the night." Then, at the end of the outpouring his Father's wrath, Jesus returns with his saints to do battle at Armageddon.

Revelation 16:17-21 reveals the day of the Lord and the Second Coming of Christ. In this passage we see things that are indicative of the wrath of God. We see lightnings, thunderings, great earthquakes, and great hailstones, and verse 19 calls it "the cup of the wine of the fierceness of his wrath." The earthquake mentioned is so great that it kills 7,000 in Jerusalem (see Revelation 11:13).

In Ezekiel chapters 38 and 39 we see a description of the armies that attack Israel at Armageddon. The nations are Persia, Ethiopia, Meshech, Tubal, Togamar, Gomer, and Lybia. When we bring these into modern times, we see that the armies the Antichrist gathers against Israel are Iran, Ethiopia, Moscow, Tubals (which is also in Russia), Turkey, Poland, and Libya. These are some of the major nations that come to fight against Israel.

> And I will plead against him with pestilence and with blood; and I will rain upon him, and upon his bands, and upon the many people that are with him, an overflowing rain, *and great hailstones, fire, and brimstone.*
> EZEKIEL 38:22

What does this verse remind us of? In Ezekiel chapters 38 and 39 we see the wrath of God being poured out at the battle of Armageddon. We also see God's dealings with a person called Gog, the chief prince of Meshech, Tubal, and Rosh (Russia).

Who is Gog? He is the Antichrist–the one against whom God is bringing his fury (see Ezekiel 38:2). In fact, the Lord kills five-sixths of the army from the North (see Ezekiel 39:2).

As Jesus prophesied, the time period immediately before the coming of the Lord will be Israel's darkest hour. However, just as the world government gathers armies to attack Israel, just as the Antichrist is about to consume Israel, something happens:

> And I saw heaven opened, and behold a white horse; and he that sat upon him was called Faithful and True, and in righteousness he doth judge and make war. His eyes were as a flame of fire, and on his head were many crowns; and he had a name written, that no man knew, but he himself. And he was clothed with a vesture dipped in blood: and his name is called the Word of God. And the armies which were in heaven followed him upon white horses, clothed in fine linen, white and clean. And out of his mouth goeth a sharp sword, that with it he should smite the nations: and he shall rule them with a rod of iron: and he treadeth the winepress of the fierceness and wrath of Almighty God. And he hath on his vesture and on his thigh a name written: KINGS OF KINGS, AND LORD OF LORDS. And I saw an angel standing in the sun; and he cried with a loud voice, saying to all the fowls that fly in the midst of heaven, "Come and gather yourselves together unto the supper of the great God; That ye may eat the flesh of the kings, and the flesh of captains, and the flesh of mighty men, and the flesh of horses, and of them that sit on them, and the flesh of all men, both free and bond, both small and great." And I saw the beast, and the kings of the earth, and their armies, gathered together to make war against him that sat on the horse, and against his army. And the beast was taken, and with him the false prophet that wrought miracles before him, with which he deceived them that had received the mark of the beast, and them that worshipped his image. These both were cast alive into the lake of fire burning with brimstone. And the remnant were slain with the sword of him that sat upon the horse, which sword preceded out of his mouth: and all the fowls were filled with their flesh.
>
> REVELATION 19:11-21

At Armageddon Jesus will return and destroy all those who attack Israel. Then, God will send the fowls of the air to consume the carcasses of all the dead in the Valley of Meggido. Jesus prophesied this in Matthew 24:27-28: "For as the lightning cometh out of the east, and shineth even unto the west; so shall also the coming of the Son of man be. For wheresoever the carcass is, there will the eagles be gathered together."

Who comes back with Jesus?

The armies of heaven! All those who have been faithful to God, and who have remained pure will be changed in a moment. Those saints will meet the Lord in the air, and they will return with the Lord to do battle alongside him.

> Now Enoch, the seventh from Adam, prophesied about these men also, saying, "Behold, the Lord comes *with ten thousands of his saints, to execute judgment on all,* to convict all who are ungodly among them of all their ungodly deeds which they have committed in an ungodly way, and of all the harsh things which ungodly sinners have spoken against him".
> JUDE 14-15

Let us look at a description of this supernatural army: Blow ye the trumpet in Zion, and sound an alarm in my holy mountain: let all the inhabitants of the land tremble: for the day of the Lord cometh, for it is nigh at hand; *A day of darkness and of gloominess, a day of clouds and of thick darkness,* as the mourning spread upon the mountains: a great people and a strong; there hath not been ever the like, neither shall be any more after it, even to the years of many generation. A fire devoureth before them; and behind them a flame burneth: *the land is as the garden of Eden before them, and behind them a desolate wilderness;* yea, and nothing shall escape them. The appearance of them is as the appearance of horses; and as horseman, so shall they run. Like the noise of chariots on the tops of mountains shall they leap, like the noise of a flame of fire that devoureth the stubble, as a strong people set in battle array. Before their face the people shall be much pained: all faces shall gather blackness. They shall run like mighty men; they shall climb the wall like men of war; and they shall march every one on his ways, and they shall not break their ranks. Neither shall one thrust another; they shall walk every one in his path: *and when they fall upon the sword, they shall not be wounded.* They shall run to and fro in the city; they shall run upon the wall, they shall climb up upon the houses; they shall enter in at the windows like a thief. The earth shall quake before them; the heavens shall tremble: the sun and the moon shall be dark, and the stars shall withdraw their shining: And the Lord shall utter his voice before his army: for his camp is very great: for he is strong that executeth his word: *for the day of the Lord is great and very terrible;* and who can abide it?

JOEL 2:1-11

How do we know that this passage is speaking of the Second Coming of Christ? It speaks twice of the "day of the Lord," and it comes with the sound of a trumpet. We also see darkness, the earth quaking, the sun and the moon becoming dark, and fire devouring people, describing the wrath of God.

In this passage we also see that "the land as the Garden of Eden" is *before* us (the Millennium), and a desolate wilderness is *behind* us. On the day when we return with the Lord to do battle we will have a glorified body. Joel 2:8 says: "When they fall upon the sword, *they shall not be wounded.*" We also see that we will run like mighty men, climb walls like men of war, and when we march *we will not break ranks.*

According to Romans 11:25-27 it is at that time that Israel will see their Messiah! Israel has been blinded for a time, but all those who survive in Israel will see Jesus.

Imagine Jesus–after he has defeated the armies at Armageddon–riding into Jerusalem. As he enters the city, some Israeli leader has the audacity to ask him the question we find in Zechariah 13:6: "And one shall say unto him, 'What are these wounds in thine hands?' Then he shall answer, 'Those with which I was wounded in the house of my friends.'"

The Jews will look upon the One whom they pierced and they will mourn as one mourns for his only son. At that time there will be great mourning in Jerusalem.

As we have already learned, God's wrath is poured out after Satan's wrath, which lasts for three-and-a-half years. We have also studied what God's wrath looks like, and we understand that it is poured out in specific places and against specific nations who attack Israel.

Is there any indication as to the length of the outpouring of God's wrath?

> And he said, "Go thy way Daniel: for the words are closed up and sealed till the time of the end. Many shall be purified, and made white, and tried; but the wicked shall do wickedly: and none of the wicked shall understand; but the wise shall understand. And from the time that the daily sacrifice shall be taken away, and the abomination that maketh desolate set up, there shall be *a thousand two hundred and ninety days*. Blessed is he that waiteth, and cometh to the *thousand three hundred and five and thirty days*. But go thou thy way till the end be: for thou shalt rest, and stand in thy lot at the end of the days".
>
> DANIEL 12:9-13

We know that Satan's wrath begins at the abomination of desolation, when the Antichrist puts an end to the sacrifices and sets himself up in the temple as a god. We also know that Satan's wrath lasts "one thousand two hundred and sixty days, forty months, or time, times, and half a time."

In Daniel 12:8, Daniel boldly asks, "My Lord, what shall be the end of these things?" Verse 11 tells us that there will be one thousand two hundred and ninety days after the abomination of desolation. This goes thirty days beyond the time period of Satan's wrath that we see in Revelation chapter 12.

On top of that, God says, "Blessed is he who waits, and comes to the thousand three hundred and five and thirty days." All together we see a *seventy-five-day* period beyond the end of Satan's wrath where something else is happening. So, in Daniel chapter 12 we see that the end does not come until seventy-five days after the conclusion of Satan's wrath.

It is very possible that it is during this last seventy-five day time period that God's wrath is poured out. According to what we have learned up to this point, it is logical to assume that the resurrection of the dead and the gathering together of the elect must happen within this seventy-five-day time period.

Once again, it is clear in Scripture that no man knows that day or hour of Christ's return. However, the Word of God does instruct us not to be ignorant of the times. We are also told that we would know when his coming is near (even at the door), and that we are children of light that that day should not overtake us unaware.

Therefore, what we see in Scripture is a seventy-five-day window of time during which it is very possible that the elect are gathered together, the wedding supper of the Lamb occurs, and then we come back with Jesus at the battle of Armageddon. (Keep in mind that heaven's time is certainly much different from earthly time.)

There are many different scenarios concerning this final period of time. It is possible that the pouring out of God's wrath takes an entire seventy-five-day time period. It is also possible that the church is raptured sometime during the thirty-day time period, and God's wrath is poured out for the last forty-five days—including the battle of Armageddon. Or, the Church is raptured immediately after Satan's wrath, God's wrath is poured out for thirty days, then Jesus takes forty-five days to set up his earthly kingdom. It is apparent that there is time that is not accounted for, but exactly what happens during that period of time is speculation.

We do understand the difference between God's wrath and the wrath of Satan. We also know that the Church is gathered together at the last trumpet. We have also seen the possible time period in which these events take place. The exciting part is that when these things begin to happen we can look up because our redemption draws nigh!

Let's Review

- God's wrath is easy to recognize in Scripture because the characteristics are always the same.
- The day of the Lord and God's wrath are the same event.
- All seven vials are the wrath of God.
- God's wrath is poured out on specific people and nations that have persecuted Israel, and the saints, and that gather together to try and destroy Israel at Armageddon.
- The armies of heaven (saints) return with the Lord to fight with him at Armageddon.
- The church is raptured sometime *after* Satan's wrath and at the *beginning* of God's wrath.
- There is a seventy-five-day time period spoken of in Daniel chapter 12 in which God's wrath might possibly be poured out.

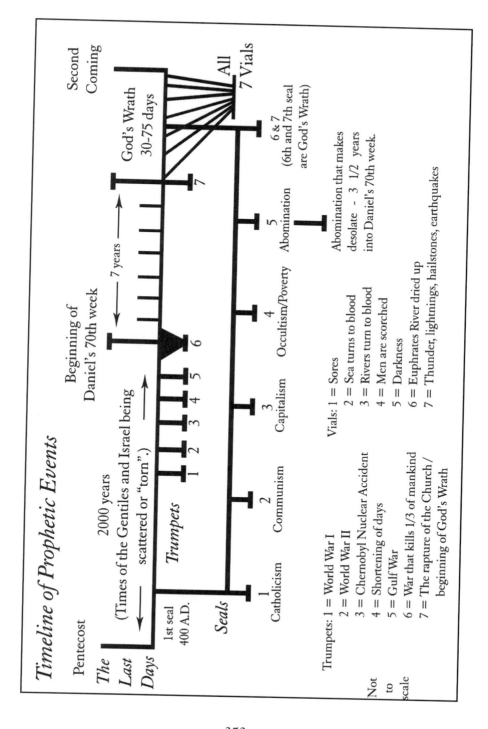

Timeline of Prophetic Events

Pentecost

The Last Days

2000 years

(Times of the Gentiles and Israel being scattered or "torn".)

Beginning of Daniel's 70th week

7 years

God's Wrath 30-75 days

Second Coming

All 7 Vials

1st seal 400 A.D.

Seals

Trumpets

1 2 3 4 5 6

7

6 & 7 (6th and 7th seal are God's Wrath)

1 Catholicism

2 Communism

3 Capitalism

4 Occultism/Poverty

5 Abomination

Abomination that makes desolate – 3 1/2 years into Daniel's 70th week.

Trumpets: 1 = World War I
2 = World War II
3 = Chernobyl Nuclear Accident
4 = Shortening of days
5 = Gulf War
6 = War that kills 1/3 of mankind
7 = The rapture of the Church / beginning of God's Wrath

Vials: 1 = Sores
2 = Sea turns to blood
3 = Rivers turn to blood
4 = Men are scorched
5 = Darkness
6 = Euphrates River dried up
7 = Thunder, lightnings, hailstones, earthquakes

Not to scale

Part
V

The Millennial Reign

In the last section we touched on the return of Christ as he sets his foot on the Mount of Olives and rides through the Valley of Megiddo–the location of the battle of Armageddon.

We learned that when Jesus returns he will come to his own people and one will ask him, "How did you get those wounds in your hands?" Jesus will reply, "I was wounded in the house of my friends."

The Jews will finally recognize that Jesus is their Messiah. They will also realize that this is the second time Jesus has come to the earth. They will weep as they discover that the Messiah who has delivered them from the Antichrist is the One whom their ancestors crucified 2,000 years earlier.

Now let us examine the millennial reign of Christ.

The Nations Repent

Before the millennial kingdom is set up, the nations will repent. At that point those who have already accepted Christ–those who were living for him before his Second Coming–will come back with him in glorified bodies. Those who were faithful to Christ will rule and reign with him for 1,000 years. On the day of Christ's return, immortal beings will come face-to-face with mortal man.

At the time of Christ's return, he will cast the Antichrist and the false prophet into the lake of fire. Then Jesus binds the devil for 1,000 years. Think about that—a world in which there is no devil to tempt mankind for 1,000 years!

> And I saw an angel come down from heaven, having the key of the bottomless pit and a great chain in his hand. And he laid hold on the dragon, that old serpent, which is the devil, and Satan, *and bound him a thousand years,* and cast him into the bottomless pit, and shut him up, and set a seal upon him, that he should deceive the nations no more, till the thousand years should be fulfilled: and after that he must be loosed a little season. And I saw thrones, and they sat upon them, and judgment was given unto them: and I saw the souls of them that were beheaded for the witness of Jesus, and for the word of God, and which had not worshipped the beast, neither his image, neither had received his mark upon their foreheads, or in their hands; *and they lived and reigned with Christ a thousand years.* But the rest of the dead lived not again until the thousand years were finished. This is the first resurrection. Blessed and holy is he that hath a part in the first resurrection: on such the second death hath no power, but they shall be priests of God and of Christ, and shall reign with him a thousand years. And when the thousand years are expired, Satan shall be loosed out of his prison.
>
> REVELATION 20:1-7

There is a specific reason for the millennial reign of Christ. When Jesus rules on the earth, he will abolish the curse once and for all. This is the time when human government comes to an end, and God sets up his government on the earth. This is called "the dispensation of the fullness of times," in Ephesians 1:10.

The Regeneration

In Matthew 19:28 Jesus said, "Verily I say unto you, that ye which have followed me, in the regeneration when the Son of man shall sit on the throne of his glory, ye also shall sit upon twelve thrones, judging the tribes of Israel."

We also see in this verse that the time of Christ's reign on the earth is called the "regeneration." According to Webster's Dictionary, to regenerate means to "give fresh life or vigor to; to reorganize." This is not the new heaven and new earth, but rather new life being given to the earth as we know it. As we will see, this parallels many Scriptures concerning the description of life in this time period known as the Millennium.

In the time of the regeneration Jesus told his disciples that they will rule over the twelve tribes of Israel. Of course we know that this has not happened yet, and that there is a time period when there are thrones of judgment on which those who were faithful will rule and reign with Christ.

Revelation 20:1-7 clearly speaks of that time–the time of the millennial reign of Christ. It is *not* the time of the new heaven and the new earth wherein the glory of God illuminates it, and the Lamb is its light. We will examine the new heaven and new earth more in the next section. However, in this section it is important that we recognize the difference between the regeneration, and the new heaven and the new earth.

In Matthew 19:29 Jesus goes on to say that in the day of the regeneration, everyone who has given up houses, land, brothers, sisters, father, mother, or children will receive one-hundred-fold *and* inherit everlasting life. Once again, just because we see the phrase "everlasting life," this is not speaking of the new heaven and the new earth. When we come back with Christ to reign with Him for 1,000 years we will have glorified bodies. At that time we will have already inherited everlasting life, and the second death will have no power over us (see Revelation 20:6).

Those who have followed Christ and given up substantive things for the sake of the gospel will have all restored (plus much more) during his millennial reign. The millennial reign is a time of blessings and restoration for all those who followed the Lord.

The Lord's One-World Government

It has always been God's purpose to have one government and one religion. That has also been the purpose of those who oppose God; however, their idea of one religion and one government is perverted.

When Jesus sets up his earthly reign, there will not be any more voting for government officials. The type of government Jesus will set up is a theocracy–a governmental state under the direction of God. Jesus will be in charge!

Daniel 7:14 describes this government when it says, "Then to him was given dominion and glory and a kingdom, that all peoples, nations, and languages should serve him. His dominion is an everlasting dominion, which shall not pass away, and his kingdom the one which shall not be destroyed." Then Isaiah 9:7 tells us, "Of the increase of his government and peace there will be no end."

What does Scripture say concerning who has authority under Jesus in his millennial kingdom? Revelation 20:6 says, "They shall be priests of God and of Christ, and shall reign with him for a thousand years." This verse is speaking of all those who take part in the first resurrection.

Jesus will establish his throne in Jerusalem. During the Millennium God the Father will be in charge, and his authority will flow down through Jesus as he rules on the earth. During the millennial reign, *Jerusalem* will be the capital of the world. The temple in Jerusalem will be the equivalent of the White House.

Another interesting biblical truth is that God promised David an *everlasting throne* in Jerusalem. King David is alive today in heaven. Like so many others, he waits for the day of the resurrection when his soul will reunite with his body.

Ezekiel chapter 37 speaks of Israel becoming a nation (see the regathering of Israel) and the millennial reign of Christ. Verse 24 says, "And David My servant shall be king over them; and they all shall have one shepherd: they shall also walk in my judgments, and observe my statutes and do them." We know this Scripture has not yet come to pass. After Christ's return, king David will rule in Israel under Christ's authority.

According to Matthew 19:28 and Luke 22:28-30, the apostles of the Lamb will rule over the twelve tribes of Israel during the Millennium. King David's throne will also be restored in Israel. All of this occurs under the authority of Jesus. Yet the Scriptures speak of another group who rule with Christ. In Revelation 20:4 the apostle John saw thrones, and judgment is given to those on the thrones. Who is sitting on those thrones?

1. Those who were beheaded for the witness of Christ and the word of God.

2. Those who had not worshipped the beast or his image.

3. Those who did not take the mark of the beast on their foreheads or in their hands.

Scripture also reveals that there will be three types of beings present on the earth during the millennial reign of Christ:

1. Angels. Angels are present today on the earth. We see them manifested many times in Scripture (i.e., at the tomb of Christ), and Psalm 91 tells us that God has given his angels charge over us. First Corinthians 6:3 tells us that we will judge angels.

2. Saints in glorified bodies. As we have learned, those who come back with Christ will have glorified bodies just as Jesus did after his resurrection.

3. Mortal beings. There will no doubt be millions and millions who are still here after the return of Christ. Immortals will be ruling over mortals. This will be a government unlike any that has ever existed.

Will everyone become born again during the Millennium?

During this millennial government there will not be any excuse for a person not to be born again. Will there be those who do not become born again during the millennial reign? Amazingly, yes! Despite the fact that the Savior himself will be present on the earth, there will still be those who will not accept him!

> And it shall come to pass, that *every one that is left of all the nations which came against Jerusalem* shall even go up from year to year to worship the king, the Lord of hosts, and to keep the feast of tabernacles. And it shall be, that *whoso will not come up* of all the families of the earth unto Jerusalem to worship the king, the Lord of hosts, even upon them shall be no rain. And if the family of Egypt go not up, and come not, that have no rain; there shall be the plague, wherewith the Lord will smite the heathen that come not up to keep the feast of tabernacles. This shall be the punishment of Egypt, and the punishment of all nations that come not up to keep the feast of tabernacles.
>
> ZECHARIAH 14:16-19

During the Millennium Jesus will require that all nations come to Jerusalem each year to worship him. It is interesting to note that of those who choose not to go to Jerusalem to worship Jesus, he does not immediately destroy them. Remember, our God is a merciful God! That means that he is very patient and kind. However, those who choose not to worship him, he causes no rain to fall on them. If they choose a second time not to come up to Jerusalem to worship, then the Lord puts a plague on them.

In this time we are living in, the Bible says God causes it to rain on the just and the unjust. What that means is, when the people of God experience blessings, the unjust also receive a blessing. During the time of the millennial reign, however, a person will not experience the blessing of rain without a relationship with the One who makes it rain.

In Zechariah 13:1-5 we see that "in that day" (the day of the Lord, the Second Coming of Christ) that all idols will be cut off and not remembered anymore. People will not be allowed to worship idols, or practice any false religion. There will be one Lord and one religion.

If any false prophets arise in that day, they will be run through with a sword. Scripture reveals that in the Millennium those who speak lies against the Lord are killed by their own family members. There will be a true fear (reverence) of the Lord. Individuals will not want to associate with false prophets.

No More War!

> But in the last days it shall come to pass, that the mountain of the house of the Lord shall be established in the top of the mountains, and it shall be exalted above the hills; and people shall flow unto it. And many nations shall come, and say, "Come, and let us go up to the mountain of the Lord," and to the house of Jacob; and he will teach us of his ways, and we will walk in his paths: for the law shall go forth of Zion, and the word of the Lord from Jerusalem. And he shall judge among many people, and rebuke strong nations afar off; and they shall beat their swords into plowshares, and their spears into pruning hooks: nation shall not lift up a sword against nation, *neither shall they learn of war anymore.*
> MICAH 4:1-3

All laws shall go forth from Jerusalem during the Millennium. Nations will beat their swords into plowshares, and nations will learn of war no more. There will be no more war after Armageddon. The agenda of national leaders will be to learn of God's rules, and how to administrate peace.

During the Millennium Jesus provides rest, peace, and prosperity as the world has never seen. Isaiah 11:10 tells us that "his rest shall be glorious." In Ezekiel 39:9-10 (after Armageddon) we see the gathering of all weapons and the burning of them with fire for seven years. During the Millennium weapons are destroyed, there is no more war, and fear is abolished. Everyone will have justice during this reign of peace on the earth.

During the Millennium the Jews and the Arabs will love and bless each other! What an amazing thing! As we view the Middle East today, this is hard to imagine. Nevertheless, Isaiah 19:24-25 says, "In that day shall Israel be the third with Egypt and with Assyria, even a blessing in the midst of the land: Whom the Lord of hosts shall bless, saying, 'Blessed be Egypt my people, and Assyria the work of my hands, and Israel mine inheritance.'"

That is true peace in the Middle East! It will be just as it was when Jacob and Esau saw each other. Instead of desiring to kill one another, the Israelis and the Arabs will desire to bless one another.

Environmental Changes

We see that during the Millennium there are also environmental changes (see Isaiah 11:6-10; 35:1-10; 60:18-20; 65:17-25). In these passages we see the desert rejoicing and blossoming. During the Millennium we will see streams in the desert and parched grounds becoming pools.

In Amos it says that all the desolate places will be gone. We will see a regeneration of the earth back to the way it was in the Garden of Eden where all the animals are plant eaters, and there is no enmity between them. The wolf and the lamb will feed together, and the lion shall *eat straw* like the bull.

Isaiah 65:20 tells us, "No more shall an infant from there live but a few days, nor an old man who has not fulfilled his days; For the *child* shall die one hundred years old, but the *sinner* being one hundred years old shall be accursed." This is a time period very different from the one we are living in now.

How do we know that this verse is not speaking of the new heaven and the new earth, or the New Jerusalem? The New Jerusalem is the believer's final place of rest (heaven) after this earth is destroyed and all sinners and satanic forces are cast into the lake of fire.

There are several indicators within Isaiah 65:20 that let us know it is a window into the Millennium and not the new heaven and new earth:

1. Men are considered old.
2. People are dying.
3. Sinners are present on the earth.

Even though Isaiah 65:20 is speaking of a time period that is very different from the present, it is obviously *not* referring to the finality of the new heaven and the new earth. As we will see, in the New Jerusalem (the new heaven and the new earth) there will be no more sin or death.

During the Millennium we see a child dying at one hundred years old. In Isaiah 60:22 it says, "A little one shall become a thousand." According to Scripture we can see that people will be giving birth to children during the Millennium, and a child who is one hundred is considered young. Old men will fulfill their days, just as Adam and his descendants fulfilled their days. However, the sinner will be accursed at one hundred years old.

Once again, we see that there will still be sinners and death during the Millennium. Why? Because the sin nature is still in existence from those who were alive on the earth after Armageddon. As long as there are still mortals, there will still be sin and death. Remember, death is the last enemy to be put under.

During the Millennium the tongue of the dumb shall be loosed, and the eyes of the blind shall be opened. Everyone will know the name of the Lord. It will be like church everywhere we go. Remember, those who are loyal to Jesus will not only be raptured, but also come back with him to rule and reign on the earth.

As we see Bible prophecy come to pass, we must keep in mind that Satan's wrath is only three-and-a-half years. On the other hand Jesus' millennial reign of peace and restoration is 1,000 years! On top of that, the Millennium is the last dispensation that involves mortal man before eternity when the devil, the sin nature, and death will no longer exist. God has marvelous things in store for all those who make him Lord.

Let's Review

- According to the Bible, Jesus physically comes and rules the earth for 1,000 years.
- The Millennium is after the battle of Armageddon.
- Those who are a part of the first resurrection are not subject to the second death, and they will reign with Jesus.
- During the Millennium Jerusalem will be the capital of Jesus' government.
- King David's throne will be restored.
- Those who remain loyal to Christ will rule and reign with him.
- The apostles of the Lamb will rule over the twelve tribes of Israel.
- Nations will be expected to come to Jerusalem and worship Jesus. Nations who refuse will be punished.
- The earth will be regenerated, and all who have given up lands, houses, family, etc., will be restored one-hundred-fold by Jesus.
- During the Millennium all weapons will be destroyed, nations will learn of war no more, and the lion will lay down with the lamb.

All Things New

We have come a long way in our study of prophecy in order to get to this point. We have gone back over 2,000 years to see how the Lord revealed events to his prophets that would occur in the end of the last days. We now have a better understanding of the nation of Israel, and how the Lord has kept (and will continue to keep) his word concerning an astonishing group of people called the Jews.

We have studied the modern nations of the Bible, the one-world government, interfaithism, the Antichrist, the wrath of Satan, the resurrection of the saints, the wrath of God, and the millennial reign of Christ. Now let's look at what happens after the millennium.

After the Millennium

And when the *thousand years are expired,* Satan shall be loosed out of his prison, and shall go out to *deceive the nations* which are in the four quarters of the earth, Gog and Magog, to gather them together to battle: the

number of whom is as the sand of the sea. And they went up on the breadth of the earth, and compassed the camp of the saints about, and the beloved city: *and fire came down from God* out of heaven, and devoured them. And the devil that deceived them was cast into the lake of fire and brimstone, where the beast and the false prophet are, and shall be tormented day and night forever and ever. And I saw a *great white throne,* and him that sat on it, from whose face the earth and the heaven fled away; and there was found no place for them. And I saw the dead, small and great, stand before God; and the books were opened: and another book was opened, which is the book of life: and the dead were judged out of those things which were written in the books, according to their works. And the sea gave up the dead which were in it; and death and hell delivered up the dead which were in them: and they were judged every man according to their works. And death and hell were cast into the lake of fire. This is the second death. And whosoever was not found written in the book of life was *cast into the lake of fire.*
REVELATION 20:7-15

After the millennial reign of Christ, Satan is set free for a little while (we do not see a specific time in the Scripture) to deceive the nations one last time. What a fascinating passage. Why would God let Satan loose? It seems as though it would have made more sense for him to throw Satan into the lake of fire along with the beast and the false prophet.

While it is true that during the Millennium Jesus rules with a rod of iron, it is also true that God has never desired to have servants who are robots. He does not *draft* us into his army. We must *choose* (as an act of our will) to come to the Lord and serve him with our whole heart. The same is true of those who do not choose to serve God, those who make that choice of their own free will.

Because God will not make anyone serve him, he graciously gives the nations one more opportunity at the end of the Millennium to willingly submit to him. The amazing thing is, after Jesus literally shows himself to the world (revealing his goodness, mercy, salvation, restoration, etc.) there are still those who do not love him!

Those who have enjoyed the prosperity and peace of the millennium, but do not love Jesus during the millennium, are not just a small remote band of rebels. Revelation 20:8 tells us the number of those who attack Jerusalem is "as the sand of the sea." For those who love Jesus it is hard to comprehend that after this enormous time period of Jesus ruling and reigning on the earth that there are so many who would desire to kill him. This is the epitome of selfishness. These ungodly people have enjoyed all the blessings and prosperity of the Millennium, yet still desire to take the prosperous kingdom away from the King!

So we see that this multitude of people band together and attack Jesus and his saints in Jerusalem. However, this time God laughs as he looks down on his adversaries. This time there is no battle. There is no war. As Jerusalem is surrounded by Satan and his enormous army, *God the Father* sends fire down from heaven and devours them!

A portion of the people that gather together to do battle against Jesus at the end of the Millennium is Gog and Magog. This should not be confused with the battle of Armageddon, which at this point has already occurred. Why then does Scripture mention Gog and Magog? When Jesus returns and sets up his earthly kingdom, He takes dominion away from nations, but the nations themselves still exist.

Once again, the battle of Armageddon occurs before the 1,000-year reign of Christ (see Revelation 19:11-21; 20:1-3). Revelation 20:7-8 explains, "Now when the thousand years have expired, Satan will be released from his prison and will go out to deceive the nations." The sad thing is that Satan deceives many of the same nations who attacked Jerusalem the first time.

After God consumes the army that surrounds Jerusalem, the earth is also consumed as God opens the book of life and judges the dead, both small and great, according to their works. At that time the earth and the heavens pass away "and there was found no place for them" (see 2 Peter 3:1-14; Revelation 20:11). Then, anyone not found written in the book of life is cast into the lake of fire with the devil, the beast, and the false prophet.

The Great White Throne Judgment

At the Great White Throne Judgment God calls up all the dead–death and Hades. Hades is the Greek word for hell. In the Old Testament sheol was the Hebrew word for hell. Therefore, we understand that there is only one hell.

In Revelation 20:12-15 we see that hell is not the final place of torment for those who have died without Christ. It is a temporary place of torment where those who have not accepted Jesus as their savior will be until the day of the Great White Throne Judgment. Hell is a holding place in the lower parts of the earth. Ephesians 4:9 says, "Now that he ascended, what is it but that he also descended first into the lower parts of the earth." First Peter 3:19 tells us that Jesus went and preached to the spirits in *prison.*

In its present state, hell is similar to what happens to a person who is arrested for a crime punishable by one or more years in prison (a felony). Typically, they are first placed in a county jail while they await their trial. For this person the county jail is a temporary holding facility. The difference is, hell is a holding place with unimaginable torment!

At the Great White Throne Judgment, all those in hell are cast into the lake of fire. Death is also cast into the lake of fire fulfilling 1 Corinthians 15:26 that says, "The last enemy that shall be destroyed is death."

At the Great White Throne Judgment there will be names that *are* found in the book of life.

Wait a minute. How can that be? The book of life is only for believers. We must remember, there will be those who are alive on the earth at the Second Coming of the Lord who are not part of the first resurrection. These individuals are either saved as they see Jesus return, or they become born again during the millennial reign of Christ. Some of those born-again believers will be alive at the end of the 1,000 years, and some will have died. All those who have accepted Jesus as their savior during the Millennium will be judged at the Great White Throne Judgment. If their names are found in the book of life, they will not suffer the second death.

The second death is a place of outer darkness and eternal torment, a place of weeping, wailing, and the gnashing of teeth, a place where "the worm dieth not, and the fire is not quenched." When the book of life is opened, all those whose names are not found in it will be cast into the lake of fire.

It is a very sobering thing to discover that the majority of people who have lived on the earth will be lost for all eternity. How do we know this? In Matthew 7:13-14 Jesus said, "Enter ye in at the strait gate: for wide is the gate, and broad is the way, that leadeth to destruction, and *many* there be which go in thereat: Because strait is the gate, and narrow is the way, which leadeth unto life, and *few* there be that find it." "Many" is obviously a whole lot more than a "few."

Also, consider the amount of people (as many as the sands of the sea) that gather to attack Jesus and saints at the end of the Millennium. All of those people are consumed by fire from heaven.

In the day of the White Throne Judgment all those who are standing before God will have to give an account for their works. In Matthew 10:26 Jesus said that there is nothing covered that will not be revealed, and hidden that will not be known. It does man no good to live with lies or try to hide things from God. All will be revealed!

The New Jerusalem

The earth will pass away with a fervent heat, and *all* things will be made new. We will literally have heaven on earth (see Revelation 21:1-27; 22:1-21).

The New Jerusalem is a type of the present-day church. Revelation 21:2 says, "And I John saw the holy city, New Jerusalem, coming down from God out of heaven, prepared as a bride adorned for her husband." Who is the bride of Christ? Ephesians chapter 5 says it is the Church. We will live and dwell in the New Jerusalem, which is also a reflection of what Christ has made the Church to be.

In Revelation chapter 21 we see an amazing description of the holy city. The gold in the city was transparent like clear glass. That is pure gold–no impurities. The gates are made out of one pearl, and the entire city is illuminated by the glory of God.

The dimensions of the New Jerusalem are 1,500 miles, by 1,500 miles, by 1,500 miles. Scripture says that its length, breadth, and height are equal. Typically, when we envision this, we picture the New Jerusalem as man would lay out a city. However, these dimensions may also describe a pyramid.

There are many mysteries in this world today, and the Great Pyramid in Giza is one of them. There have been many speculations concerning why the Great Pyramid was built. It is the only pyramid that does not house the body of one of Egypt's kings. Another interesting feature is that it has no capstone (or cornerstone) at the top.

Some have even suggested that aliens built the Great Pyramid. If God's people did have a hand in building this pyramid (to reveal the glory of the gospel and foreshadow the New Jerusalem), it would be just like the devil to try to pervert its meaning. New Age religions have also used the pyramid as an occult symbol.

Some have suggested that Joseph, Daniel, or even Noah built the Great Pyramid. With that in mind, consider the following Scripture:

> In that day shall five cities in the land of Egypt speak the language of Canaan, and swear to the LORD of hosts; one shall be called, the city of destruction. In that day shall there be *an altar to the LORD in the midst of the land of Egypt,* and a pillar at the border thereof to the LORD
>
> ISAIAH 19:18-19

When Egypt was divided, the Great Pyramid was right on the border. Isaiah 19:19 speaks of an altar as a pillar to the Lord on the border in Egypt. Could the Great Pyramid be that altar? Bear with us while we speculate.

There are sixteen other pyramids in Egypt and the Great Pyramid is by far the largest. It is ninety times the volume of the Sears Tower. It covers thirteen acres of land, and when it was built, is was not more than one-tenth of an inch off being square.

They say that if you connected every locomotive in the world to the Great Pyramid, you could not move it one inch. Napoleon calculated that from the stones used in the pyramid he could put a ten-foot-high wall around all of France. It is so enormous that no one can say for sure how it was built.

Another fascinating aspect is that there were 144,000 stones used to build the Great Pyramid, many weighing seventy tons each. Archeologists have discovered that when it was originally built, those 144,000 stones had been sealed so well that you could not even put a piece of paper inbetween the stones. Revelation 7:3-4 tells us that God has 144,000 living stones who are sealed.

The Great Pyramid was built perfectly upon longitudinal and latitudinal lines. The earth's highest point of latitude and longitude crosses at the center of the pyramid. In other words, it sits perfectly upon the center of the earth. Primitive man did not build the Great Pyramid. It was built with forethought and purpose.

The Great Pyramid had been sealed so well that archeologists did not realize there was actually a doorway leading inside. When they finally found this doorway, what they discovered was amazing.

Within the passageways of the pyramid they discovered a type of a 6,000-year clock. The way the Great Pyramid is set up may not mean much to secular archeologists, but to the Christian it is very significant. In Matthew 7:13 Jesus tells of the broad path that leads to destruction and the narrow path that leads to everlasting life.

When a person enters the Great Pyramid, they have a choice to make. They can either take a broad path that leads downward to a pit, or a narrow stairway that goes upward.

About two-thirds of the way up (around the 4,000-year mark) you can go into a room in which there is an empty tomb. It was 4,000 years after creation that Jesus died and rose from the grave!

Then, if you continue up the narrow stairway you come to a king's chamber (2,000 years later–the 6,000-year mark). As a person enters the king's chamber by the narrow way, they find a polished granite box that is the exact measurements of the Ark of the Covenant.

The broad path leads downward to the 6,000-year mark and drops off into a pit, then drops off again signifying a bottomless pit.

The height of the Great Pyramid is the same as the length of its sides, and the capstone is missing. Archeologists cannot figure out why the builders of the Great Pyramid (which is built so precisely) left off the capstone, which on a pyramid is called the *cornerstone.*

In Matthew 21:42-44 Jesus explained that the stone *that the builders rejected* has become the chief cornerstone (speaking of himself). He went on to say that whoever falls on this stone will be broken, but on whomever it falls, it will grind them into powder.

The Great Pyramid has been a symbol of the New World Order, and it is even on the back of the U.S. dollar bill. As we have already discovered, on the back of this bill we also see the "all-seeing eye" capping off the Great Pyramid and the Latin words *Novus Ordo Seclorum,* which means New World Order.

The builders of the New World Order believe they are the saviors of the world, and yet the cornerstone that was rejected by the builders symbolizes Jesus himself. In Matthew 21:42-44 Jesus identified himself as that cornerstone, and he spoke of a day when he will return, conquer the nations, and rule with a rod of Iron. Can you see how the devil has taken what God has created and attributed it to himself?

One day we will find out whether our speculations concerning the New Jerusalem are correct. In the meantime we should not worship with pyramids, attaching to them some sort of power and spiritual significance.

The fact remains that what born-again Christians experience in this life in the spiritual realm (e.g. freedom from the curse and rivers of living water), they will experience in the natural realm in the new heaven and new earth (Revelation 22:1-3). Furthermore, they shall live forever with the Father, the Son, and the Holy Spirit. A place where God is the light, where there is no more curse, no more nighttime, no more sorrow, no sickness and disease, and no temptation or sin. A place in which everyone loves each other, and Jesus reigns supreme as the chief cornerstone. That is the reality of the new heaven and new earth.

The key is to be ready to meet Jesus. Our studies have revealed that time is growing short, and all prophecies will be fulfilled in their time. Jesus sums it up as only he can in Revelation chapter 22:

> And, behold, I come quickly; and my reward is with me, to give to every man according as his work shall be. I am the Alpha and Omega, the Beginning and the End, the First and the Last. And the Spirit and the bride say, "Come." And let him that heareth say, "Come." And let him that is athirst come. And whosoever will, let him take of the water of life freely (verses 12, 13, 17).

Let's Review

- After the 1,000-year reign of Christ the devil is released for a short time.
- The devil gathers armies together (as the sand of the sea) to attack God's people at Jerusalem.
- God sends fire down from heaven and consumes all those who are attacking Jerusalem.
- Satan is cast into the lake of fire with the beast and the false prophet.
- After the Millennium is the Great White Throne Judgment of God.
- Death and hell give up their dead. The dead are judged and all those not found in the book of life are cast into the lake of fire.
- Death and hell are also cast into the lake of fire.
- The new heaven, the new earth, and the New Jerusalem become the dwelling place of all those who have made Jesus Lord of their lives.

Revelation Unveiled

Now that we have examined prophecy all the way to the new heaven and earth, let us take a closer look at the book of Revelation to see how it all ties together.

Revelation simply means the act of revealing. Revelation 1:1 explains whom it reveals when it says, "The Revelation of Jesus Christ." In this book Jesus reveals himself and tells of some of the most magnificent promises we see in the entire Word of God.

> The Revelation of Jesus Christ, which God gave unto him, to show unto his servants things which must *shortly come to pass;* and he sent and signified it by his angel unto his servant John: Who bare record of the word of God, and of the testimony of Jesus Christ, and of all things that he saw. Blessed is he that readeth, and they that hear the words of this prophecy, *and keep those things* which are written therein: *for the time is at hand.* John to the seven churches which are in Asia: Grace be unto you, and peace, from him which is, and which was, and which is to come; and from the seven spirits which are before his throne; And from Jesus Christ who is the faithful witness, and the first

begotten of the dead, and the prince of the kings of the earth. Unto him that loved us, and washed us from our sins in his own blood, and hath made us kings and priests unto God and his Father; to him be glory and dominion forever and ever. Amen. Behold, he cometh with clouds; and every eye shall see him, and they also which pierced him: and all kindreds of the earth shall wail because of him. Even so, Amen. "I am the Alpha and Omega, the beginning and the ending," saith the Lord, which is, and which was, and which is to come, the Almighty.

REVELATION 1:1-8

The Lord promises that we will be blessed as we read the book of Revelation. He also desires that we understand what we read so that we may act upon the words that are written.

At the same time, it is interesting that the book of Revelation has a curse attached. Revelation 22:18-19 tell us that if anyone adds to the words of this prophecy, God will add the plagues to them that are written in the book. It goes on to say that if anyone takes away from the words of the prophecy of this book, God will take away his part from the book of life.

How the Book of Revelation is Laid Out

In Revelation 1:19 John receives instruction from Jesus concerning how to document the thing that he sees:

Write the things which thou has *seen*, and the things which *are*, and the things which shall be *hereafter*.

This is a key verse to understanding the entire book of Revelation. We see three main categories or divisions:

1. The things which John had seen
2. The things which are
3. The things which shall be hereafter

Revelation 1:12 says, "And I turned to see the voice that spake with me. And being turned, I saw seven golden candlesticks." Then, John goes on to describe the things that he saw:

- Seven golden candlesticks
- One like unto the Son of man
- His head and hair were white like wool
- His eyes were as a flame of fire
- His feet like fine brass
- In his right hand seven stars and out of His mouth went a sharp sword

John followed the instructions of the Lord, and in Revelation 1:12-17 he wrote a description of what he saw.

The next things John is told to write are the things that are. We find this in Revelation 1:20: "The mystery of the seven stars which thou sawest in my right hand and the seven golden candlesticks. The seven stars are the angels of the seven churches: and the seven candlesticks which thou sawest are the seven churches."

God had specific instructions for the seven literal churches that existed in John's day. The "are" John was instructed to write had to do with seven literal churches over which he was the apostle. The word "angel" used in this passage means messenger. John was told to give a message to the messenger (or pastor) who was over each of these individual churches.

Historically, some of the churches John wrote letters to failed. Nevertheless, he had a burden for seven churches and he fulfilled what the Lord asked him to do when he sent these messages to those seven churches.

The messages given to the seven churches in Revelation are extremely valid for churches today. Are there lukewarm churches today? Of course there are! Are there loveless churches today? Of course there are! The instructions remain timeless, but the context is specific to that time period.

Now we understand that in the first chapter of Revelation John wrote the things that he had seen. Then, in the second and third chapters of Revelation he wrote about the things that are.

Now we come to the next instruction John received, and that is to write the things that must take place *hereafter*.

> After this I looked, and, behold, a door was opened in heaven: and the first voice which I heard was as it were of a trumpet talking with me; which said, "Come up hither, and I will show thee things which must be *hereafter*."
>
> REVELATION 4:1

In this verse John hears a voice like a trumpet speaking to him saying, "Come up hither, and I will show thee things which must be hereafter." He is now beginning to write about the things which will take place hereafter, following God's instructions to the letter.

In Revelation chapter 4 the Lord begins to reveal what will take place in the last days (the last 2,000 years–or hereafter). It is important to realize, however, that the book of Revelation is *not* in chronological order. If we believe it is, it will not make sense.

Although Revelation is not chronological, there is an order: the things which John had seen, the things which are, and the things which will happen hereafter. We have looked at the first two, but what about the things hereafter?

In order to drive home the point that Revelation is not chronological, we will ask a simple question: How many times can a city (Babylon) fall? The answer is quite simple–one time. Yet, Revelation 14:8 and 18:2 speak of Babylon falling.

Several other examples are:

- The powers of heaven being shaken (see Revelation 8:5; 11:19; 16:18).
- A great earthquake as the world has never experienced before (see Revelation 6:12; 8:5; 11:13, 19; 16:18).

- ◆ The sun becomes black and the moon becomes as blood (see Revelation 6:12; 16:10).
- ◆ Great hailstones (see Revelation 11:19; 16:21).
- ◆ The mountains being moved and an island passing away (see Revelation 6:14; 16:14).

As we learned in a previous lesson, all of these events listed are indicative of the outpouring of God's wrath. Does he pour out his wrath on the earth three or four times in the book of Revelation? No. If he did he would have to keep re-creating the earth so that he could pour it out again and again.

As we study the book of Revelation we can think of the events of "hereafter" like the four Gospels. The gospel (or good news) of Jesus was written through the eyes of four separate men—Matthew, Mark, Luke, and John. Each of those men wrote from a different vantage point, and each Gospel is slightly different while not contradicting each other.

John saw Jesus as the One who came down from heaven. Luke saw him as the perfect man. Mark saw him as the servant, while Matthew saw him as the coming King. The point is, each Gospel writer saw Jesus from a different perspective, but it was the same Jesus.

The book of Revelation is like putting Matthew, Mark, Luke, and John together in the same book and calling it "The Gospel." What we would end up with is four accounts of the death, burial, and resurrection of Jesus in one book. In "The Gospel" we would see Jesus feeding the same multitude several times, Judas would betray Jesus several times, and we would find the same parables told anywhere from one to four different times.

Unlike the Gospels, one author wrote the book of Revelation. Yet, in this book we see many of the same events told from several different perspectives. That is why we see five outpourings of the wrath of God. It is the same event told five different times. It is important to remember that from Revelation chapter 4 to the end, all has to do with the *hereafter* (after John received the vision, or from approximately AD 95 forward).

There are three sevens that are the backbone of Revelation (of the hereafter):

1. The seven seals
2. The seven vials
3. The seven trumpets

We have already learned that several of the seals, trumpets, and vials are the same events, and that they helped establish a timeline.

Between the seals, trumpets, and vials are what we call *parenthetical* chapters. These chapters help give us additional information concerning the events "hereafter."

Now we will go chapter by chapter and look at how the book of Revelation is put together. Since we have come so far in our study of prophecy, you should find that the pieces of the puzzle will fall right into place.

Chapter 1

In chapter 1 John tells of the purpose for which he was instructed to write: "To show unto his servants things which must shortly come to pass." We also see the way in which John was to write these things: "Write the things which thou has seen, and the things which are, and the things which shall be hereafter."

Within this chapter are the things which John had seen: "I turned to see the voice…" "I saw the seven golden candlesticks…" "and when I saw him…"

Chapters 2-3

In chapters 2 and 3 John writes those things which are. These things concerned seven literal churches over which he was an apostle. God had specific messages for each of the seven churches.

Chapter 4

From chapter 4 onward, John writes about those things which must be hereafter: "Come up hither, and I will show thee things which must be hereafter." The hereafter is obviously from John's lifetime (the time of his vision) forward to the culmination of all things. In other words, the events of the hereafter take place in the last days (the last 2,000 years), and not just a final seven-year period.

In chapter 4 John is taken up in the spirit (not raptured, nor is it symbolic of the rapture) and he records the activities surrounding the throne of God.

Chapter 5

In chapter 5 we see a book sealed with seven seals. John wept because no one had been found worthy to open the book. One of the elders told John, "Weep not: behold the Lion of the Tribe of Judah, the Root of David, hath prevailed to open the book, and to loose the seven seals thereof." Within chapter 5 we get a beautiful glimpse of our Savior, the conquering King who is from everlasting to everlasting.

Chapter 6

At the beginning of chapter 6 the Lamb (Jesus) begins to open the seals. As we have already learned, the first four seals are extremely different from the last three.

We learned that the first four seals in Revelation verses 1 to 8 parallel the four horsemen in Zechariah 6:1-8. The first four seals are:

1. Catholicism
2. Communism
3. Capitalism
4. Occultism

At the fifth seal we see the souls of those who are slain for the word of God, and for the testimony that they hold. In verse 10 we see these souls crying out to God saying, "How long, O

Lord, holy and true, dost thou judge and avenge our blood on them that dwell on the earth?" These are the souls of those slain for their testimony during Satan's wrath.

The sixth and seventh seals are the outpouring of God's wrath. We know this because in each of these seals we see great earthquakes, the sun becoming black, the moon becoming as blood, voices from heaven, and thunder and lightning.

When we examine chapter 6 we are seeing a *long* version (in terms of the length of time covered) of many things that have happened, and will happen in these last days. The seals cover a period of time from around AD 400 (the beginning of Catholicism) all the way to God's wrath being poured out at the last trumpet.

The trumpets are an even *shorter* description of the "hereafter" events. The possibilities of the seven trumpets (as we have already seen) cover little more than a 100-year time period.

The vials are a *real short* account of "hereafter" events. All of the vials are God's wrath being poured out, which happens in a very short time span at the end of Satan's wrath.

The seven seals, the seven trumpets, and the seven vials all begin at different points in time, but all of them end at the same event.

Chapter 7
Chapter 7 is a parenthetical chapter. In this chapter we see 144,000 Orthodox Jews who are sealed by God, 12,000 from each tribe of Israel.

Chapter 8
In chapter 8 the Lord finishes describing the seals (the seventh seal), and begins describing the seven trumpets.

Chapter 9
All of chapter 9 deals with trumpets five and six.

Chapter 10

Chapter 10 is also a parenthetical chapter. In this chapter we see the seven thunders which were sealed up and no one knows what they are. Also, John ate the little book that tasted sweet as honey, but when he ate, his belly was bitter.

Chapter 11

Chapter 11 is a parenthetical chapter as well, in which we see events that will occur during the last three-and-a-half years of Satan's wrath. We see that the outer court is not measured, the holy city is trodden under foot for forty-two months, and two witnesses prophesying for one thousand two hundred and sixty days. All these events pertain to the last three-and-a-half years.

Within this chapter we also see the seventh trumpet sounding as there is a great earthquake, great voices in heaven, and the kingdoms of this world becoming the kingdoms of our Lord, and of his Christ (see Revelation 11:13-15). In verse 15 it says, "And he shall reign forever and ever." This is the last trumpet when the church is raptured and God's wrath is poured out, after which Jesus returns to rule and reign on the earth.

Chapter 12

In chapter 12 we see the woman clothed with the sun, the moon under her feet, and the crown of twelve stars on her head. As we have learned, this represents Israel. In verses 1 to 5 we see a period of time covering from Genesis (when Satan fell) all the way to when Christ was caught up to the throne of God.

In this chapter we also see the devil cast to the earth, and he comes down having great wrath because he knows he has a short time. Then the devil persecutes the woman who gave birth to the child. The woman is given two wings of a great eagle as she is flown into the wilderness where she is nourished for three-and-a-half years. At the end of this chapter we also see very clearly that the devil also persecutes those "which keep the commandments of God, and have the testimony of Jesus Christ."

Chapter 13

All of chapter 13 speaks of the Antichrist and the false prophet. We see the one-world government (the four separate beasts in Daniel chapter 7 come together as one beast) out of which rises the Antichrist and the false prophet.

Chapter 14

In chapter 14 we see the 144,000 again. This chapter goes into more detail about this massive group of people. It also speaks of the vine of the earth, which are unbelievers who are cast into the winepress of the wrath of God.

Chapter 15

Chapter 15 is an introduction to the seven vials which are the outpouring of the wrath of God. We see, "Seven angels having the seven last plagues; for in them is filled up the wrath of God" (Revelation 15:1). Then, in verse 7 we see again, "And one of the four beasts gave unto the seven angels seven golden vials full of the wrath of God."

Once again, we see that the seals, trumpets, and vials all begin at different points in time, but they all end at the same place—the wrath of God. The seals cover the longest time period (around 1500 years). The trumpets cover a shorter time period (a little over 100 years), and the vials a very short time period (possibly thirty to seventy-five days).

Chapter 16

In chapter 16 we see God's wrath (all seven vials) poured out on specific places and people. The wrath of God is not poured out on the entire earth. In this chapter we see that the wrath of God is poured out upon:

- Men that had the mark of the beast and worshipped his image
- The sea that became blood
- The rivers and fountains of waters that became blood

- Men who blasphemed the name of God, not repenting or giving him glory
- The seat (the headquarters) of the beast
- The great city, Babylon. Rome will suffer a great earthquake that divides the city into three parts.

Chapter 17 and 18

Chapters 17 and 18 give a description of Mystery, Babylon the Great, and the judgment God will bring upon her. We learned that the Catholic Church fits the description of the Mystery, Babylon the Great, the harlot. Here are several key elements of the description of Mystery Babylon:

- She sits on a scarlet colored beast (she is partnered with the socialistic one-world government).
- She is described as a great whore with whom the kings of the earth have committed fornication.
- The harlot is arrayed in purple and scarlet, decked with gold precious stones, pearls, and having a golden cup in her hand full of the abominations and filthiness of her fornication.
- The woman was drunken with the blood of the saints, and with the blood of the martyrs of Jesus.
- The woman is a great city on seven hills who reigns over the kings of the earth.
- All the nations have drunk of the wine of the wrath of her fornication, and the kings of the earth have committed fornication with her, and the merchants of the earth are waxed rich through the abundance of her delicacies.
- She possessed the souls of men.
- In her was found the blood of the saints.

Chapter 19

In chapter 19 we see the Second Coming of Christ and the battle of Armageddon.

Chapter 20

Chapter 20 speaks of the 1,000-year reign of Christ on the earth.

Chapter 21 and 22

In chapters 21 and 22 we see the new heaven, the new earth, and the New Jerusalem, and we are given warnings not to add or subtract from anything that is written in this book. It also tells us not to seal up the message of this book, but rather to make it known. Why? Because Jesus is coming back soon!

ARE YOU READY?

Final Note

The most important thing in this day and age is a solid relationship with Jesus Christ. If you've never accepted Jesus as your savior, you can right now.

Salvation is not based upon how many good things you do, or how good you become because we will never be good enough to meet a perfect, holy savior face-to-face. Man needs something else. Fortunately, God gave us a free gift! It is called salvation.

Romans 10:9-10 tells us, "If you confess with your mouth the Lord Jesus and believe in your heart that God raised him from the dead, you will be saved. For with the heart one believes unto righteousness, and with the mouth confession is made unto salvation." Second Corinthians 7:10 tells us, "For godly sorrow produces repentance leading to salvation."

If you desire to make that decision, pray this prayer from your heart:

"Lord Jesus, I repent! I turn from the way that I am going and I desire to follow you. Lord Jesus, I believe in you! I confess with my mouth, and I *do* believe in my heart that you are Lord, and that God raised you from the dead. And right now I make you Lord of my life."

If you just prayed that prayer, congratulations. We would encourage you to find a good church family where the pastor preaches the truth of God's Word. Most importantly, do not *ever* turn back!

About the Authors

Jeff Canfield is the pastor of Word of Life Church in Sullivan, Indiana. The author of two other books *A Call to Honor*, and *Life Isn't Rocket Science*, Jeff is a graduate of Rhema Bible Training Center, and has a Bachelor of Religious Science from Logos Christian College. To contact Pastor Canfield e-mail him at:
isiradio@juno.com

Dan Dyer is the founder and senior pastor of Whosoever Will Full Gospel Church in Dugger, Indiana. He is the author of an end-time workbook entitled *Understanding the Last Days*, a supplement to a series of teaching on the last days, which is available on CD. To order CDs and workbooks, contact Pastor Dyer at:
Whosoever Will Full Gospel Church
P.O. Box 624
Dugger, IN 47848
(812) 648-2188.

Together Jeff Canfield and Dan Dyer host a monthly radio program called Iron Sharpens Iron. This program is broadcast in 120 countries outside the U.S. through the World Prayer Broadcast Network.

To order additional copies of

What

LEFT BEHIND

Left Out

have your credit card ready and call
1 800-917-BOOK (2665)

or e-mail
orders@selahbooks.com

or order online at
www.selahbooks.com